A Steelheader's Way

LANI WALLER

Photos by
KEN MORRISH

*With a chapter
on steelhead biology
by Bob Hooton*

STACKPOLE
BOOKS

Guilford, Connecticut

Published by Stackpole Books
An imprint of Globe Pequot
Trade Division of The Rowman & Littlefield Publishing Group, Inc.
4501 Forbes Boulevard, Suite 200, Lanham, Maryland 20706

Distributed by NATIONAL BOOK NETWORK
800-462-6420

Copyright © 2018 Lani Waller
The first edition was published by Headwater Books and Stackpole Books in 2014.
Photos by Ken Morrish, Fly Water Travel, unless otherwise credited
Illustrations by Dave Hall

British Library Cataloguing in Publication Information available

The Library of Congress has catalogued the first edition as follows:
Names: Waller, Lani.
Title: A steelheader's way / Lani Waller; photos by Ken Morrish ; with a chapter on
steelhead biology by Bob Hooton.
Description: New Cumberland, PA : Headwater Books ; Mechanicsburg, PA : Stackpole
Books, 2009. | Includes bibliographical references and index.
Identifiers: LCCN 2008935116| ISBN 9780979346064 (hardcover : alk. paper).
Subjects: LCSH: Steelhead fishing | Steelhead (Fish) | Steelhead fishing—Pictorial works.
Classification: LCC SH687.7 .W35 2009 | DDC 597.57—dc23 LC record available at
https://lccn.loc.gov/2008935116

ISBN 978-0-8117-3660-2 (hardcover/paperback)
ISBN 978-1-4617-5062-8 (e-book)

♾™ The paper used in this publication meets the minimum requirements of American
National Standard for Information Sciences—Permanence of Paper for Printed Library
Materials, ANSI/NISO Z39.48-1992.

Second Edition

Printed in the United States of America

Contents

Acknowledgments

It is impossible to thank all those who have helped with this book, but here are four who deserve special thanks.

Jay Nichols of Headwater Books has been both editor and publisher, and he brought much to the project, including a patient ear for some things I wanted to say—things not ordinarily discussed in books of this kind. His enthusiasm was also unstoppable, and when I told him one day that I thought the book was finished and that I had said what I wanted to say, he congratulated me—and then asked me to double the volume of writing. In the end, I think our priorities and values came together in a way that made this project much better than it otherwise would have been.

Ken Morrish also brought something to this book that I could not have done on my own. Kenny is a gentleman and a steelhead addict with the eye of a poet. His photographs speak for themselves, and I am happy that they are included here. I owe him a special thank you, and it will be obvious to the reader that his images are indeed one of a kind.

For over twenty years Bob Hooton has been a trusted source for information on the biology and science of steelhead. He is regarded as one of the most informed and knowledgeable of all those who study both the art and science of wild steelhead, and if Bob says something is true you can go to the bank on it. He is also an expert steelhead angler, and I am delighted and honored that he contributed a chapter on the life cycle and biology of steelhead.

Dave Hall is an expert angler and fly tier who spends a lot of time chasing steelhead all over the Pacific Northwest. His paintings document his love of the activity and hang in some well-respected collections. Dave's illustrations bring a lot to this book, and I thank him for his time and effort.

Over the years, I have had the best teachers and mentors possible. Bob Hulsey, whom I met in 1956, is one of the best anglers I've ever seen in action. Thanks to Bill Shaadt and all the West Coast boys for lessons on focused energy and for an unyielding commitment to success. The patient guiding and explanations from guides Gary Miltenberger, Bob and Jud Wickwire, Keith Douglas, Billy Labonte, Jeremy Dufton, Jimmy Allen, Aaron Henderson, Gordon Wadley, Donny Williams, Bob and Jed Clay, Dave Holland, and Mark McAneeley filled in a lot of holes.

The writings of Joseph Brooks, Trey Combs, Dave Whitlock, and Bill McMillan helped keep the dream alive on days when I could not chase my own. Silver Hilton Steelhead Lodge deserves special mention for giving me the opportunity to fish one of the greatest rivers in the world, a perfect testing ground for over thirty years now.

Thanks to John Randolph, who was instrumental in getting me started in writing. Thank you also to Tom Pero for supporting me over the years, and to longtime friends Mike and Chris Fong and Mel and Fanny Krieger for all their stories and support.

Sage Rod Company has been an ally for over thirty seasons. They are a great bunch of people who make the best fly rods in the world. Thanks also to Howard West and Bruce Richards of Scientific Anglers 3M for their faith in a young and energetic steelheader's desire to "get the word out," and "make a couple of movies," and at the same time give him more great fly lines than he was capable of using.

Thanks, too, to those who chipped in the ideas, energies, and dollars needed to protect the great rivers of the north. Yvon Chouinard of Patagonia Corporation has an unyielding desire to make a real and sustained difference and has shown many the way to a greater reality and better way of doing business. Thanks also to Mary Lou Burleigh and Bruce Hill of the Wild Steelhead Campaign, and to Stephen Myers of Silver Hilton Steelhead Lodge, Pierce Clegg of Babine Norlakes Lodge, Chick and Marilyn of Babine Steelhead Lodge, Gordon Moore of Intel Corp, and Tony Stellar, Chris Travis, and Dave and Kathy Larsen of the North Coast Steelhead Alliance. Thanks also to Richard Overstal, the Smithers-based attorney behind so many of the good ideas we have at our disposal today.

Author's Notes

The conclusions and observations on the following pages have been gleaned from a long time marching up and down a lot of steelhead rivers with varying degrees of success, but with little of that in the beginning. The process began in 1956, with home-grown worms and sugar-cured salmon eggs—"Pautzke's Originals," the label read.

Over the years, I have gone through so many convolutions and evolutions it would be impossible and rather boring to drag someone through all of that in an effort to tell the whole story and present all the possible options for catching steelhead. In any event, that's already been done by very good anglers and writers who have brought more zeal for that kind of thing to the table than I could.

Here's what matters to me. Out of the chaos and complications of my prolonged effort to get to the core of the whole enchilada, a systemic perspective and way of

No one looks at a river quite like a successful steelheader, and no other kind of angling brings the same rewards. It is the end game for those who love moving water and wild fish.

fishing for steelhead emerged for me that eventually included not only the essential elements of strategy and equipment but an appreciation for some things not ordinarily seen as having anything to do with "how to catch 'em." This connection began to come into focus in 1979 when I ventured to the waters of northern British Columbia. The summer-run steelhead I found there were unlike any other fish, and they seemed to represent who I was and who I wanted to be for the rest of my life.

Now, after many seasons, I believe we can make fishing as complicated as we want by collecting all the facts, opinions, and tackle our hearts desire, or we can simplify, distill, and condense—or even ignore—much of this information and still be good anglers if we are good hunters. But no matter the path we take, success ultimately depends on the fish.

This didn't really hit me until one bright day about eight years ago on, of all places, the clear flats of southern Belize, as I stood next to David Westby, one of the world's true experts on fly fishing for permit. At the time, David had been guiding for these most difficult fish for over fifty years, and he had seen all there was to see. Much of this information he shared with me over the seasons we had fished together, providing patient answers to my endless questions about tides, flies, tippets, weather, fish behavior, sun tan lotions, line tapers, rod lengths, the benefits of fiberglass push poles versus those of wood, rod lengths and actions, motors and boats, best time of day, and whether we had any more orange sodas in the cooler.

This particular morning, three large singles were coming in like heat-seeking missiles, and David asked me if I could see them. "I see them," I answered. "I see them." I remember how their tails looked like black swords, cleaving the shallows as they came toward us rooting in the sand and mangroves, unaware. "Well,"

My own seasons as an angler have passed with a growing appreciation of wild steelhead and the rivers they ascend each year. It wasn't long before I realized I had found something special worth saving.

LANI WALLER

Rivers have been called the arteries of the forest. Steelheaders knows this better than most, and the relationship between moving water, the landscapes through which it flows, and the wild salmon and steelhead that live there all become a part of the journey. When you stand in a steelhead river, you stand in a story with many chapters.

David whispered, "then, if you can see them, I'll stay here. You go make the cast, and just remember this—they either bite or they don't, and that's all you have to know."

Lastly, I'll add this. If I jump around a bit when I write, it's because none of this really happens in a straight line. Time changes places in the mind as you contemplate, describe, or go fishing, because our hopes emerge, in part, from a desire to relive past events. The present thus becomes both the past and future simultaneously, and as long-time angling companion John Ferguson said, "We are always in the middle of it, aren't we?"

Well, yes and no. Sadly, some things do end, and John's words now resonate in a different way for me. He took his last fish this past fall when we were on a two-week odyssey to the Kispiox and Babine rivers in northern British Columbia. All was well the night before at Bearclaw Lodge, as we assembled our gear in preparation

Silver Hilton guide Mark McAneely holds a wild September steelhead for John Ferguson, one of many fish the two anglers took from the storied pools of the magnificent Babine River. LANI WALLER

for the next day. "I think I need more studs on my felt soles," he said as he screwed in another dozen or so in each sole. I took what was left and added a few more on my number fifteens. We slept, dreaming of the big fish the Kispiox River was famous for.

The next morning at breakfast, for some reason, Ferguson told lodge manager Joy Allen, "It isn't often that we get to choose the way in which we go, but if I had my choice, I would do so with a wild steelhead on my line." That very thing happened that afternoon at 3:30 P.M., as John slipped away with guide Donnie Williams and close friend Frank Giacobbe as his honor guard. As Williams beached John's twenty-two-pound buck, Frank took photos of what would turn out to be the last moments of John's life.

So I dedicate this book to John and what he stood for. I don't remember how many we actually landed over the twenty-some-odd years we fished together, but he made each and every one of them better than they would have been without him. His life and accomplishments and our friendship were a constant reminder that there is so much more to fishing than winding them in. I have tried to tell that part of the story here, as well as some of the other stuff. I hope I have succeeded in combining the two.

Novato, California
September 5, 2008

The best casting positions and effective presentations can be anywhere; sometimes you do not even have to get in the water. The goal is to be in the right place at the right time.

1

Steelhead are not only the fish of a thousand casts; they are also the fish of a thousand questions and the fish of a million words. The mystery of their biology, life, and journey only add to their magic. To those who hunt them, they are beyond simple definitions.

The Fish of a Thousand Casts:

A Steelhead Biology Primer

by Bob Hooton

Two underlying principles govern steelhead. First, no rules stand the test of all times and places. Second, anyone reading these pages has almost certainly crossed the threshold from being consumed by passion to catch steelhead to that other place where curiosity and the quest for knowledge is insatiable. The fish of a thousand casts becomes the fish of a million words.

Most steelhead anglers want to know more about their quarry's life history and the factors governing their distribution and abundance. Any of these could be the subject of an exhaustive treatise that would likely bore most readers. The purpose here is not to try and regurgitate the full spectrum of knowledge on steelhead; rather to offer up enough material to bracket the subject without requiring the reader to hold a science degree to understand it. Call it a primer.

So what is a steelhead, other than a gorgeous creature that is the stuff of angling mythology? Stated simply, it is a sea-going rainbow trout. In the lexicon of science it is an anadromous fish, or one that is born in fresh water but matures at sea before returning to spawn in its river of origin. It was first described and classified as a member of the trout family, belonging to the genus *Salmo* and the species *gairdneri*, in the mid-1830s. More than 150 years later, as evolutionary science became increasingly sophisticated, the American Fisheries Society's Committee on Names of Fishes re-assigned steelhead to the genus *Oncorhynchus*. The biological name *Salmo gairdneri* that existed for most of the recorded history of steelhead ulti-

mately became *Oncorhynchus mykiss*. *Mykiss* trumped *gairdneri* because in 1792 a German taxonomist described the western Pacific steelhead from the waters of Kamchatka as *Salmo mykiss*. By the strict rules of scientific nomenclature the species name is determined by the person who first described it. When the Kamchatkan trout of 1792 was broadly accepted to be externally indistinguishable from North American steelhead at about the same time as the assignment of steelhead to its new genus *Oncorhynchus*, both the genus and species were adjusted to give steelhead the scientific name it now bears.

Inclusion of steelhead in the same genus as all other Pacific salmon disguises one highly significant life

In total, the natural production of steelhead along the Pacific Coast of North America today is around one-quarter of what it was when anglers first attempted to document the population. There is an obvious strong inverse relationship between wild steelhead abundance and human population.

history feature. Unlike Chinook, coho, sockeye, pink, chum, and cherry salmon (the western Pacific analog of our chum) that all die shortly after spawning, steelhead can live to spawn multiple times. More on this later.

Now, just to emphasize the rule that there are no rules, steelhead (anadromous rainbows) and resident

A steelhead's size, shape, and color vary according to strain, gender, time in the river, and other individual differences. This fresh-run fish certainly deserves the description "polished steel" and is a good example of what the fuss is all about.

rainbow trout are entirely capable of being each other. Steelhead sometimes produce offspring that never go to sea. Conversely, steelhead have been shown to have originated from one or more parents that never left fresh water. These variations are a big advantage from an evolutionary perspective. They provide a great deal of flexibility in terms of adapting to catastrophic events, human-induced habitat alterations, and constantly changing environments.

There is more to consider. Different rivers support what we refer to as different races of steelhead. Three are recognized among the wild populations of the native North American range—coastal summer and winter steelhead and inland summer steelhead. The coastal summer- and winter-run fish tend to be creatures of rivers draining the westward or outer slopes of the coastal mountain ranges. The interior summer-run fish generally originate from rivers inside the coastal ranges, often several hundred miles inland. In the major Pacific drainages such as the Columbia, Fraser, and Skeena, a rough guideline is that winter steelhead dominate in tributaries within 100 miles of the ocean. Tributaries beyond that distance tend to be the exclusive preserve of the interior summer race. Coastal summer steelhead distribution

Steelhead expert and professional photographer Kenneth Morrish holds up one of his best friends. For some anglers, the bigger they are the more they are loved, but every steelhead is a trophy, and each one is special. Ken's smile says it all.

tends to mirror that of the winter fish, although populations of the former are comparatively infrequent.

The contrast between a winter steelhead from a small coastal stream in southeast Alaska and an interior summer steelhead from the headwaters of the Columbia system in southern Idaho is stark, to say the least. That winter fish of the outer coast may never journey more than a few hundred meters from the ocean terminus of the river it calls home, and it may spend only days or weeks in that river in the business of replacing itself. Prior to hydroelectric development on the Columbia, interior summer steelhead cousins of that coastal fish traveled 800 miles and occupied fresh water for eight or ten months to do likewise.

More on rules to be broken. Summer steelhead, whether coastal or inland, enter fresh water in an immature state. By *technical* definition, summer fish are those that arrive between May and October. Winter steelhead are those that enter fresh water between November and April. The latter are relatively mature at that time. It isn't hard to imagine the world of gray between a fish that shows up near the end of October versus one that arrives in the early days of November, but a line had to be drawn somewhere. Then there are the situations where fully mature winter steelhead arrive only days before spawning in late April or early May, along with summer steelhead that won't be spawning until the next calendar year. Anglers can be forgiven for sometimes being confused about technical details of stocks and races of steelhead. Many anglers define their fish according to the time of year they catch them rather than the time a fish may have left the sea or how advanced its state of maturity.

Steelhead are late winter or spring spawners, but "spring" to a fish is more related to water temperatures and biological clocks than to the calendar. Thus, over their natural range, steelhead can spawn from as early as December to as late as June. In coastal streams that support both summer and winter steelhead there is usually an obstruction or falls that creates reproductive isolation. Summer steelhead are commonly the only anadromous fish present in upstream reaches in these situations. Again, however, this pattern is not complete or perfect. The fish sorted it out for themselves prior to human intervention or we wouldn't be recognizing them here. Unfortunately there are too many situations now where either hatchery intervention or removal of nature's selectively permeable migration obstacles (or both) has foreclosed options for fish and science.

Sometimes you can't walk, fly, or drive to the river. An angler rides into the sun, somewhere on the Kamchatka Peninsula of Russia, looking for the perfect run. Hope springs eternal. Maybe this will be the day when that elusive twenty-five-pounder will finally come to the beach.

RANGE

The historic range of wild steelhead extended from northern Baja California, north along the eastern Pacific coast to the Bering Sea. In the western Pacific, steelhead exist through Russia's Kamchatka Peninsula and the adjacent mainland bordering the Sea of Okhotsk. The Russian populations are small by North American standards and thought to be discontinuously distributed over their range of occurrence. North American populations are, by far, the most studied and understood.

Steelhead live on the northern side of the Alaskan Peninsula, but the North American rivers at that latitude represent the limit of the steelhead's range and none of them are known to sustain significant production. Resident rainbow trout are the exclusive *Oncorhynchus mykiss* representatives in Bristol Bay streams, even though those same streams contain large populations of other anadromous salmonids. There is no parallel to the Bristol Bay resident/anadromous circumstance at the southern limit of distribution of the rainbow trout.

Kamchatka is the last frontier for wild steelhead, and the Russian fisheries community has adopted a science-first policy. The rivers on the west side of that stupendous volcano-riddled peninsula and some on the mainland side of the Sea of Okhotsk are still home to impressive populations that are the most biologically diverse of all. Baseline scientific information no longer

Steelhead return to streams and rivers of all kinds and sizes. In very small streams such as this Great Lakes tributary, it is best to think of a steelhead as a wise and cautious resident rainbow trout. Avoid heavy lines, short leaders, large flies, or careless maneuvering. Stay out of sight when you cast, and leave your bright shirt at home.
JAY NICHOLS

available anywhere else continues to produce fascinating insights into population features that likely once existed within and between North American rivers.

The steelhead's range has been extended dramatically courtesy of hatcheries. Rainbow trout or steelhead have been introduced to every continent on the planet, except Antarctica. In North America the most heralded introductions involve the Great Lakes. Historical records are less than perfect, but it is generally accepted that the earliest releases were to the Au Sable River, a tributary of Lake Huron, around 1876. The stock origin was the McCloud River in northern California. It is not certain that the original introductions involved anadromous rainbow trout. The debate whether present-day Great Lakes populations qualify to bear the name steelhead (remem-

ber, by definition a steelhead is a rainbow trout that grows to maturation in the ocean) may hold some significance academically, but trying to alter angler perception on this point is not a worthwhile investment of anyone's time. Through the latter part of the nineteenth century and the entire twentieth century, the number and source of rainbow/steelhead introductions was mind boggling. Pedigrees aside, the Great Lakes support an immensely popular sport fishery among eight states and one province that border the lakes. Many of the fisheries remain dependent on hatchery production, but there are several examples of colonization and creation of naturally sustaining populations, especially along the Ontario shorelines of Lakes Superior and Huron.

POPULATION

How many steelhead are "out there"? It depends. The variables are many, not the least of them the reference period, the location, and the distinction between wild and hatchery fish. Every animal population has its center of abundance where the suite of environmental conditions it requires is optimal. With increasing distance from the center, those conditions deteriorate steadily and abundance diminishes accordingly. For North American steelhead the center of abundance was the Columbia River basin. Arguably it still is, although artificial propagation now sustains a majority of the Columbia's production. The Central Valley streams of California once supported enormous numbers of steelhead by today's yardstick. Northern British Columbia and southeast Alaska may be revered destinations for today's steelheading aficionados, but the natural productivity of those areas and the number of fish they can generate pale to insignificance relative to the Columbia River of the nineteenth century.

By the time there was any serious attempt to document steelhead (or salmon) abundance it was already too late to define precisely what historic populations looked like. However, one thing is clear: The older the baseline, the higher the level of depletion evident today. The evidence of yesteryear paints a very different picture of habitat capacity and fish production than most fisheries managers or anglers seem to fathom or are willing to acknowledge.

Archived records of commercial fishery catches and cannery packs are partially instructive. So are dam counts and native and sport fishery harvest records, where available. Those sources lead to estimates of at least two million (and likely three million) wild steelhead annually ascending streams bracketing the North American

The Great Lakes provide anglers with the opportunity to catch large numbers of steelhead.
JAY NICHOLS

Sometimes two heads are better than one, and friends only add to the magic and excitement of taking a wild steelhead on the fly. In this case British Columbia guide Jimmy Allen agrees—his client holds a fresh-run Kispiox River steelhead.

Steelhead that return to their natal rivers in the fall come at a time when the weather is restless and changing. The fish themselves seem that way, and anything can happen at any time and on any cast. The colors only magnify the excitement and pleasure of a taking fish.

steelhead distribution. Presently, even with unprecedented hatchery intervention, a liberal estimate of total abundance is about half of what it was. The spawning population in California today probably doesn't exceed 25 percent of historic levels, and the number of individual stocks or populations continues to decline. The Columbia, above Bonneville Dam, does not appear to have reached more than half of historic wild steelhead abundance any time in the last decade, and 80 percent of what has shown up began life in an artificial incubator. Washington's Puget Sound, perhaps the center of the longest and most intensive hatchery steelhead program and the home of up to 800,000 wild steelhead in the late nineteenth century, is irreversibly mired in endangered species issues and consequences.

The steelhead spawning population (95 percent wild) over the vast geography of British Columbia today is estimated to be well below the most recent ten-year average (335,000) of the Columbia. Rivers of the Skeena River system in northern British Columbia dominate steelhead angling folklore, frequently creating an illusion of abundance. The reality is, even in the best year in the last fifty, the estimated number of those world-famous summer steelhead reaching the mainstem Skeena did not exceed 70,000. It seldom reached even half that number in all the other years. Alaska and Kamchatka, whose river habitats are much closer to historic quality and quantity, have not fallen victim to the ubiquitous downward spiral, but their total contributions do not begin to match those from the North American center of the steelhead's range.

No one can predict with absolute certainty how many steelhead will return to the rivers of the Pacific Coast of North America this year or next. The natural fluctuation in abundance is frequently in the five- to ten-fold range, and the reasons for that remain easier to explain after the fact. If you want to be wrong, just make a prediction. That said, I'll offer that, independent of absolute numbers, about half of the steelhead that do show up will be attributable to hatcheries between northern California and Puget Sound. In total, the natural production of steelhead along the Pacific Coast of North America today is around one-quarter of what it was when first attempts at documentation were made. There is an obvious strong inverse relationship between wild steelhead abundance and human population.

To put the Great Lakes scenario into perspective one might consider that the tributaries to those lakes and the hatchery weirs that exist on many probably see a cumulative total steelhead population similar to that of all the rivers along today's Pacific Coast of North America. Those returns come after an intensive, harvest-oriented sport fishery on the lakes themselves. No one familiar with high-seas drift-net fleets from far western Pacific bases would deny some level of harvest of North American origin steelhead by vessels targeting other species, but the focused and intensive sport fishery for steelhead (and salmon) in the Great Lakes before those fish enter their river of choice has no parallel in the Pacific Ocean.

LIFE HISTORY

And now for a necessarily simplistic overview of steelhead life history. Freshwater residence followed by physiological transformation to adapt to an entirely different external environment at sea is common to all steelhead and other anadromous fish. What sets steelhead apart is the multiple ages at which that seaward emigrating or smolt stage occurs. Smolt size tends to be independent of age and geographic location and usually falls between six and eight inches. Given that steelhead are spring spawners, the beginning of life occurs in the same season throughout their range. The significant differences in what might be termed spring in central California and spring in northern British Columbia—or spring in coastal streams near sea level as opposed to those hundreds of miles inland and thousands of feet higher—manifest themselves in smolt age. The colder the temperature, the shorter the season over which juvenile steelhead will grow and the older the average smolt will be. The longer it takes to get to that predetermined smolt size, the fewer smolts there will be.

Juvenile steelhead are not gregarious, unlike their Pacific salmon relatives. They won't be found in schools in river habitats. As they progress through their freshwater life history stages from fry to parr to smolt, each individual's demand for territory and food increases. There is only so much suitable steelhead rearing habitat

The Egg Sucking Leech does it again. This large male just couldn't resist. I've often wondered if any steelhead has ever seen a leech with an egg in its mouth, but it doesn't seem to matter. This fly works in almost all circumstances, and many anglers consider it essential. LANI WALLER

in any given stream; therefore there is an upper limit on what can be produced. The best habitats are those with the combination of preferred physical features (porous substrate, suitable stream gradient, and sediment-free water), a long growing season, high nutrient levels, and water temperature that stays within the optimal range (10 to 12 C, or 50 to 55 F). That suite of conditions can produce steelhead smolts in a single year. More commonly, however, it takes two or three years of stream residence to achieve smolt size. Hatchery steelhead programs are designed specifically to fast-track the achievement of smolt size in one year and thus avoid the prolonged freshwater residence that would otherwise reduce production and eliminate cost effectiveness.

The oldest steelhead smolts originate in habitats such as the upper Sustut River in northwestern British Columbia. There, in waters described as "steelhead paradise," spawning occurs in late May and June when the ice and snow a mile above sea level and 400 miles from salt finally opens up. By the time the eggs hatch and fry emerge from gravel, the growing season is all but over and the fry go right back into the substrate until the following "spring." It takes four, five, and occasionally even six years for those fish to achieve the threshold smolt size. Small wonder such stocks are at the low end of the steelhead productivity scale and extremely sensitive to any force that reduces the number of spawners reaching home.

The best habitats for steelhead have a combination of porous substrate, suitable stream gradient, and sediment-free water; a long growing season; high nutrient levels; and water temperature that stays within the optimal range of 50 to 55 F.

At the other end of the spectrum are the streams whose natural features support smolt populations dominated by two-year-olds and even occasional one-year-olds. Many of the storied streams along the central and northern California coast are in that category. Younger average age means more smolts and thus a potentially greater supply of adults from the progeny of a spawning pair. These are the populations best able to withstand human-induced mortality.

Life at sea compounds the complexity of their overall life history. Whereas all steelhead smolts emigrate at similar times and under similar conditions in spring, the differences between populations and races manifest themselves at immigration. River-bound steelhead vary widely in age, size, and time of return. They are comprised of everything from the unique half-pounders originating only (in North America at least) from streams along 120 miles of coastline between southern Oregon and northern California (Rogue, Klamath, Mad, Eel) to the more common six- to twelve-pound fish that dominate most populations. Those half-pounders are fish that return in an immature state in the fall of the same year they left weighing, on average, what their name implies. They emigrate a second time the following spring and return as mature fish after their second summer of ocean feeding. The six- to twelve-pound fish are those that spent some or all of two or three summers respectively at sea before returning for a first or maiden spawning. Of course summer steelhead, or those that return to fresh water between May and October, depart their ocean feeding grounds before the winter fish. The contrast in productivity between fresh water and ocean environments is underscored by the fact that steelhead commonly take two or three years to achieve smolt size, while equal time at sea will produce fish that average three to four times as long and thirty-five to fifty times as heavy.

The largest steelhead spend the greatest number of summers at sea before commencing a spawning migration. The interior summer steelhead populations originating from rivers in the northern part of their distribution tend to support a higher frequency of fish that spend greater number of years at sea before spawning. Tributaries of the Skeena River and some of the Kamchatkan Peninsula streams are well known in this regard. The fish that is the stuff of every steelheader's dreams is the one that stays at sea continuously and leaves only enough time at the upper limit of its life expectancy (eleven or possibly twelve years) to spawn

The largest steelhead spend the greatest number of summers at sea. This Skeena buck is a good example of a wild steelhead with multiple summers in the ocean. LANI WALLER

once. That is the long-odds lottery winner most likely to top forty pounds.

The remarkable thing about the overall life history of wild steelhead is the multiplicity of age combinations the species exhibits. Interpretation of scales removed from maturing or mature fish reveals six different age groups for each of fresh water and ocean life. The observed combinations of those fresh water and ocean ages total twenty. When multiple spawners are added to the mix, that number rises to at least twenty-seven. Whereas the abundance of steelhead is highly constrained by their

"Hero shots" are a part of the game, but never hold a steelhead out of the water for over thirty seconds. It can suffer irreversible brain damage. Get the photo, and let it go.

Silver Hilton guide Mark McAneely holds a female Babine steelhead taken in mid-September. Female steelhead here can exceed twenty pounds and can lay as many as a thousand eggs in the spring spawn. Like steelhead everywhere, only around 1 to 2 percent of her prodigy will return as adults.
LANI WALLER

dependence on river habitats as juveniles, the complex life history inherent in any given stock positions it to compensate for depressed freshwater or ocean survival conditions that could easily erase species with fixed and simple life histories (e.g., pink, sockeye, and coho). Repeat spawning female steelhead characteristically produce more and larger eggs and substantially buffer a weak return of maiden fish in any given year. They are disproportionately valuable contributors to steelhead population maintenance.

Most hatchery programs produce steelhead that reflect only a small fraction of the natural life history variability inherent within and between wild populations. The numbers of steelhead that can result from carefully administered hatchery programs may be impressive, but those fish represent only a narrow segment of the diversity and adaptability of wild fish. Such prod-

A solitary angler makes one of the thousands of casts said to be necessary to catch a steelhead. The search for a fish on a river of this size can be intense, but it is never boring. Effective presentations for steelhead are, in some ways, their own reward.

ucts cannot be relied on to sustain natural populations over the longer term.

The ocean movements of steelhead have been reasonably well established through cooperative high-seas research programs involving Canada, the United States, and Japan. The data compiled through those programs involved the recovery of tagged adults that originated from two sources. The first was fish that were initially tagged and released by researchers themselves. Some of those fish were recaptured at sea during the same research initiatives, while others were recovered in rivers in North America. The second was fish that were originally tagged as juveniles in North American hatcheries. This latter group bore adipose fin clips and data-rich coded wire tags (CWTs) that had been injected into their cartilaginous noses prior to release. Additional revelations came from observers aboard foreign fishing vessels, from

analyses of foreign fleet catch records, and from examining steelhead for specific parasites that serve as naturally occurring biological tags. The latter involved two trematodes that occur only in steelhead from the Pacific Northwest region of the United States. Kidney tissue from maturing fish captured at sea were sampled for the presence of those trematodes to establish the prevalence of steelhead from that region.

Through the late 1970s and well into the 1980s, most of the North American hatchery steelhead program administrators cooperated with the CWT protocol and the common objective of furthering the collective understanding of steelhead biology. Highly specific data such as stock origin, size and time of release, age, and migration routes and timing was readily obtained through retrieval of CWTs from ocean-caught steelhead. Unfortunately, fiscal considerations took precedence over

No one—scientist or angler—knows for sure just why steelhead take flies. All you can do is put the fly in front of them and hope they take it.

science at what we now appreciate as the most inopportune moment. The increasingly costly CWT programs became a distant memory at virtually the same time that high-seas research programs for steelhead and other species were finally being funded at a meaningful level. Not the least of reasons for the enhanced sampling was the allegation that foreign fleets drift-netting flying squid were devastating North American steelhead. Had hatchery operating budgets not been the only concern, our knowledge of steelhead at sea would have been enhanced significantly.

The generalized pattern that emerged from the high-seas research on steelhead revealed a number of interesting features. First, steelhead smolts, unlike salmon, move quickly away from fresh water. They do not linger in estuarine or near-shore environments. Second, they tend to move north and west through near-surface waters progressively farther into the central-north Pacific in spring and summer and then reverse that route in fall and winter. This annual counterclockwise cycle is repeated until fish are

approaching maturation, at which point they spin off and move directly to their river of origin. The multiplicity of stocks, races, ages, and life-history stages of steelhead results in fish traveling in opposite directions. Emigrating smolts and post-spawning steelhead (also called kelts) are moving offshore in spring while passing immigrating late winter and early summer steelhead. Steelhead originating from the Columbia Basin south tend to be distributed more southerly at sea and not as far west as those from coastal Washington northward. Known origin fish were recovered as far west as longitude 160 E, almost due south of the southern tip of Kamchatka and nearly 3,500 miles from home. Rates of travel among near mature steelhead were equally impressive, averaging thirty (and reaching as high as fifty-three) miles per day.

Sea surface temperature was the primary factor defining ocean distribution. Most steelhead were captured far offshore in waters that ranged from a low of about 4 degrees C (49.2 F) early in the year to a high of 12 degrees C (53.6 F) in mid to late summer. The seasonal shift in sea surface temperature tends to define the living space available. When the southern boundary of the preferred temperature zone moved north in spring and summer, steelhead were more concentrated in the northern part of their distribution. If one looks at a map of the north Pacific Ocean and considers that the Alaskan Peninsula serves as at least a partial barrier to the northern distribution of many North American populations of steelhead, it isn't hard to imagine that intrusion of warmer ocean waters (uninhabitable for steelhead) from the south could have significant impacts on growth and survival. Under a scenario of increasing sea surface temperatures, especially near shore, steelhead stocks originating from the southern part of the range could be at a distinct disadvantage in having to travel through inhospitable waters for increasing distance both as emigrating smolts and immigrating adults. Summer steelhead making their homeward migration in mid-summer would be worst off. The good news is that the squid being sought by foreign drift-net fleets prefer water temperatures higher than those where steelhead are likely to be encountered. The bad news is that the frequency and severity of elevated sea surface temperature events are not diminishing.

An accounting of steelhead life history and behavior is endless and, to reiterate, this is not a treatise. Much could still be said about survival rates, fecundity, food and feeding, repeat spawning, sex ratios, straying, harvest rates in various fisheries, and on and on. There is no shortage of information available for those with an appetite. Perhaps the message to leave here is that everything we have come to understand about steelhead emphasizes just how diverse and adaptable these animals are. Unfortunately though, resiliency only goes so far. Extended freshwater residence prior to ocean life does not work to wild steelhead's advantage in a twenty-first century where rivers are regularly victimized by higher socio-economic purposes than fish and fishing. The number of places where nature prevails is shrinking at a disturbing rate, and the opportunities lost within a single human life span continue to rise commensurately. Add to that global warming, and all the signals indicate the vast ocean pasture, once thought to be virtually limitless, isn't.

The next time you bring a wild steelhead to hand, think about the forces conspiring against what you have just experienced. Floods and droughts, winter's harshness, summer's heat, and predators (two legged or four) didn't claim it in the years it took to hatch and grow large enough to make it to sea. Predetermined annual circuits over thousands of miles in an ocean environment replete with another suite of uncaring predators, some with miles of nets, were navigated successfully. Estuaries and lower river reaches may have been strained by more cork lines hung with web while a ravenous population of marine mammals now conditioned to institutionalized living hovered beyond. From several thousand eggs and the struggles of a single spawning pair the return of two of their kind means the resource is hanging on. Remember that.

The wild and free rivers to which steelhead return are in danger. One of our responsibilities as anglers is to join in the effort to protect those still left and the wild steelhead that return to them each season.

CHAPTER

2

The magic of steelhead comes from many sources—unspoiled rivers, pristine forests, mountains of solid ice and stone, and the fish themselves. It started this way, and if we help preserve our rivers and landscapes, it will always be this way. It also helps if you make a great cast now and then.

The Magic

I pulled my first rainbow trout from the spring-fed waters of California's East Walker River at the ripe old age of nine. That event, in 1949, was as exciting as shoving both hands into the jelly-bean jar at Macfarland's Five and Ten, and sitting next to Betty Graves during the class picnic. Something else was there that day, a mysterious blend of vague yet powerful signals, which came from some unknown and distant source. In the end, the little fish was a revelation and a message—one that has continued unabated for fifty-five years and that has become a big part of my life as an angler and outdoorsman.

Some years later after that first trout, I discovered a host of other species including permit, tarpon, and bonefish. But wild steelhead remained a favorite. Tarpon, sailfish, and marlin are obviously larger and much more

powerful, tuna are more stubborn, and salmon more tenacious. Permit? They are almost always more difficult, and their neighbors on the flats, bonefish—especially the larger ones—are also difficult and as quick as bullets. But none of these species, with the possible exception of Pacific and Atlantic salmon, roam the open seas with a steelhead's wisdom and knowledge. Nor does any fish, including salmon, return to rivers more beautiful. When a steelhead at last reaches the gravel at your feet, everything seems to come with them.

Steelhead are also among the most graceful and beautiful of the creatures we hunt with a rod and a reel. They are at times pure silver and steely blue, brick or blood red, black, and sometimes olive or pewter. To those who pursue them, their image alone would seem sufficient for cold withdrawals from warm sheets and dark, pre-dawn rides along wet or frozen highways to the rivers of choice.

The great difficulties of their own brave journey only add to their uncommon stature. Only days after their birth and emergence from spring gravel, a two-inch fry negotiates its new environment with purpose. Even newly hatched individuals, who have not yet begun to feed, are superb and careful swimmers. They hold steady and true in an atmosphere of cool spring-time water, and in a few weeks neither the cold flood of

rising currents nor, later in summer, the warm trickle of a miniature pool evaporating in a small tributary only a few feet wide and inches deep seems to matter. Some of them will survive.

In a year or two, or perhaps three, their compass is set, and even a thousand-mile downstream journey will be a reasonable proposition. Then come the months of gypsy wanderings across the open sea, the constant gorging, their amazing growth, and then, at precisely the correct time, their unerring return to their birth rivers. If this is suddenly impossible, as it was when Oregon's Mt. St. Helens erupted and polluted certain streams with unbearable levels of volcanic ash, they simply ignore thousands of years of evolution and go somewhere else where the pickings are, for the moment at least, better. Not a bad idea. Darwin never said, "Only the strongest survive." What he said was, "Only the most adaptive will."

Some of the excitement is about size. Steelhead in some river systems can be over thirty pounds. This is not bad for a trout that, when first hatched, could hide in a thimble. And in my non-scientific opinion, the word "trout" is not negotiable. I was—admittedly without any real knowledge of the rationale—surprised when, a few

The spirit of a steelhead can be seen in its eyes, and in the way in which it comes to you and then leaves forever. No creature is more beautiful and deserving of your best efforts.

LANI WALLER

Steelhead have the strength and power of salmon and the beauty of rainbow trout. To a dedicated steelheader, no fish can equal them for excitement or appreciation. They are worth every effort and every cast you have to make.

LANI WALLER

The rivers and forests of the Pacific Northwest seem the perfect home for a fish such as a steelhead. Fishing in such places is a reminder of the spirit of our landscapes and an opportunity to escape the pressures of ordinary time and routine. It is also a good way to re-connect with forces both powerful and real. As one steelheader remarked, "I go to church in places like this."

years ago, the scientific community proclaimed steelhead to be a closer relative of the Pacific salmon than they were of rainbow trout. I've done no scientific investigation and none seems needed. In my opinion, a steelhead's behavior and appearance seems to be more like a rainbow trout's than any Pacific salmon, most certainly when the rising fish first breaks the meniscus, closes on a dry fly skittering on the surface, and sucks the tapered leader into a spiraling boil. The executive summary arrives a few moments later when at last you have the apparition in your hands.

This fall season, I was searching the eye of a quick run in a northern British Columbia summer-steelhead river with a skittering dry fly and a series of short, flicking little casts of no more than fifteen feet. A first fish

showed in the seam between rough and tumble currents and the adjacent, slower moving flat. The fish came to the floating pattern with its white mouth yawning, then quickly withdrew without touching the fly. I raised the fish eight more times—twice on two different dry flies and twice on two different wet flies—pricking it both times with one of the small wet flies. I changed flies once more and the fish finally took firmly, after plucking the pattern three times. It was a beautiful male of about eleven pounds, complete with a rainbow stripe and pale-olive back hammered with spots.

Four downstream steps later, a mercury-bright female took a submerged dry when I deliberately cast into the rough water, using the current to get the line perfectly straight to set up the drift into the flat once more. The fly was, for a moment, lost in the churn and foam of strong currents, but she took it anyway. Though I have no proof, I maintain it was the trout in both of those steelhead, and not the salmon, that inspired their reaction, and when I had them by their tails their images clinched the deal. When I released them, I could see the door closing.

Steelhead, when unmolested, can live in a staggering variety of watersheds. The Great Lakes tributaries of the midwestern United States have one expression of them; thousands of miles away, good numbers of untouched and unnoticed strains of steelhead inhabit the wilderness streams of Alaska and Russia. Others still hold fast against civilization's pressure, deep inside the roar of the magnificent watersheds of British Columbia.

You can even find them just outside the city limits of coastal villages in California, Oregon, and Washington where they hide like ghosts in the dark shadows of concrete bridges and buildings, only a breath away from the gathering storm of high-rise buildings and long ribbons of asphalt. A few remain in southern latitudes, which may seem absurd to those who think of steelhead as a

To know something of steelhead and to be successful catching them requires an intimate comprehension of the water in which they are born and return to spawn.

The steelhead's appeal seems also a matter of seasons and time, and they are a reminder of our place in the living and changing process of nature. Fall-run fish are in transition. They turn orange and blood-red, the colors of deciduous trees in September and October.

northern fish only. Malibu Creek in southern California, for example, still has a remnant of a wild run. A few still survive in the mountain streams of Baja, and some return to a few of the rivers in Argentina.

To know something of a steelhead and to be successful catching them requires an intimate comprehension of the water in which they are born and to which they return to spawn. And this is some of the best of it. If you love fishing in rivers, it is the end game, and I would argue that no other freshwater fisherman can surpass a successful steelheader's grasp of hydraulics and the shifting moods of complicated currents. When the rise or

pull to the fly comes, it seems one of the most meaningful validations possible of your level of understanding and skill in dealing with moving water.

Their appeal seems also a matter of seasons and time, and they are a reminder of our place in the living and changing process of nature. A spring-run fish on Washington's Kalama River feels like spring. They are cold and quick, their colors fresh and young. A summer-run fish from the Klamath or Dean River is different. They are always active and full of purpose, leaping beneath blue skies and clouds as white as cream. Fall-run fish are in transition. They turn orange and blood red, the colors of deciduous trees in September and October. And steelhead returning in winter carry the drama of rainy skies, cold, rolling thunder, and deep currents impossible to wade— a time when only the green spindles of pine and spruce sparkle in the rain and gathering mist.

Theirs is also a story of value and "appreciation," both financial and philosophical. These great game fish are becoming rarer with each passing season. Our rivers and streams have been polluted, channelized, dammed, and over-logged, and while resident trout have suffered, steelhead and salmon have suffered most. Not long ago, even rivers fairly close to our cities held staggering numbers of fresh-run wild steelhead. Northern California's Russian River, for example, only a short distance from San Francisco, once held a run of wild fish that numbered in the tens of thousands. Today that run is one-fifth the size. The loss of these great fish extends far beyond the edge of our rivers and our own personal desires and dreams as anglers. It is a great tragedy and wake-up call for all of us, whether we fish or not.

Fishing for steelhead, like all good and decent angling, should become, over the seasons, an appreciation of the mystery and power of the natural world and our place in it. In this sense it is not sport at all, and one could argue it becomes religion. It has for me, and my own doctrinal perspective includes a great faith in what is powerful, mysterious, and unpredictable in nature—the hope that our natural world, including our wild, un-

Be careful when you release your fish. Always point them into the current and never let go until they are so strong you have to work a little to hold them still.

Some say that steelhead fishing is for lunatics. I agree. Only the insane would want to get up at dawn, drive for ten hours, and then stand in a wet and cold place with your rod in the air and no strikes for the next two days. But when the fog clears and you see where you really are, the rest of the world suddenly seems to need medical attention.

dammed rivers and wild steelhead and enough of our wildlife will somehow survive and find a way to withstand our own worst efforts at civilizing the planet.

And now, years after I drew that first wild trout from the clean pull of unspoiled waters, the implications seem clear: our submersion in technology, accompanied by our withdrawal and separation from nature, come at a great cost. We journey effortlessly and reach into distant landscapes once impossible to imagine, and yet in the end many of us remain homeless.

So perhaps the best of the magic is that it brings an understanding of our belonging to the natural world. When a steelhead fisherman reaches the river at dawn and wades through the shadows of mountains carved in stone and ice, he feels tied to the earth and water as surely as any creature may be. Order has been restored. The past has been re-gained. And the future? That all depends. I suggest it looks pretty damn good if the leader holds and you make it through the fourth jump.

CHAPTER

3

Steelheading is not fishing. It is hunting. Your job is to stay focused and pay attention to details. This includes your tackle, your wading, casting and presentations, and the conditions of the river. You also have to know something about a steelhead's habits and preferences. All of this takes some time and patience, but once learned it pays the greatest and most reliable dividends.

The Successful Perspective

During my early years as an aspiring angler, I often wondered about something I had read: 10 percent of anglers catch 90 percent of the fish. *Was that really true?* I wondered. *If so, why? What was it that made the difference?* Most of my curiosity was personal—in that way when you love something and want to be very good at it, yet you know you are not. There was no doubt where I stood in the lineup. I was up to my ears in the water occupied by the 90 percent group.

I started looking for reasons. Perhaps it's a matter of tackle, I thought, as I collected every tackle catalog I could find and memorized all the statistics, the numerical descriptions, and sizes of everything made for fly fishing. I purchased things I didn't need, believing that the more I owned the better I would become. Owning and collecting tackle is its own reward, and the ability to know and use it is critical, but as I learned over the

years, one day at a time, it remains only one part of the formula for success.

My pursuit continued. Perhaps it all hinged on the design of the fly, I reasoned. All I needed was the right combination of irresistible features to capitalize on the greed, hunger, and territorial response of any fish in the water. I memorized fly patterns and tied flies late into the night.

My reading began and continued unabated for decades—Joseph Brooks, Al McClane, Lee Wulff, Ted Trueblood, Carl Richards and Doug Swisher, Ernie Schwiebert, Trey Combs, Bill McMillan, and the other obviously successful figures who illuminated the pages of wonderful publications became my teachers. I used them constantly throughout and during my "formal" and civilized education, not only to learn more about angling, but as relief from more traditional intellectual pursuits.

Years later, after pounding waters both near and far, reading between the lines of these anglers' books, buying and selling gear, and jealously watching those 10 percent succeed, something slowly began to come into focus. One day, I had it. It wasn't the gear, and you couldn't buy the knowledge and wisdom. You simply had to find it in yourself. I know now that in some cases you can improve success by traveling to unfished waters and out-of-the-way places, but even in these locations some anglers still consistently do better than others under a wide kaleidoscope of changing conditions.

I eventually learned that those who succeeded consistently had the yearning of a certain kind of heart, the focus of a certain kind of perspective, observation, and sensory interpretation. They weren't fishermen at all. They were hunters.

These hunters see the environment, including our steelhead rivers and those dark shadows that suspend in its currents, as a living process, one to which they belong and one that can be defined, anticipated, and used for opportunities to succeed. And in this way, the rivers we

Globe-trotting angler Brian Gies of Fly Water Travel holds a great winter-run steelhead, taken from a secret place of his. Brian has patience and a keen eye for details—hallmarks of steelhead experts.

love finally enter the soul and hand of who we really are. It is not history; it is not detached scientific observation, or a photograph, a painting, or even art itself. It is more than that. It's alive and close at hand. In the end, the cognitive processes and values of civilized men and women become useless and fall painfully short of measuring any reality other than their own.

Learning to fish successfully comes from the recovery of those senses that have been dulled by the constant ingestion of most of our technological accomplishments. Time? Forget it. There is no future and no past, only the immediate connection to the current and pool, the fish, and nature's signals, signs, and revealing patterns.

When I left the sacred grounds of traditional trout fishing for the unmanicured exploration of wild steelhead, I floundered, crawled, then waded into a newfound world where science and rational inquiry were things I needed least. The ever-changing conditions of the West Coast salmon and steelhead rivers, coupled with the comings and goings of a nonresident migratory animal, required a different focus. One day at a time, my urban mind began to shrink as one piece of information after another yielded to new and remarkable "data." I found new ways of seeing and interpreting such things as water temperature, air temperature, available light, the glassy currents, and I had the vague feeling that I could become a part of the mysterious process unfolding before my eyes. I began to notice details such as the small seam of water just a little different from the others or that dark split of water pouring around the smooth shoulders of a submerged boulder that emerges as a single current flowing with perfect direction and speed. And I began to catch more fish.

The second and more obvious requirement for success is sufficient physical conditioning. You must be able to see well, move quietly, and use your tackle proficiently. I am most reminded of this when I go saltwater fishing on the flats. My vision is no longer up to the task of seeing the great subtleties there, and without the superior eyes of a good guide, I am left with little more than the easy stuff and the pleasure of simply being there. That's not a bad deal, however, and I appreciate what I can get.

And this confession illuminates one more truth. Some of us will always be better hunters than others, and there is always more to learn. My own attempts at finding and catching steelhead have not yet been perfected, and I am, even after all these years of fishing, still study-

Move and fish slowly when you are in the right place. In this shot I am holding my mend by keeping the rod upstream of the swinging line. This slows the fly down as it comes into the sweet spot.

ing, watching, and trying to get my nose deeper into the center of it.

A small stream near my home in northern California has a run of wild winter steelhead. The upper stream and all tributaries are off limits and no angling is permitted. I stalk these small pieces of water in December, January, and February, when the fish return to spawn only a short distance from nearby civilization. Observing their movements into their natal currents has given me insight into their habits, their choices of traveling lanes, and their choices of cover. This careful study has been invaluable to me and has helped form a core of information that remains relevant on other rivers and at other times. A steelhead's habits are not accidental. They reflect

natural processes and conditions. Understanding this has given me the ability to predict their behavior, and thus organize strategies accordingly.

In March and early April, the adults in this little stream have returned to sea. Their young lie silently beneath the gravel, developing one day at a time. By late April or May, the young fry have emerged, swimming up through the roof of their rocky nest. It is interesting to watch them closely after they take their place in the water and begin their freshwater residency. After only a day or two, they begin to select certain times and locations to swim about and inspect their new home, to rest, to hide from danger, and to feed. It is a perfect laboratory, because the pools are miniature versions of larger streams. Boulders are the size of walnuts. Tailouts are only two to four inches deep. Rapids and riffles are also small, and the center of the pool is no deeper than a foot or two.

These two-inch fry hold in exactly the same kind of places I catch their relatives as adults. They want their water coming in a straight line and not churning; they hold steady in front of small stones, covering their flanks from a blind attack. Some hold a little farther downstream in a current seam that has re-joined itself, after splitting around one of the walnut-size boulders. Some hold steady on miniature ledges only an inch or two high. When they rest, they select neither the fastest currents nor "dead" water. Just like the adults, they prefer water with moderate speed.

Their preferred lies changed as water temperature, depth, and speed changed throughout the spring and summer. When they fed, or reacted to the sight of food, they seemed like ordinary trout, at times aggressively chasing caddis, mayflies, and other aquatic insects with reckless abandon. Other times they were careful, selective, and tentative. And feeding would start without warning and end as quickly. Danger was constant and they learned quickly. When they first hatched, I could stand up and my shadow would not frighten them. Several days later, they instantly fled for cover when I waved my arm over the small stream.

One season, I watched one pool almost daily and counted forty-one fry that had hatched in the spring. By late July and early August only two had survived the

Sometimes the hunt takes you into deep water, a good place to find a willing fish that others may have missed. It is also a good way to take a swim, so wade carefully, and if in doubt bring a wading staff with you. Polarized glasses help you spot underwater obstructions.

Memorize the places where you hook steelhead because those kinds of places exist on all rivers. As time goes by you will develop an inventory of recognizable water types. The more of these you know, the more effective your hunt will be.

warm summer temperatures and the feeding birds and snakes. It was then that I realized how indelible and predictable their habits were. Life itself hung in the balance, and I left with a deep sense of appreciation of their hardship and the implications for me as an angler. When you add the rest of it—their downriver migration, their season (or seasons) in the open sea, and the difficulties of their return to the river—you begin to see the magnitude of their odyssey. Our hunt for them must include this knowledge and awareness of their habits and reasons for behavior.

Fifteen seasons later, I am fishing in a great pouring of currents. It has been raining for several days, and the visibility is less than twelve inches. It is so bad no one wants to go out, but four of us can't stand sitting around camp. So it looks as if it's me and three long-time companions: Bill Morris, Lou Rago, and Linus Niedermeyer. I do the calculations. There's a chance. Five days ago,

before the rain, it had been good. So they are here; that one fact alone would seem sufficient motivation to put on waders and give it a go. As we pull up to the first pool, the river looks like mud. It's moving, but it isn't the way we'd really like it. Morris turns to me and asks, "Well, Waller, what in the hell do we do now?" The question was flattering. Bill has caught a lot of fish.

"I don't know," I reply. "We'll think of something." I pause. "How about a little cognac?

"Nope," Bill answers. "Later."

When I look at the water, it all comes back—the need for straight-line currents going at the right speed and depth. In this case, cover is not an issue. The dirty water provides that, and thirty pounds of fresh-run summer steelhead can lie invisible in twenty inches of water. As I wade, I watch my feet. The depth at which they disappear will be the shallowest in which I might find a fish, because the fish always know, under all condi-

Steelhead love shadows. Not only can they hide in them, but they can see better there than in the glare of a high sun and cloudless sky. Knowing a steelhead's strengths and weaknesses is important. You have to fish with knowledge.

tions, just how much water it takes to hide them. I also know that not all will be close to shore, and that some fish will be holding in the pool's deeper sections. But what difference will it make if I can't get my fly close enough for them to see? *Fish the water you can cover,* I remind myself. So, I deliver the four-inch long, hot pink fly on a short cast into depths of two to three feet with a slow sinking line. And wouldn't you know? He's on. All twenty-two pounds of him. Morris smiles.

The rest of the day went almost this well. Many of the steelhead had moved close to shore in their search for the right current speed. At the end of the day we had hooked fourteen in conditions some said were impossible. That we were fishing a river fabled for its runs of

fish is beside the point. The steelhead did exactly what any would do, on any river, under such conditions. They changed their position, and buoyed by the security of cover (in this instance, dirty water) they seemed willing to respond. Without this kind of basic understanding, we lose. Just ask those who had not gone out that day. As the hours passed and the currents slowly cleared, the steelhead moved into progressively deeper water. After two days had passed, anglers could only catch fish in water three feet or deeper with rippled currents or shadows that provided cover for the fish.

Water temperature does the same thing. As it becomes colder, fish move into slower seams; as it warms, they move closer to the center of deeper and stronger currents. Why not? If my own blood were the same temperature as my atmosphere I would be careful where I walked, how much I exerted myself, and when and where I rested. I often remind myself and new anglers that when a steelhead moves into the river, it constantly looks for two things. First is cover, a good place to hide. The second comes from the need to find places to stop and rest on the journey upstream. In the end, I divide all places where steelhead will be as either resting or holding water. Resting water tends to be smaller and shallower; steelhead will normally only stay there for a few minutes to perhaps an hour or so before moving on. Holding water is larger and deeper. Steelhead can stay there for months if they have to.

Both resting and holding water provide cover. Fish mostly use resting water to take an opportunistic breather as they migrate upstream on their way to their spawning areas, or back downstream after spawning. Resting spots are the fish's equivalent of our rest areas along a highway—they don't have to be perfect, but they have to provide minimal levels of comfort, in this case sufficiently slow current speed. These spots are temporary because they are usually relatively shallow and thus more likely to change quickly in response to changes in light, water clarity, and temperature.

Fish seek holding water when they have to remain in a section of the river for a longer period of time, either during their migration upstream when the water

This is perfect steelhead water. Steelhead love this depth and current speed and configuration, and it is easy to fish. Fish these places hard and well, and memorize them. You need all of these you can find.

Silver Hilton guide Billy Labonte holds a fish I took in November, two feet from shore. Most steelhead get a little lazy in cold water and will move closer to shore to find easier currents to hold in. LANI WALLER

drops and clears to the point that they lose most of their cover and they have to hide for days or weeks, or at the end of their journey as they wait days, weeks, or months for spawning to begin.

This all sounds easy enough, but there are some variables and deciphering them separates successful hunters from the rest of the pack. The first wild card is that an almost infinite number of possible lies, each one unique, may all have sufficient depth and tolerable levels of light and current speed. You have to look at all of these possibilities and choose the place in each run or section of river that will most likely hold the most fish. Steelheaders call this place "the bucket." Identifying the subtle differences between these lies, the ability to "read water," can be the part of the game most difficult to learn. The river has many pages, and many of them look almost identical.

To further complicate the issue, a fish may temporarily stop in a less-than-perfect place because the current speed and depth of nearby options are even less favorable. That same kind of place would be ignored in

another section of the stream with better options. Steelhead always seek the piece of water that suits them most, given the surrounding conditions.

The second wild card is that steelhead are not "behavioral clones." There are differences in their willingness to accept certain conditions and to adapt to changes. Some will tolerate more light than others. Some accept faster currents than others. Some linger a little longer as the water drops or rises. Generalities are risky, but often the females seem more willing to hold in faster water and colder currents. The males seem lazier, especially as they grow larger. But not all are. Their health and conditioning matter.

As I write this, I am reminded that only a few weeks ago during the first week of November, I was fishing in snow and water temperatures that hovered around 39 degrees F. Most of the fish had indeed moved closer to shore, and the word was out that you should let fly swing all the way around into the slow and shallower seams near shore. I knew that some of the big fish, the trophy bucks, had sufficient strength and reserves to hold in quicker water, so I didn't spend all my time fishing near the bank. I hooked, but lost, four very large males in lies more typical of autumn temperatures. Two of them stayed on for over a half hour before the hook pulled. We saw one of them—an immense tail broke the surface just as the drag on my reel slipped and backlashed. The fish snapped the 15-pound-test leader as if it were 6X. "That's a big tail," Aaron Henderson said as the fish broached and he held the boat steady in the heavy water. "Well over twenty."

The second one also seemed well attached. But thirty minutes later, after taking the fly in the middle of the river, it still had not shown and held steady, deep beneath the roar of three-foot standing waves. My guide Dave "Beano" Holland simply said, "Man, I would have loved to have seen that fish. Look at where he was. How could he have done that? The waves are three feet high and the water is 39 degrees."

The other two were nowhere near the shore, and I never would have found them if I hadn't known that not all steelhead are created equally. In the end, they are where you find them. It's as simple and as complicated as that. But the hunter's eye, the ability to suspend other mental processes and merge with the processes of nature, and the ability to remember past experiences and conditions that resulted in a hooked fish, are all at the heart of the matter.

BUSTING STEELHEAD MYTHS

Today's modern anglers know more than any previous generation. What follows here is a chronological listing of myths I have encountered in the past fifty years, which provide an interesting map of our learning and progress.

"Steelhead don't take flies. They only take bait and lures."

For decades the largest and most vocal segment of the Pacific Northwest steelhead angling "culture" mostly fished with bait and lures. If you don't use flies, how can a steelhead take one? Sometime around the early 1950s, fly fishing for steelhead began to be accepted in northern California, Oregon, and Washington and some parts of British Columbia. Nonetheless, I still hear this myth from time to time, mostly from those who have never tried fly fishing for them, or who tried it once or twice, failed, and gave up.

"Steelhead will take flies, but only if they look like salmon eggs."

In 1978 when I first journeyed to northern British Columbia, egg patterns were all the rage, and if you tied on a fly that did not look like an egg or small gob of roe, everyone thought you had one oar out of the water.

continues on next page

A fish like this busts the myth that "Great Lakes steelhead really aren't steelhead at all." JAY NICHOLS

"You have to fish all flies right on the bottom."

This myth began to die when line manufacturers started making shorter sinking-tip lines that did not usually scour the bottom. Previously we used 30-foot shooting heads or Teeny lines with 22-foot sinking heads. When anglers began to see the effectiveness of shallower presentations, they slowly began to change their minds. Once I learned how much fun it was to take steelhead on a more shallow drift, with a wet-tip line, I did all I could to help push the cause. This included the Type 8, 15-foot tip from Scientific Anglers. No one liked the way they hinged on the cast, but the lines were effective.

"The farther you can cast, the more steelhead you will catch."

I learned the truth about this one the hard way, fishing with anglers who knew better and who were experts at reading water. My own strategy before this was to wade out as far as I could and cast as long a line as I could—all day long. I soon learned better and found out that there can be steelhead only fifteen feet away if you know where to look.

"Steelhead stop feeding when they enter the river."

Years ago, I would kill a steelhead now and then and found aquatic insects, sculpins, and both salmon and steelhead eggs in their stomachs. I've seen both winter- and summer-run steelhead take caddis and stoneflies in front of me as I fished, and I've had several summer-run steelhead regurgitate parr when I picked my catch up for a photo. They may not feed with the regularity of a resident trout, but it happens.

"Steelhead never take dry flies."

By the early eighties a lot of us late-comers knew this wasn't true, especially for summer-run steelhead, and I've taken a few winter runs on dry flies on northern California's Feather River. I've also talked to knowledgeable anglers who have duplicated this on winter-run fish, but they certainly are not as willing to take on the surface as summer-run fish. Roderick Haig-Brown was instrumental in getting the dry fly accepted as a legitimate option, especially for summer-run steelhead. When we made the three original Scientific Anglers 3M videos in 1986, we got footage of several Babine steelhead rising and taking my dry fly. Interestingly enough, I had several anglers tell me, face to face, that the footage was "faked, and that we were throwing rocks on top of the fly to mimic a splashing take."

"You can use any color of fly as long as it is black."

This was popularized by a few articles that proclaimed that black was the most visible of all colors and that since black flies worked under all conditions, black was the best color. Now, I am not sure if color matters at all. Steelhead have incredible vision, and I have caught many fish on lighter colors, even in dirty water.

"Wet flies for summer-run steelhead will always outfish dry flies."

The key word here is "always." Sometimes the dry fly can be better, if pressure is not excessive and the water is warm and clear. The dry can sometimes even hold its own against the wet on pressured water, if you use a very small, buggy looking fly and fish it on a long leader of fifteen feet or so and a very slow waking swing. It seems that some steelhead just like to look up.

"Light tackle is more sporting than heavy tackle."

"Light" and "heavy" are relative terms. The biggest issue is the breaking strength of your leader. Light leaders force you to take it easy and not really lean on the fish, exhausting the fish past the point of no return over a long period of time. Use the heaviest leader you can get away with and put as much pressure as you can on the fish. You'll be doing them a favor, and the sooner you land them, the more reserves they have to recover and swim away unharmed. Nothing is worse than playing a steelhead for too long.

"The longer the rod, the better it fishes."

During the two-handed rod renaissance of the early 1980s, most manufacturers started selling the long two-handed rods that had been used by European anglers for a very long time, so we inherited some of the old salmon myths about rods. I put up with the 14 ½- and 15-foot rods because they were all you could get, and because they are somewhat easier to learn with, but I never fell in love with them. Casting them felt like fishing with a tree. This myth is slowly dying, and more anglers are learning the advantages of the shorter and lighter rods.

"Great Lakes steelhead really aren't steelhead at all."

The origin of this myth is obviously a West Coast sentiment. Rick Kustich, a long-time steelheader who divides his time between the Great Lakes steelhead fishery and the British Columbia summer-run rivers, knows better. Rick has had several discussions with Canadian biologists who state unequivocally that there is no anatomical difference between West Coast steelhead and those of the Great Lakes. Stocks of Great Lakes steelhead came from West Coast brood stock, and fish from Great Lakes watersheds with good natural reproduction show clear and continued DNA evidence of their West Coast origins. In addition, in the successful Great Lakes hatchery programs, the genetic origins of Great Lakes steelhead continue to show DNA evidence of their West Coast biological origins.

Successful steelheading is not rocket science, but it takes concentration, effort, and attention to detail. Don't worry if you are not a great caster or strong wader. Concentrate on being a great hunter. Find those places where you can fish with confidence, according to your abilities and preferences.

CHAPTER

The best steelheaders are not ordinary anglers. They are something else: they are hunters. They think like a hunter, they see as a hunter, and they act like a hunter. And the best of these are predators. This kind of psychology can be explained, described, and defined, and it has nothing to do with gender.

The Hunter's Eye

Not long after I started my angling life and endeavors, I noticed that some anglers always caught more than others did, and I wondered why these anglers always seemed to succeed. What did they have? What did they know? Where did their success come from? Could it be learned? How long would it take?

I finally understood their success when I began to see a common thread in all the best anglers I fished with and observed. I could hear it in their stories, both published and unpublished. Despite differences in specific techniques, different choices in their tackle and equipment, and different target species, it became obvious that the consistently successful anglers shared a certain kind of perspective, psychology, and commitment.

These anglers were more than fishermen. They were hunters. Their strategies were, for the most part, hunting

strategies, and their tackle and gear were not recreational toys purchased because they looked good but rather the tools and weapons of a hunter's focused pursuit. And when they talked, in magazines and books or around the campfire at night, I listened.

As time passed it also became obvious that their knowledge took some time, patience, and a focused effort and desire to develop, but in the end led to an understanding and consistent success available in no other way. I will also add this: It also took me some time to see, hear, and understand what they had and knew. Much of it was complex and interrelated, and it took a while for me to really focus and let it "sink in."

Here are some of the elements of this hunter's perspective that I have witnessed and tried to make my own.

The great anglers find a way to step aside, at least temporarily, from the ordinary cognitive processes of their daily habits, routines, and perceptions and "reclaim" or "return to" the psychology and perceptions of a hunter. This may sound like a stretch to the reader, but in a very real sense I believe the hunter's eye is a "reversal and return" to the past, to the remote origins and beginnings of human history and cognitive perspectives. In other words, they turn off their cell phones or social media receptors and much of their daily habits and responsibilities, and start watching and listening to something else.

They become connected to something else. Success then depends upon the angler's ability to see nature and natural processes and to become a part of that process.

Once inside this mindset, civilized routine, distinctions, and categories that ordinarily separate and isolate humans from the natural world are temporarily forgotten, replaced by an active and focused interaction between the hunting angler and the world he or she is hunting/fishing in. This view and perspective appreciates the importance of careful and sustained observation that eventually leads to an understanding and awareness of the psychology and habitual behavior of the prey. In other words, if you know where the prey most likely is, and why it is there, and what it is most likely doing, you are more than likely to catch it.

I also believe that this kind of mindset in this kind of environment connects the hunting angler with the universal force contained in all life. It is rediscovered and the hunting angler is transformed from a passive and disconnected human being to a connected participant. When hunting anglers are fishing, they do their best to "get inside of time" and stop looking at their watch or appointment book, and start looking at the world they are now standing in. What they are looking for is not inside their watch or appointment calendar.

This kind of mindset also contains a curiosity about the natural world and how it functions. Hunting anglers are truly interested in what is going on all around them when they are fishing. They see patterns and cause-and-effect relationships and connections most would not. They watch these processes carefully, and they draw conclusions from them. And when something unusual occurs outside of normal events, they look for the inference and effect of that event.

These kinds of anglers also remember past successes and failures and use both as guideposts for the future. This includes both their own performance and that of their tackle. They are also well organized and structured. They know what to keep, what to throw away, and what to leave behind. This sentiment includes both their physical equipment and any bad habits or shortcuts in their angling they may have tried.

The best are also extremely competitive. Many anglers claim that this kind of attitude can ruin a good experience and violates the best principles of our endeavors as anglers. At times it certainly can. Nonetheless, all of the consistently successful anglers I have fished with have a sustained and unrelenting focused commitment

and drive to prevail at all times and under every condition. In my opinion, the dark side of competition lies in one principle: If you want to compete, if competition is in your blood, I suggest you compete against yourself and your past accomplishments and leave other anglers out of your personal drive to conquer and prevail.

I also believe successful anglers know the importance of believing and keeping the faith. This includes

their aspirations for the future and their dreams of past successes. These sentiments become, in effect, not aimless reverie but an important part of the preparation and focus. They are reminders and are real evidence of success and accomplishments. I say dream about those whenever you want, and keep them wrapped around your waist like an invincible belt. For a long time now I have described this process as: "What an angler fishes for

We really aren't fishing *for steelhead, we are* hunting *them, and the best of us have what I think of as the 'eye of a hunter.' This means a willingness and patience to keep on going no matter what the weather is, what time of day it is, or how tired we are.*

comes to the mind first. Then if all goes well, the hand has them."

It seems to me that this "recipe" for angling as hunting may well include other elements, but the ones just outlined do not stand alone. The lines between them are sometimes blurred, and in the end the processes of the "great" anglers are a seamless collection of many different parts. I have often thought of this kind of consciousness as "changing channels." Ordinary thoughts and perceptions still exist—they are alive and well, waiting on another channel. In the meantime the hunter/angler is no longer focused on these modern or civilized processes. They are not in the office. They are hunters once again, and they are going for the throat even if they are not going to cut it.

And what about this? One of the most interesting thoughts I have considered over the years centers around the question of whether these traits are something you either have or do not have. And if you don't have them, you can't learn them. Maybe. Mother Nature never puts all her eggs in the same basket and it seems certain that not all of us are created equal, and not all of us have evolved in exactly the same manner. Some of us are smarter, some are more sensitive or more curious, some are stronger physically or have better hearing and sight, some will work harder and some will not, and some don't even care, ad infinitum.

Time spent on the water? It helps, but I'm not sure this is the most important part. Here is one example: I have fished most of the world's truly great steelhead rivers for many decades. Because steelhead are migratory and return to the rivers of their birth, they are almost always on the move and seem to come and go like ghosts. For this reason alone, when they are returning to the rivers of their birth, this kind of angling has been described as hunting as much as it is fishing, and the comparison seems not only appropriate but necessary for success.

I also have had the opportunity to fish for many seasons on the same river, side by side with anglers who had many years of experience on that river. And yet they always seemed unaware of just what they should do, and how and where they should do it. Many would ask the guide, "What pool is this? Where is the best place to start, and where should I finish? Where is the bucket, and what kind of line should I use?"

By comparison I have seen first-time anglers show up on that same river, anglers who had never fished for steelhead anywhere, and yet they learned the answers to these kinds of questions after being shown the pool only once. Somehow they "learned fast" and seemed to have a feeling for where they were and what they had to do in order to succeed, even without prior experience.

And what about gender? Here is the answer: I was giving a talk one evening in Smithers, British Columbia, about the hunter's instinct and how much that mattered. How it was everything. At the end of the talk, a woman raised her hand and asked me if that ancient instinct was primarily a masculine trait and perspective. She added that she knew that traditionally men were the hunters and women stayed home cooking, cleaning, and taking care of the children. She looked at me carefully, with no trace of any emotion or private agenda, and continued, "Do you think therefore that only men have the instincts of a hunter and that these instincts are missing in women?"

The room suddenly became very quiet. One hundred and eighty eyes rotated toward me. Ninety pairs of ears leaned forward. As I stood there looking back at the lady standing in front of me, time suddenly reversed and went spinning backward, year after year in a rapid blur of memories, and a young woman suddenly reappeared, sitting quietly in the living room of a steelhead lodge on the Skeena River. Her husband, Brad Zeerip, and I were talking about steelhead fishing, about our favorite rods and lines, our favorite steelhead flies, and the rivers we knew and loved.

I remembered the way the woman—Brad's wife, Kim—had leaned forward and her intense focus as she watched and listened without speaking. When it came time for Brad and me to decide where we would fish the next day, she moved closer to the edge of the sofa and said that we should go on our way alone as she had "so much to do in the kitchen." Her disappointment was evident, however, and I didn't know what to say other than, "Well, maybe that can wait, and it would certainly be OK with me if you want to go with us." She smiled and excused herself and disappeared into the kitchen.

Nothing more was said. The next morning Brad and I went on our way over to a favored riffle on a small tributary of the Skeena River. As it turned out, we didn't catch anything, but it didn't seem to matter. The river was perfect and the October trees were burning in brilliant shades of gold, orange, and red leaves that shook like tambourines in the cool fall air. When we arrived back at the lodge, Kim heard us in the driveway and came running out of the front door to hear what had happened. "Nothing, Honey," Brad said. "We didn't get a bump."

That night at dinner I tried to help but I think I only complicated things, though Kim never complained about my clumsiness. Over coffee and dessert in the living room, Brad and I continued with our fishing stories. Kim was still there, listening intently. By the time we got around to the big fish we had hooked and lost on the Skeena, I knew what I was going to do. I excused myself and went into my room.

I took the rod and reel I had used that afternoon from the edge of my bed and went back to the living room. I walked over to where Kim was sitting and looked at her. "This is for you," I said. "I know you are interested, and I want you to have this and use it. I hope you get hundreds of steelhead on this rod, and the next time we meet, whenever that is, you can tell me some stories." Her delight was obvious and so was mine, and I couldn't help but notice the way she held the rod in her hands. Her grip was steady, and I watched as she looked at it and moved it slowly and carefully from side to side. It was one of those moments I've never forgotten.

I said good-bye the next morning and boarded the flight from Smithers to Vancouver then on to San Francisco one rod and reel lighter than I had started with, but I knew it had found a good home. I also remember that it was a favorite, but that made the gift only more special to me.

Years went by. How many I can't remember, but when I eventually returned to their fishing lodge, at dinner the first night Kim had some interesting stories of her own. Her ideas about fly patterns, the best lines and reels, and her favorite strategies were interesting. It was also interesting to see Brad's reaction. He was obviously proud of her, and I was more than glad I had given her the equipment. But men can be blind sometimes, and I confess to wondering if she could have possibly developed into a truly seasoned angler so early in her life.

"I think we should go fishing," Kim suddenly said. Brad agreed. So did I. "Where should we go?" Brad asked. She mentioned a river I had heard of but had never fished, a small tributary of the main Skeena. I went to my room and got my gear together, and as we climbed into the car, Kim looked at me and said, "Remember this? You gave it to me a long time ago. Remember? I've caught a lot of fish with this outfit and it isn't over yet." Her eyes were steady, full of that certain kind of light, and away we went.

"What rivers do you like the most?" I asked her as we drove to our destination. "Oh, I don't know," she replied. "They're all good if you know how to fish them and you're there at the right time. I guess I like them all." My ears perked up. So did my eyebrows.

When we reached the tributary she wanted to fish, I looked at the water as its currents moved steadily toward the main Skeena. The mountains were painted with a fresh coat of snow, and the late September air was clean and cold. The stream seemed a bit cloudy to me, but I didn't say anything. We pulled up to the edge of the river, got out on the gravel bar, and started the ritual of getting dressed and ready. Kim had the rod I had given her clutched in her right hand, and I noticed a quick agility and adeptness in the way she pulled on her waders, a sweater, a well-used fishing vest, and a fuzzy wool cap—the kind with ear flaps.

The three of us walked for a while until she stopped. The run before us was a real beauty almost two hundred yards long. The current speed and depth were perfect. The surface texture revealed the presence of some large boulders scattered along the run, mixed in with the smaller rocks and gravel. "Looks good," I said.

"It is," Kim replied. "This is one of my favorites." She pointed with her rod. "See that tree down there, the one with the dead branch hanging over the river's edge?"

"Yes," I answered. "I can see it."

"Well, that's the bucket," she said. "And there is always a fish there. You and I should start well upstream from that point and fish our way down into the good part."

"What about Brad?" I asked. Kim replied that he would walk downriver a ways and fish one of the runs near the estuary and that she and I would cover this particular run together.

"OK," I said. "You go first and I'll follow you down."

"No," she answered. "I don't want to do that. You're our guest so you go first and I'll fish behind you."

I thought about the offer as I looked at her all dressed up and ready to go. "Now what?" I asked myself. I didn't know what to do. Here I was, eating their food, sleeping in their best guest room, drinking their Scotch, and having a great time as they drove me around fishing. I also thought about the fact that the first fly a steelhead sees usually has the best chance of taking the fish. Everyone knows that, I thought. I wondered how I would feel when I caught something and she didn't. The run looked easy to cover with a forty-

Never keep a steelhead out of water for more than twenty-five seconds. Get your photo in a hurry and then get the fish back where it belongs—in the river.

five- to fifty-foot shot into the currents. Even the wading looked simple.

"I can't miss," I told myself. "It's just too easy. If anything is here, I'll get it, and she won't have much of a chance."

"Sometimes the truth can be hard to see, and sometimes it isn't," someone once told me. "On all kinds of rivers, including those you've never fished before." What in the hell does that mean? I remember thinking.

"Listen," I said to Kim, "I really want you to catch a fish with that rod I gave you. That would mean a lot to me. So I want you to go first and I'll come behind you.

And besides, I would love to have a photo of a woman angler in my slide show. Right now I only have one."

"Well, do you fish with many women?" she asked.

"No, not many at all," I replied.

"Well, maybe that will change someday," she said. "But you are our guest today, so you go first. This is my favorite stream and I live here and can fish it anytime I want, so that means I get to have my way."

I gave in. "OK," I said. "I'll use a black fly and you can use a different color. Maybe a Popsicle."

"I don't like Popsicles," she answered. "Do you like them?"

I thought about it—about the time I caught seven in a row on that pattern, all of them out of the same pool. "Oh yeah," I answered, "I like them. I've caught a lot of fish on a Popsicle."

"OK," she said. "Then here's the deal. You go first with the Popsicle, and I'll come behind you with a black fly."

Well, now she's done for, I thought, looking at the water. I can't miss. "OK," I finally answered.

And off we went, the two of us down the river. Even now I can remember the way I fished that run. I went through that water with the proverbial fine-toothed comb and whenever I looked back at Kim, there she was and I thought, Damn . . . that woman really knows how to cast. I tried to move a little faster than usual because the rules say that the lead angler going down a run should go a little faster. I looked again at her casting. It was perfect. "Maybe it's the rod," I told myself. "It's a hell of a caster."

About forty-five minutes later, with the dead tree branch hanging down somewhere in back of me, I knew I was out of it and that I had finished the pool. "Now what?" I asked myself. "Maybe I should sit down and just watch for a while." This thought was suddenly shattered by one of the loudest screams I have ever heard. It came shooting up the river toward me like an arrow and circled my head and ears like a hurricane.

Kim screamed again, louder this time. Much louder. "YAASSSSSSSUHHH!" she howled. "I'VE GOT HIM. HEE'S MIIIINE!"

I turned around to see her fly rod bent in an almost impossible arc. I could see the well-used reel, but not the handle. How could I? The handle was a blur. Worst of all, she was standing right where I had stood and fished as well as I could—right in the bucket just opposite the hanging branch. The place where I never had a touch. The place I had slowed down and pounded with what must have been five dozen casts. The place where I had even changed line densities, just to be sure. The place I had then abandoned, absolutely convinced there was nothing there because if there had been, I would have caught it.

Goddammit, I thought. How in the hell did she do that? What happened? I thought the first fly they see is the one they take. What happened? Then, it hit me . . . the fish had just moved into that part of the run and wasn't there when I fished it. Yeah, that's it, I thought.

That's what happened. He simply wasn't there when I was.

Brad heard the scream too and was running up to Kim with his camera. I didn't know what else to do, so I did what I was supposed to: I wound up my line and went running down to the place where Kim was standing. Her smile was a mile wide. Her eyes were blazing and her hands were wrapped around the cork handle of the rod I had given her, in a grip that could have crushed the skull of a lion. It was obvious she wasn't in the kitchen anymore. She wasn't cooking, ironing, or setting the table. She wasn't putting any diapers on a child. She was doing something much different. And she wasn't kidding.

Thirty-two minutes and forty-five seconds later, after three or four of my nervous cigarettes, the fish finally came to her steady hand, giving up the ghost and rolling over on its immense side in twenty inches of cold water. It radiated a beautiful fluorescent silver that seemed to be dancing in the falling light. Its flanks were firm and thick, its back seemed made of cold steel, and its perfect eye looked up at us from a world lost in time and yet one still with us. It was transcendently beautiful, and there are no better words for it than those.

The camera clicks were quick—a series of bright flashes. The measuring tape came next, unrolling down the heavy side of the fish, then again, this time circling its girth. "Forty-two by twenty-three," Brad said softly. "My God, it's forty-two by twenty-three." Good Lord, I thought, looking at Kim, in her almost worn-out woolen hat—it looks bigger than that. And maybe they do if someone else catches them, but that should be beside the point.

"Measure it again." I said. "It looks bigger than that." They did. "Forty-two by twenty-three" they both agreed.

Kim knew what I was thinking. She looked up at me and said simply, "Well, Lani, you know what they say. The first fly wakes them up. The second fly gets 'em." She was smiling. So was Brad, and once the ocean of male ego in my chest dried up a bit, so was I. In truth, I don't think I have ever been more excited. And for all the right reasons.

As the great steelhead slowly disappeared back into the darkening currents, I looked at Brad and Kim and something came back to me. And it was all good. And I've never forgotten it.

CHAPTER

5

Some anglers believe a steelhead strikes out of anger, territorial imperative, curiosity, or imprinted behavior. Your job is not necessarily to answer that question but to fish in a manner that makes it easy for them to see your fly and take it with minimum effort—and to fish in places where they are most likely to be. When the strike comes, you won't care why it happened.

Why a Steelhead Takes a Fly

After three days, the rain stops. By the fourth, the river is clearing and the sun sends yellow shafts of light cracking through steaming branches of pine, spruce, and balsam. The river recedes, and the mood in camp lifts. "Well, I'll say this," someone remarks, "you can bet the grab is really going to be on now. Hot damn." Everyone's face suddenly relaxes after seventy-two hours of fervent prayer.

My personal choice for fishing in dropping and clearing water is an upriver run I had first seen almost ten years ago. Nameless and beautiful, it eventually came to be known as "Mystery Canyon Pool," because that was the only thing I could think of, no one objected, and because the landscapes and water there almost defied description.

After a twenty-minute ride upstream, I am out of the boat and on the hunt. As the boat disappears around

the corner, the river seems to expand. Sixty feet away on the far shoreline, just past the first gut I want to fish, nearly vertical granite walls frame the mouth of a cave and gnarled trees hang like deformed spindles over a dark seam of current that unwinds like a snake.

Down below, the tailout spreads nearly seventy feet. The surface is shiny and slick, almost oily looking. A few boulders crease the surface; trees are upside down in the reflection. Underneath this languid, zebra sky are steelhead so large I wonder, "How can I live without them?" Given the numbers and size of fish, even in this color of water, I decide to try a floating fly close to shore, even though a wet might have been a more rational choice.

I deliver the first fly—with stiff moose, white wings, and umber hackle—on a short cast. Beneath the floating

pattern, portraits of medieval faces sculpted by time, water, and ancient lava look up at me. The vision is inescapable. I remember the autobiographical stories about an Italian Renaissance painter who saw them everywhere, even on smoothly plastered walls. At least I'm not yet that far gone. The fly rides on—a triangle of light creasing the surface—ignorant of my reverie. For several feet there is nothing on it or under it. Only the faces.

Then, a solitary form emerges into sunlight, smoothly and with great caution, riding on an invisible umbrella of current. Fifteen feet away, the eyes become visible, followed by the wet roll of strong shoulders and the coat of silver and red. It seems odd, I think, to see how much you can see if you look, how fast it is and

Cold water may slow a steelhead's strike response, but it will still take a fly under those conditions. Fish slowly and methodically. Some anglers feel a large fly will trigger a response better than a small one.

If a steelhead responds to your fly but does not take it, it may take a fly of different size and color. So carry several sizes, colors, and styles.

Some anglers feel that bright light and clear water may reduce a steelhead's willingness to move far to intercept something they do not have to eat in order to survive. On the other hand, overcast days are believed to be good because steelhead feel somewhat hidden in low light and thus will be more aggressive and willing to take.

yet how slow. The black rainbow spots are there, and then leopard flanks as the fly disappears into a yawning mouth. I do nothing, and the moment hangs.

She tilts sideways as she descends and returns to her lie. The gesture seems expressive, as if she is considering that the insect she has just ingested is somehow all wrong, strange, and out of place. I'm hypnotized and curious. Why did she decide to take it? What will happen if I continue to do nothing? I throw slack, the line sags, and an instant later she answers. Her mouth opens again, and I watch as she quietly exhales the fly and descends into darkness. She seems puzzled and absolutely beautiful. The fly lifts and floats to the surface. I remember smiling at her.

Moments like this, when you can get them, reveal much. At the least, they remind me of the steelhead's remarkable character, their willingness to take a fly that looks like nothing and to refuse carefully sculpted patterns that look absolutely real to me. At the most, I also learn about my own life as an angler, and the two seem

An old steelhead myth says that the bite is best when mist is over the water. That's one reason why many steel-headers want to be the first one on the pool in the morning. I'm not sure it is the mist. More likely, it is because the first fly a fish sees usually has the best chance of taking that steelhead.

welded. About the cavernous, medieval faces? At my age and after all these years of looking, I'll leave it at this: If you have to ask, I can't tell you.

Several steps downstream, I find her again in a different place. Floating through her atmosphere, she looks and rises to four different flies with those same curious eyes, only to reject each one. First came a large fly of my own dressing, then a low-water, riffle-hitched purple Muddler, then the black plume and bright body of a small Signal Light. On a last attempt, the Signal Light

does it. I remember looking at my watch just after I felt the hook slide in. Only twenty minutes had elapsed from the time I first raised her, yet it seemed impossibly long, one of the advantages of fishing over the ticking clock of ordinary time and life.

This fish seemed typical of one of the three kinds of steelhead I believe we have out there. The first will, at any given moment, take the first fly they see. The second will not take anything. And the third? They hang on the edge. You can take them if you know they are there and

50

stay with them. Sight-fishing anglers earn a living at this, and I have seen resting fish ignore over thirty casts and over ten fly changes before they finally took—like the bucking female I landed after three other fly choices. Sometimes, the take can be induced.

It is cat and mouse, trial and error. And the reason why a fish refuses one fly but suddenly takes another remains beyond me. I select a fly, one that I believe in, that meets the conditions of light and water clarity. The colder and dirtier the water, the larger I prefer my flies to be. Fish have to see it before they can take it. My other fly choices are just attempts at triggering the strike once I have raised or spotted a fish that has refused my first offering.

To date, we have not succeeded in cloning the spirit of a wild animal. Each is different. I have watched a group of steelhead schooled in the shallow water of a tailout as I fished a floating fly over them. Some eyes rotated toward it and some did not. Several casts later, one becomes "nervous." Its pectoral fins quiver and the fish moves forward, then settles back without taking. After another cast a second fish may move up toward the fly, but refuse it. Another cast with the same fly and that steelhead lifts through the meniscus, inhaling the pattern as if absolutely nothing could have changed its mind. Perhaps nothing could. What made the difference is a mystery.

Winter-run steelhead are in some ways the most frustrating. When the bite is on, they often seem uninhibited and take anything reasonable. If the bite is off, nothing works. There seems little middle ground. They do not play with or investigate a fly like a summer- or fall-run steelhead. I have not seen many winter-run steelhead that will come three, four, or five times before finally taking the seventh or eighth fly—something not uncommon for a summer-run fish. My guess is their winter minds and their psychological clocks are different. The coastal rivers I have fished for winter-run steelhead have periods of low water, punctuated by quick flooding or surges and then quick drops again in water levels. These steelhead come quickly, spawn quickly, and then begin heading back toward the saline lagoons of their river mouths. I've always wondered if the uncertainty of their environment and their relatively hurried schedule produces a different temperament.

Fishing from a small skiff, I have also seen winter-run steelhead schooled in tidewater pools. Some, sadly, had so many flies on their bodies they looked like submarines strung with lights—snagged on the back, dorsal, tail, or pectoral fins by usually well-intentioned anglers who threw everything at them, including some things they shouldn't. An hour later, these same steelhead suddenly come alive and respond with eager takes. The reason? I'm still not sure. I am convinced that steelhead are at times motivated by agitation, anger, territorial protection, curiosity, actual feeding or instinctual feeding response, or a combination of these things.

Spring-run steelhead seem relatively reluctant to rise predictably to a fly. It could be snow-cold water

Atlantic salmon angler Sondra Boley holds a Babine female above the surface of Triple Header pool. Salmon anglers make good steelheaders as long as they slow down the swing of their flies. JUD WICKWIRE

Expert steelheader Ed Ward brings the mesh to another steelhead. Ward's large and swimming style of fly called The Intruder does a great job of triggering a strike response from a steelhead.

It went over them in a teasing sputter that stalled at the end of the drift without producing a flicker of recognition. A dozen or more drifts with five different dry flies produced absolutely no response.

At this point I turned the fishing over to John. Thirty or more perfect casts to them with an assortment of wet flies also produced nothing. "Well boys," the guide remarked, "maybe the bite is off. But don't worry, I know how to find out." From out of the helicopter's pontoon came a large spinning rod with a bass jig the size of a small bird hanging from its tip. The guide presented the lure with an enthusiastic casting stroke that reminded me of cutting wheat. As I watched, the blood-red, lead-headed marabou jig landed to one side of the school. Five turns of the handle produced a reaction from at least ten of the resting fish, and the fastest sucked in the lure with a take that raised our eyebrows. The guide released the fish, then hooked and landed two more on two consecutive casts before we had to leave due to an approaching storm. The guide smiled, and said, "Well, boys, it looks like the bite wasn't off after all." We returned two days later; John and I looked at one another's choice of flies. The red in them looked the color of bright blood. Underneath all of that lay several wraps of heavy lead wire—the obvious choice of true angling expeditionaries and unbridled opportunists.

For the past twenty-seven years I have fished the major Skeena tributaries from late August though mid-November. Each fall, usually in September, if water conditions are stable with temperatures in the high 40s to mid 50s, good numbers of aquatic insects can hatch in the late afternoon when air temperatures are warm. Juvenile steelhead feed actively, hurling themselves at these emerging bugs, even those hovering a foot or so above the surface. Sometimes the river is alive with silver darts and quick splashes as young steelhead gorge themselves. Their instinct seems brave and strong.

In my opinion, steelhead never forget this troutlike feeding—and neither do I—which sets the stage for a remarkable opportunity when we both return. They are now older, but I approach the river with childlike enthusiasm. Fishing becomes rhythmic, a gypsy dance along cold stony shorelines, singing to myself waist deep in the throat of a green seam or tripping through shadow riffles with grasshopper legs and heart in a wad, always waiting for the pull.

Some anglers also suggest barometric pressures as a possible trigger for fish striking a fly (or an impediment

temperatures in March and April. One such spring day in April, publisher John Randolph and I stood on the banks of a small coastal river in northern British Columbia, staring down at almost a hundred steelhead holding in the center of a six-foot-deep run. Nothing moved. The first fly I fished to them was a waking dry. Why not?

OPTIMAL WATER CONDITIONS

Steelhead have both a specific feeding instinct or impulse and a basic survival instinct. The feeding impulse loses some of its biological imperative when the fish enters the river but does not usually disappear altogether. Sometimes they actually feed, sometimes they respond to something that looks like food even if they do not ingest it, and sometimes the feeding impulse seems absent. The survival instinct, however, remains in place throughout their entire lives. Ever-changing environmental conditions also affect a steelhead's willingness to take a fly. As water conditions change, so does the "mood" and the survival/feeding response of a steelhead. Water clarity, temperature, and volume (water flow) are the most important river conditions that determine a fish's willingness to take.

Clarity

Steelhead are most responsive when the water has a clarity of at least a foot and a half, because like all animals, they are more comfortable when they can see their surroundings. Secondly, they have to see the fly before they can take it. On any given day, even on the best of rivers, there may not be many fish around. The more fish that see your fly, the more you are going to hook.

Temperature

Water temperature is relative. Some rivers are always colder than others, and the fish in them have adjusted. There are limits, however, and it's hard for me to be optimistic when water temperatures drop below 36 degrees F or climb as high as the low 60s, on any river. On rivers that normally run relatively cold throughout the season, the fish will adapt and will still take in temperatures as low as the high 30s. On warmer rivers, these same temperatures (approximately 38

degrees) reduce a steelhead's willingness to take and leave them shivering. A quick and sudden drop of four to six degrees in a day or two, either from a sudden flood of glacial runoff or the loss of sun on the water seems to put the fish off more than a slow and steady drop in temperatures that continues over a period of several days.

Flow

Water flow can change things as well, and a sudden increase in volume may make the fish go off the bite. In these cases they seem to have other things on their minds. For example, they may start moving again. Almost universally, dropping and clearing water can really turn them on. This is my favorite set of conditions, and I have had some of my best days fishing when the water has been high and dirty, followed by a drop in flow and a clearing of the currents.

Long and slinky pink marabou flies have become a favorite of mine in all kinds of water color, and this Skeena-system buck agreed. Jed Clay put me on to this one and does the hoist as I snap the shutter.
LANI WALLER

Fish on! This leaper took a dead-drifted fly fished on a floating line with a yarn indicator. This system works well when fish have been pressured, or when you can see the steelhead, because a dead-drifted fly doesn't seem to alarm them and gives you multiple opportunities to entice them to take.

to it), and although that might have an effect, I never plan my fishing based on a barometer. Generally, other issues seem more relevant, but not always. One late fall Bob Clay and I were haunting the Bulkley and Kispiox rivers in northern British Columbia. The weather had been steady for two weeks with bright blue skies and no wind. Water conditions were excellent with five to six feet of visibility and temperatures that hung steadily at 43 degrees F. Those temperatures are warm enough for Skeena steelhead because colder rivers have produced a more tolerant strain. On this day, Bob and I were fishing dry flies. The rivers were deserted; the fish essentially unmolested. We had steady and reliable dry fly fishing on both rivers and were averaging a total of five or six fish a day, for four days.

On the fifth day, we were on the Bulkley and planned our day so we would end up at one of Bob's favorite pools. My first dry sailed over the upper riffle of

the run, dropped into place, and as it began its waking crawl, a beautiful fifteen-pound hen took it. Bob came down. His first cast, several feet below, took a male about the same size. Two hours later, by carefully picking our way through the run several times with different patterns, we had taken six fish from the same piece of water, raised four or five others, and went home with a twenty-two-pound buck Bob landed tucked neatly into our memory and my camera. I sent the photo to Trey Combs, and bearded Bob Clay, with a young smile and a woolen hat groomed from the neck of a Peruvian alpaca, ended up on page 392 of Trey's monumental book *Steelhead Fly Fishing.* It was a great day.

What I remember about this fish was that he first rose to a Waller Waker, then refused it. Bob changed flies as I stood next to him. The fish came once to each new fly Bob used, only to refuse a second cast with that same fly. Eventually Bob ran out of new goodies and said,

"Well, now what?" Not knowing what to do, but enjoying my chance to guide a guide's guide, I replied, "Put the Waker back on . . . the one he first responded to." The fish took immediately with a shattering rise Bob refers to as the "Alligator Snarf."

That night, the wind came up and changed direction in a cold howl from the north until the moose hide stapled to Bob's barn door rattled like a leather tambourine. The barometer went nuts. The next day came over the mountaintops like a cold razor. We hit the river at ten and started fishing again. For eight hours. Nothing. Not to worry we thought . . . yesterday's miracle run was still ahead of us, and all hell would surely break loose. "What I like about this place," Bob said when his raft hit the shore, "is that the fish are always here."

"No kidding?" I said.

"Yup."

One hundred casts later, in swirling wind and gathering clouds, only two fish had responded. On any kind of fly. Neither fish took, and we quit at dark, skunked. For two more days the weather stayed unstable. We hooked no more, even in the miracle pool, and at the end of the third day, I had to leave. "Call me," I said to Bob, "when the bite goes on."

Bob called on November 4. "Man," he said, "you missed it. I went back to the miracle pool and took eight fish. It's still good, up and down the river."

"What happened to the weather?" I asked.

"Well, it's been the same after that storm blew through. The barometer has been steady."

Dropping and clearing water after a period of high dirty water also seems to inspire a change in a steelhead's reactions. One of my best days ever came on a summer-run stream after two weeks of high and unfishable water levels. Water temperatures were good, around 46 degrees F or so, and no other anglers were on the water. You never know when it will happen, and you have to believe in each cast, irrespective of conditions. But on this day, nothing could go wrong, and I hooked fourteen fresh steelhead from one run. Nine took on the first pass through the pool. The others came the second time through after I had changed the color and used a smaller fly. There could have been other variables, but it seemed something in the dropping and clearing water inspired them.

Rising and clouding water may diminish a steelhead's willingness to rise, but I make less of this than most. If they can see the fly, I believe I have a good

chance of taking a fish or two. One week in mid-September the visibility was so poor—no more than eight inches—that no one was fishing, and yet with careful exploration with a large black fly, my partner and I took four fish in conditions most thought hopeless.

Ambient light is also a factor. I prefer lower levels of light, such as in early morning or late in the afternoon or if there is some color in the water. I believe this makes a steelhead feel more secure and less exposed. Perhaps because of that sense of security, they are more willing to rise. If the water is very clear, with a visibility of five feet or more, steelhead lose the protective cover provided by low levels of light, and this can make them reluctant to respond. Remember their priorities; they are not in the river to feed. They are returning to spawn, and surviving long enough to do so is at the top of their list. A worried or alarmed steelhead in clear water illuminated by high levels of light is almost always a poor candidate for your fly, though some anglers take fish with small patterns dead-drifted on a floating line and long leader. Under these circumstances the fish move to the security of deeper water.

Ambient light not only varies day by day, but by time of the year. For example, on some rivers that I fish, many steelhead, if undisturbed, sometimes lie much closer to shore in shallower water in late October than

This small but perfect September female took a slowly drifted fly on a floating line. These strikes are among the most exciting because the energy of the strike is instantly transmitted to the rod and hand. LANI WALLER

This angler is in a good place to get a pull because the water has the right depth and speed. I believe that a steelhead is more willing to take if it feels comfortable and safe. Fish carefully in places like this. If they are there, you have a good chance of hooking one.

they will in August. Because of the low sun in late fall, the water near the shore is darker.

Territorial "protection" may also be a factor, and steelhead most likely view a large, swimming fly as an intruder to be dealt with. In this sense, Washington steelheader Ed Ward's great fly The Intruder is well-named. Over the years I have, when conditions allow, grown fond of fishing a large, three- to four-inch fly that looks alive and animated as it swings through the water. Given the steelhead's propensity to take small fish, both in the

salt and when they return to spawn, I believe this type of pattern plays on their territorial impulses and imprinted feeding responses. When the water drops and warms, and when angling pressure increases, I use a smaller, more sparsely dressed version of that same kind of fly.

The more fishing pressure there is on a river, the harder it is to get steelhead to bite because they soon learn that all those funny looking creatures splashing up and down the river are up to no good. The most willing fish are always undisturbed fish. On pressured rivers, I try to get to the water first or arrive after everyone has left. I'll also focus on fishing those places other anglers overlook, including shallow riffles and out-of-the-way pockets.

Steelheaders sometimes refer to a fish that won't bite as being a "stale fish." Some say that the longer a fish is in the river, the more likely it is to go stale; conversely, freshly arriving fish will take almost anything they see. This is sometimes true, but you can't always go to the bank with that one. A steelhead can go "stale" at any time, as a response to the factors mentioned above. But, a stale fish can suddenly light up and go on the bite even if it has been in the river for many weeks or months.

My own belief is that the willingness of a steelhead to take ultimately rests securely in biological necessity, a need that soon becomes an indelible part of their behavior. This begins almost as soon as they lift through the gravel of their embryonic nest and continues unabated for their entire freshwater existence as a youngster. It continues, and escalates, during their life in the ocean. If they do not eat, they die. When a steelhead returns to spawn, the need for actual feeding is usually reduced, more so in some strains than others, but I think their

attraction and response to our flies reflects their life-long need to feed. Their rise to the fly is genuine.

It is easiest for me to understand why summer runs take flies. Their aggression and willingness to strike is troutlike, and I have seen them take caddis and mayfly adults in swirling rises on many occasions. I do not believe it was "necessary" or "imperative" feeding in the sense it would be for a resident rainbow. They have enough fat stored in their bodies to sustain them for several months without the need for daily feeding. Not a bad idea, when you stop and think about it.

Eighteen seasons ago I was hiking along a summer-run stream in British Columbia a mile or so upstream from my companions, and as I approached one particular pool, it suddenly broke open with several large and boiling rises. Some caddis were flying in the air, and I soon discovered that all the rings were made by a single female, a bright fish of about fifteen pounds who was gliding back and forth like a shark, sucking in the bugs one after the other. I put my rod down and watched her take four or five more. Fearing her mood might change without notice, I took the shortcut and cast the fly I already had on, a moose-hair floater of my own design,

I believe that a steelhead's strike response rests most solidly on biological needs. If they do not feed, they die. I don't think they ever forget this. It forms the basic element of their response to your fly when they encounter it during their return to the river.

Trey Combs has one by the tail, taken in a pool called "Double Stripe" on the Babine, while he was doing research for a book. Later that week, Trey was fishing next to the large boulder behind us and had to swim for it with a twenty-five-pound buck leading the way. We landed it, but it was hard to determine which of them was the wettest. LANI WALLER

even though it looked little like the small caddis she was taking. She rose to it twice, refusing each time, and then disappeared. I clipped the fly off, sat down, and waited quietly in the shadow of a spruce.

Several minutes passed. She reappeared and began taking the naturals again. The first cast with a sparsely dressed number eight (that still looked nothing like the real thing), riffle-hitched and dragging, had her. Fifteen minutes later, after several searing bursts and high, cloudy leaps, she lay at my feet like a silver ship in a cradle of water and stone. She was, in a word, perfect. Other things were with her, impossible to ignore, and they floated to the surface as surely as she had.

It was one of those angling moments that, for some reason, seem to come suddenly and unexpectedly, bringing an awareness normally hidden from ordinary perception. As Stephen Ward, a West Coast angling companion, wrote in a recent communication in which he described one such moment in his life: "It felt like I was on an accelerated journey through life with seemingly unrelated incidents suddenly pulling together to provide clarity where there was none before."

So I looked at her again, this magic fish, and at myself—both of us tired and breathing in the shallows on some river in the middle of nowhere and yet in the center of it all—and I paused, and asked her: "Just why did you take that fly? It was such a poor imitation of what you were feeding on." Her transparent fins were extended like wings, pulsing. A galaxy of stars swirled on her pink cheek. Her gills were heaving. No answer. She was getting ready to disappear. Forever.

I cleared my throat, and sat down on a rock and looked at the moss. There were diamonds of water in the coils of its spores, and in the fading light of day they danced like mercury in the waves of a green sea. Far above, a dark curtain shifted, throwing shadows across the pool as the sky cracked open with bolts of lightning. I could smell the coming rain, and I watched her regain her strength and dissolve in a swirl of clean water. As she swam away, I thought again of some of the advantages of wading around out there, year after year, from ocean to river to pond and back again, catching them and then letting them all go. Though I return home with nothing visible to show for the effort, I am somehow stronger and wiser than I was when I shuffled out the front door in the first place.

If all this seems out of place in a chapter on why a steelhead takes a fly, I respectfully suggest the following. The more you see, the more you know, and the more you know, the more successful you will be. Open your eyes as you cast and wade, find the colors and shapes in the river, watch the leaves falling, and smell the blowing wind. When the next hard pull of a wild fish shoots you in the heart, and your next inhalation arrives, always remember that neither came in the daily mail or over the Internet.

Dropping and clearing water can really turn on the fishing. Some of my best days fishing have been when the water was high and dirty, then it dropped in flow and the currents cleared. LANI WALLER

CHAPTER

6

The slower section of current just below the incoming rapids and in the center of the river offer a steelhead a place to pause and rest before it moves upriver—and it is deep enough to provide cover. This kind of current configuration, depth, and speed can be found in a lot of places. Keep your eyes open and hunt for these kinds of conditions.

The Taking Lie

Over the years, my experience with steelhead and the places they take has taught me that there are as many exceptions to the rules as rules themselves. Many different types of water have their time and potential, and when someone speaks of a taking lie, they are usually talking about a piece of water they are familiar with, one they have the ability to cover, and places where they have succeeded before. And there is nothing wrong with that, for now we find ourselves where I think we should be. Success breeds confidence, confidence inspires faith, and having faith brings our best efforts.

Only two weeks ago I was fishing a certain pool on my favorite river. I had a film crew of six with me shooting for a steelhead film, and we needed a large fish for the camera. The river was out, and the toes of my wading shoes disappeared by the time the tops of my boots were in the current. The crew had little idea of the

implications of this, but I knew what it meant. I had not taken a fish in three days of trying.

Nonetheless, I soon hooked up, but instantly lost the fish. Pilot error. The fish just stopped the fly, and I thought the take was only a snag. For the next three hours I made my way through the muddy currents, setting the hook on about fifty rocks and three or four tree limbs but found nothing. Near the end of the day, some of the lodge's other anglers had stopped fishing and pulled in to see how it was going. "No good," someone said. "No good at all."

The anglers waved, and after watching for awhile, said, "Well, hell, it's just for a film, so why doesn't Waller have a guide fishing behind him to double the chances of getting a fish?" So the director shouts, "Well, Lani,

what about it?" I thought about it. And something clicked, some interminable stubbornness, and my search for a fish, for better or worse, seemed a matter of faith more than anything else. I believed in that piece of water, and I believed if it could be done, I could do it. There was time and money on the line, and so many other things. Shaking my head and yelling, "No!" to no one in particular, but mostly to three days and three hours fishing in the mud without a take, I went back up to the heart of the run.

Five casts later, he took. Twenty minutes later the crew was filming a twenty-two-pound wild male that I slid on to the beach with a roar in my ears and a lump in my throat. As I watched the tape roll down the flanks of that steelhead and stop just short of forty inches, I

I am fishing in water where the currents are running in a straight line, are about the pace of a fast walk, and the water is deep enough (around three feet) to provide cover for a resting steelhead. A steelhead could be anywhere in the section below me, from midriver to that point directly below me.

If you can't believe they are there, you will fail. Fish without faith and you're in for a very long day. They come first to your mind before they reach your hand.

JAY NICHOLS

wondered just what I would have had to live with, for whatever time I have left, if I would have given up and let someone else take my place in that spot. The last thing I remember is the way my voice broke as the camera moved in for a close-up.

Later that night, my roommate and co-producer Marshal Bissett and I were having a shot of whiskey by the fire, talking about my decision to go back to the lie and give it another shot. He smiled and said, "Good call, Waller. Good call."

"Lucky," I replied, "just lucky."

The difference between success and failure in fishing can hang on a thread, one that runs through every move and decision you make out there, including where you stand and where you cast. If you can't believe they are there, you will fail. Fish without faith and you're in for a very long day. They come first to your mind before they reach your hand.

Some of my favorite places to hunt steelhead are areas with current speed about the pace of a brisk walk, with straight currents and a depth anywhere from three to six feet. I also find it hard to resist a three- to five-foot-deep tailout studded with boulders and singing in the warm light of late afternoon. It is also difficult not to get excited when I enter the head of a pool and see that soft section of slower current just to the side of hard running water or an arrangement of several boulders just breaking the surface of a long run.

If pushed for a more universal truth—and these kinds of statements make me nervous—I would say that when it comes time to find them, their mood matters most, but an inclination to strike may occur more frequently in some kinds of water than others and may be best triggered in a lie that is much like the ones they sought to feed in when they were youngsters in the river. I don't think they ever forget this, and neither should you. At that time of their life they have to learn quickly or they perish, and when it comes time to feed, they are essentially looking for three kinds of circumstances: (1) places where the ambient light provides sufficient illumination, (2) currents where they can easily suspend with little effort, using the flow of water under their fins to hover and suspend as they look for food, and (3) places that offer immediate cover in which to hide, should they sense danger.

One fall day, on the cold and stony shoreline of a long pool, three of us sat in a boat beneath an umbrella sky of cotton clouds and crisp, clean air, watching the

A well-deserved fish of a lifetime for Jon Dee of Stuart, Florida. Giant steelhead prefer the same water types as other steelhead but at times they can hold in stronger currents. MARK MCANEELEY

river go by. The pool just looked good—a vague term that could have meant almost anything I suppose, but given my perspective in 1984, it meant something as long as my arm with a head as big as a shark and a tail like a small plane's rudder.

Cottonwood and sloping hills of spruce and pine rimmed the pool. Across from us on river right, a tangled pile of twigs, small trees, and fresh mud lay plastered along a short and sandy beach—a beaver's den, all set for the coming winter. What held my attention was the slow and steady push of water on river left that traveled downstream in a line as straight as an arrow. The water appeared to be between five and seven feet deep. Here and there, beneath the arrow of current, I could see the dark shadows of several large boulders. So I asked the guide, "What's the name of this pool?"

"Beaver Pond," he answered. "That's their den over there on the beach."

"Yup," I said, "I can see that."

Dave, my angling partner for the day, asked, "Is it any good?"

"You bet," the guide answered. "A good place for a big fish. We got one about twenty-six pounds the first

TAKING LIES

To me, a taking lie is a place in the river that offers a steelhead an opportunity to stop and regain strength. Once in this safe and comfortable resting place, some of their other behavioral characteristics, necessarily muted during the hardships of their migration, suddenly emerge. In my opinion, these emerging behavioral patterns include curiosity, confidence, territoriality, and perhaps even a "playfulness." While they are fattened from their ocean feedng, they do continue to eat. Back in the days when I killed them, I found all kinds of real food in their stomachs.

At this moment in their immense journey, the resting steelhead is no longer a wandering oceanic creature. It is back in the place of its birth, renewed by the flow of clean, fresh water. Even without a biological imperative to feed, can the instinctive impulse to respond to those things that look like food be far behind? So, if pressed for a definition, I would say a taking lie is any place where a steelhead becomes, once more, what it really is—a trout. There are always many places on a river where a steelhead can become a rainbow trout once again, but many of these are very difficult to fish. So, as eager and opportunistic anglers, we pass these by and go on in search of the familiar, the convenient, and the manageable.

Someone once advised me to not waste my time on the river and "only fish the best places, because you can't fish all the water." Good advice. Several kinds of places on a steelhead river almost always have a fish or two in them, or more, if the water is at least two feet deep and moving at a moderate speed approximately equal to a fast walk. The bigger such a place is, the more fish it can hold.

Steelhead will pause and rest in any slower water that is off to the side of a fast moving current. In a typical run or pool, there is usually some current coming in at the upper part of the run, which is often called the "head" or "eye." Steelhead like to congregate here before they move upstream. Almost always there is a section just off to one side of the main current in the head of the run that is slower. This spot offers a good place for steelhead to rest and test the currents before they swim into the fast water and begin the next step in their upstream journey. Most anglers are aware of the slower water on the inside of a curving run, but there is also slower water on the outside of that curve, and steelhead will hold here, especially if it has a few large rocks and boulders in it.

The middle section of the pool is usually the deepest, and it may have enough volume and room for many steelhead. These areas are even better if they have large rocks and boulders, or a ledge-rock drop-off to provide extra cover if the water is extremely clear or if there is a considerable amount of angling pressure. In these circumstances steelhead will often seek shelter in the middle of a pool, especially if the sky is cloudless and clear.

Steelhead like to hold in sudden and steep drop-offs that slow down the push of uncomfortably fast current. These drop-offs can be almost anywhere, from the top of a run or pool down to the tailout. Where ledge rock runs parallel or almost parallel with the currents, steelhead will line up in single file along the edge. Cast toward the center of the river and let the current swing your fly into the drop-off, or cast above the drop-off and give slack as your fly leaves the edge and begins to swing into deeper water. Sometimes much of the bottom section of a pool may be ledge rock. Ledge-rock bottoms usually have deeper "slits" or trenches in them, where steelhead will locate even if the water on either side

I love it when the good guys get a big one. Long-time companions Gale House and Silver Hilton guide Billy Labonte hold a Babine buck that Gale took "greased line"—using a floating line and wet fly delivered on a 14-foot leader. LANI WALLER

of the trench is too shallow. This is especially true early in the morning and late in the evening when the light is changing and the fish are moving around, either looking for a place to hide or for a good route upstream.

A single boulder (any rock at least two feet high and two to three feet wide and long) is another one of my favorite places to fish. The larger the boulder, the more resting positions it usually offers. Steelhead will hold to one side of the boulder (in the trench formed by high water swirling and scooping out the gravel around its base), behind the boulder in the slower triangle of water called "a slick," and where the currents behind the boulder come together. Last but not least, a steelhead will lie in front of a boulder to protect their rear flank. A steelhead has a 30-degree blind spot behind it, and because it doesn't have time or energy to keep turning around in the current, it covers this blind spot by holding in front of a boulder.

Water in shadow, especially with high sun and clear water, is another good spot to fish. A steel-head's eye has a pupil that cannot enlarge to gather available light when it is low, and it cannot contract when the light and glare are intense. So when the light is bright and the water is low and clear, steelhead often move to the shadows so that they can continue to see effectively.

The tailout, the downstream end of a pool just before the water spills into the rapids or riffle below, is one of the best places of all. If they have sufficient depth, moderate current speed, and are shaped correctly, tailouts provide steelhead with a resting spot after leaving the pool downstream and negotiating the rapids. The best tailouts are those with rocky bottoms, depressions, ledges, or drop-offs that also have boulders to break the current's flow and provide cover.

Anywhere a tributary enters the main river can be good. Steelhead sense the difference in water temperatures and clarity and will lie just off the mouth of a tributary. Often the runoff from even a small creek can push out a hole in the main river that provides additional depth and cover for a resting steelhead.

time we fished it. And lots more big ones after that." I found that statement interesting, for obvious reasons.

So, Dave gets out. From the tip of his rod a silver, four-inch-long spoon hammered from solid steel hangs like a pendant. Now I know what you're thinking, because a lot of fly anglers don't like lure fishermen, but I learned almost from the start that if you want to know how many fish are really in the river, give a good angler a level-wind reel and a spoon and turn him loose. I've seen ten or more steelhead come out of a run after I went through with a fly and thought I had done a good job by taking two or three fish.

"I told you, I ain't messing around," he says, as he sees the look I am giving his spoony rig.

"I need a smoke," I say. "Anybody got one? It's too damn cold for anything to bite right now. Maybe we should have lunch and then hit the pool."

No answer. Just glaring eyes. I'm outnumbered. And smokeless. I consider my options and remember that the better part of valor is knowing when to retreat, so I put the pressure on the guide to get me out of there and take me to another run because there is no way I am going to fish behind some guy with a four-inch spoon who knows what he is doing.

So, we take off to the next pool upstream, which is just around the corner. When I get out of the boat and study the water, the configurations of current do not have the same music as the pool we just left. It's too fast on the shallow side, and I don't see any rocks bigger than a basketball. Maybe I should have gone behind Dave after all, I think. There is one decent looking lie near the tail. Maybe it will happen down there.

An hour later, the boat comes to pick me up. Dave is eating his lunch, smiling. As they approach, he puts his soup down, tilts his head, and then moves his arms horizontally in and out, in and out, and then in and out again, as if he was playing an accordion. The gestures are a question: Did I get anything? "Nope," I answer as I crawl over the frozen gunwale. "Never got a touch. You?" Dave just looks at me and says, "Thirty-two pounds."

The story is true, and the guide carefully measured and weighed the fish. That night at dinner, after listening to all the stories inspired by the capture of Dave's Pig, I suggested that we rename Beaver Pond and call it Pig Pen. The name stuck because, at the time, a lot of us called any really big steelhead, a fish over twenty pounds, "a pig." But a pig is not to be confused with a monster. And Dave's fish was one of those, but I always hated to admit it.

A year later, in 1985, I agreed to move heaven and earth in order to capture on film a steelhead taking a dry fly and a large fish over twenty pounds, on any kind of fly. "The more over twenty, the better," Scientific Anglers CEO Howard West said. The dry fly take was relatively easy and was recorded on a pool named "Goose," but when it came for the big one, I took the film crew back to Pig Pen. On the fourth cast I had him and knew from the instant he took that he was the one I wanted, but the hook pulled and I was left alone in front of the cameras with my hands over the top of my head and something like "Ohhh man" dribbling out of my mouth.

This past September I attended the annual Smithers, B.C., steelhead fundraising banquet. The guest speakers were Yvon Chouinard, owner of Patagonia Corporation, who has done more for conservation in one year than most of us do in a lifetime, and screen writer and novelist Tom McGuane. Both said some important and necessary things, given the threat of Atlantic salmon farms inside the mouth of the Skeena River. Just before the banquet began, someone began passing around a photograph of one of those eye poppers you dream about. The fish looked immense, and soon the room was buzzing. "What a steelhead," everyone said.

"How big?" someone asked, as a group of us gathered around the image. The flanks of that steelhead were pure silver, with a wash of bright red down its gill plates and lateral line. It looked as long and as heavy as a small tarpon, and its belly hung over the water's edge like a bag of wheat. The veins in the guide's temple were almost popping as he strained to hold his client's fish and smile at the same time.

"Thirty-two pounds. Maybe thirty-three."

"Where'd they get it?"

Take a close look at this run. The colored water and large submerged rocks provide lots of cover and protection for a resting steelhead, giving it a feeling of safety and comfort. In my opinion, a comfortable fish that feels safe is a good prospect for taking your fly.

Steelhead like the cover provided by a riffled or choppy surface. They can hide there, even if it is relatively shallow. A lot of anglers pass up this kind of lie. Unfortunately, in this case the hooked fish turned out to be a rock. But for a moment even Jimmy Allen, on the left, thought they were into a good fish.

Buckets change as water rises or drops or as it clears or becomes cloudy. So pay attention to the changes in conditions. Yesterday's taking lie may be too fast, too slow, too dirty, or too clear to fish well.

BUCKETS

Steelheaders use the term "bucket" to point out that section of a major run or pool that holds the greatest numbers of fish. The word is not usually used to define a steelhead's choice of a place or places to rest in a shallow riffle or in sections of river that contain a mixture of many different and faster currents. These potential resting places are called "pockets."

I first heard the term used by steelheaders who fished the winter-run rivers of Northern California, especially in relation to the larger sections of the stream, and its lower tidewater pools. Since steelhead are usually on the move when we fish for them, it becomes critical to be able to have at least an educated guess of where they might stop, rest, and accumulate on their journey. Since not all steelhead will bite at the same time, or with equal intensity, fishing in the bucket usually offers a shot at the most fish.

There are an almost infinite number of variations on the term "bucket," though all buckets have sufficient depth to hide a resting steelhead and a moderate current speed, which allows them to rest and conserve their energy. Sometimes a steelhead run or pool looks almost the same, from one end to the other, with the same essential current speed, depth, and structure—all of which look good to the angler's eye—and yet for some reason the fish choose only one place to rest and hold. Finding these places can therefore require some time and experimentation, but it is time well worth spending, since successive generations of returning steelhead will continue to favor those exact places.

However, events such as severe flooding can relocate, eliminate, or even create new buckets. When this happens you will have to learn the pool or run all over again. The bucket can also change, or move, as water levels rise or fall. And some runs always have more than one bucket. The great runs are, for lack of a better description, almost "all bucket."

"Dunno. Somewhere on the Babine. You know how it is. They're where you find them."

"Hmmm," Yvon says quietly. "I don't know. That's a nice fish."

McGuane says nothing, but I can see the wheels turning. I knew the guide holding the fish and I knew the river, but from my position in the crowd I couldn't see what pool it came from.

About a month later, I get a package from the guy who caught the fish. Jon Dee, longtime friend and client, from Stuart, Florida, had signed the photo for me, thanking me for "Helping make his dreams come true." Now I'm not sure just what I had to do with it, as Jon is a fine angler, but I will say this: He had one hell of a smile on his face. When I looked at the background, it took a moment, but soon focused. The stony shoreline seemed larger due to the abnormally low water that year, but there it was, as clear as the river itself: the sloping hills of pine and spruce, the uneven and rocky shore line of river right, the slow and steady beat of the arrowed currents just beyond Jon's right's elbow. Pig Pen had done it again.

So I call him, and after he tells me the story, I tell him how the pool got its name. Then I ask Jon just what he will be thinking the next time he goes back to that pool. For a long time he doesn't say anything, but I could hear his breathing in my ear three thousand miles away in Florida.

"Big," he says. "From now on I'll be thinking big. But in a way it doesn't matter. I love them all, don't you?"

CHAPTER

7

All good presentations are nothing more or less than attempts to present the fly in a way that makes it look alive and easy for a willing steelhead to take. It is your responsibility to make these elements part of your fishing. In the end, presentation is your best ally, or your worst enemy, and if you can't make an effective presentation you won't take many fish.

Elements of Presentation

The presentation that you choose should be part of a plan that attempts to capitalize on the water conditions and the "mood" of the fish (fresh run, stale, lightly or heavily pressured) and your favorite way of doing business, including choice of equipment. By favorite way of doing business, I mean fishing dry or wet flies with floating lines or sinking lines fished downstream on the swing. No matter the particular way in which you deliver the fly to the fish, all good presentations get the fly close to as many resting fish as possible, with a minimum of wasted time and effort. Since steelhead do not feed like ordinary trout, you cannot depend on their hunger to inspire a strike. This central theme should determine and define almost all of your presentations.

In the broadest sense, choosing a presentation should rest upon three criteria. In the first place, you should

enjoy it. Fishing in a way you like breeds confidence and faith and helps you stay with it when the catching is really tough. Secondly, your presentation should put fish on the bank. I have never been one of those who can fish day after day for the act of fishing alone. For example, I admire but cannot emulate those steelheaders who fish only the dry fly, even under circumstances that offer almost no chance for a catch. Going without works for a while, but at some point I want a pull on my line. The third basic consideration is your skill and experience level. Beginners should realize their limitations and should cast and wade within their abilities.

Presentation actually encompasses many different elements besides the basic way you choose to cast and present your fly. These elements should be a part of all basic strategies no matter which basic presentation or system of fishing you prefer. They include the way you decide to approach the run or pool you are about to fish, your wading strategies and maneuvers once you are in the water, whether you are searching for only large fish, whether you are sight-fishing or blind-casting, how quickly you decide to cover the water, and your ability to stay focused. All of these items on this long list matter. A good cast by itself may look and feel good, but you should remember that its effectiveness depends on more than a tight loop or smooth casting stroke.

All presentations begin where you do. Choose a starting point that provides the best possible position given the way you want to fish.

APPROACH

Plan your approach to each pool in a way that maximizes the potential of your presentation. All good steelhead water shares certain characteristics such as sufficient depth of three to seven feet and moderate speed and currents moving in a relatively straight line. But each run has critical differences, and each always has a "bucket," the place that holds the most fish, even if it is only a single steelhead. So take the time to evaluate the run and find the best possible position from which to begin fishing.

If you already know the run and understand its requirements, then you can begin fishing without a lot of reconnaissance, but if you have never fished the pool before, walk the run to identify prime places for your fly and to try and understand the best approach and posi-

tion from which to begin. This research in the beginning puts you over more fish more quickly.

This initial appraisal of a run also helps you determine the length of your casts. Shorter casts give you more control over your line, which allows you to mend and set the hook more effectively. Longer casts to a steelhead are more exciting to me personally, but the amount of line on the water delays the sensation of the strike, which can result in not hooking up at all or hooking the fish poorly, only to have the hook come loose during the fight. Never wade any deeper than you have to, and this includes not getting in at all if the fish is close to shore. If I am fishing in a large run that looks good from one side of the river to the other, I fish the water closest to me first with a short line to cover the fish directly below me and close to my shore. If this produces nothing, then I go back for a second approach with a longer line.

POSITION

Your wading position creates an "angle" in relation to the target, which you always need to consider because each basic type of presentation has an optimal position that will produce the best drift and increase your chances of hooking a fish. For example, when casting upstream and dead-drifting a fly down through a seam or to a sighted fish, it has been my experience that the best position for delivery is almost directly below the target. This angle gives you better line control because the line is essentially traveling straight toward you. You can gather slack as the fly drifts toward you, and when you set the hook, you pull it toward the corner of the fish's jaw. When you can see the fish, it can be more effective to dead-drift your flies to a target that is more directly opposite you, because you can then measure your casts to avoid lining the fish.

On a down-and-across presentation, I prefer a position that puts the fish anywhere except directly below me. I want to be standing above and off to one side of the target so the sideways swing of the fly helps set the hook. A steelhead holding directly below you is more difficult to hook because even a sideways movement with the rod will often pull the fly out of the fish's mouth, and not toward the side of its jaw, especially on casts over thirty feet or so.

One essential element is the speed with which you fish. Make sure you move slowly enough to cover the water. Don't leave any good-looking spaces untouched, and minimize unnecessary movements and careless wading. Keep your eyes where they belong—on the water and on your line. Steelhead don't live in trees.

WADING SAFETY

Steelhead are not worth drowning for. Wade carefully and with respect for the power and strength of a river. Watch your step (I always wear polarized glasses to help me see the structure just ahead of me) and do everything you can to stay safe and balanced as you walk in the water. A wading staff is a great help when the wading gets tricky, and my favorites are made from ordinary bamboo garden poles. They are light, very strong, and they float. Mine are usually attached by the handle to a spring-loaded retrieval device clipped to my wading belt. This keeps the floating staff next to my waist or hip, and all I have to do is reach down, pick the staff up, and steady myself. When I am finished, the retrieval device pulls the staff back and holds it in place next to my hip in the water's surface. Since I am a right-handed caster and usually make my presentations off my right shoulder, the staff floating by my left side is out of the way and yet instantly available should I need it. Trouble happens quickly, and you may not have time to withdraw a collapsible wading staff from its scabbard and assemble it.

If the stream bottom is slippery and full of boulders or sudden drop-offs or divots in ledge rock, I keep the staff in my left hand for support and stability as I move downstream. If I am casting from an especially precarious position, I stabilize myself with the staff with my left hand and cast with my right. The 11- or 12-foot switch rods can be cast with one hand, and they keep you fishing when the going gets tough, which allows you to cover water others may not have. It's hard to remain focused and confident if you are afraid and unsure of your footing. I recommend always carrying a staff, but if you do not have one, a stick will work in a pinch.

I find wading in shallow water more difficult than wading in deep water. When you wade waist deep, the water provides support and stability, and since you are lighter on your feet you can maneuver easier around large rocks and across uneven bottoms. Plus, if I fall, I would rather only fall two feet and be cushioned by the water than fall five feet and land on rocks.

Steelheading is not a numbers game and fish like this are special. If you need to catch a lot of fish to feel good, you are standing in the wrong part of the world.
LANI WALLER

Touch is also important—especially when wet-fly fishing—because the line is your probe and your messenger. Keep it under control at all times and use it not only to know how your fly is swimming and where it is, but also when a fish has taken your fly. In placid currents, I often drape my staff over my shoulder; when the wading gets tough, I let it float in the water beside me where I can grab it quickly.

75

BIG FISH

On the rivers I fish, most anglers define a trophy as a fish of twenty pounds or more. These kind of steelhead take more time and focus, because even on the best of rivers there are fewer twenty- to thirty-pound steelhead than ten-pound fish. On these rivers, a twenty- to thirty-pound steelhead can come on the first cast, the five hundredth, or on the last cast of your life.

Through my own experiences and talking with other fortunate anglers who have landed large fish, a perspective eventually emerged for me. Taking a big fish, on any kind of presentation, starts by being on those rivers that have the trophies, and being there at the right time. When I decided to transform my fishing and my presentations from those aimed at "ordinary" steelhead to the capture of truly large steelhead, I looked north to the waters of British Columbia.

If there is such a thing as a "big fish presentation," and I think there is, it includes not only being on the right river at the right time but also a necessary kind of perspective. You have to believe you can do it and present your fly with that kind of attitude—on each and

The fish of a lifetime never comes easy, but it can be had if you are in the right place at the right time. Carrie Labonte was, and took this Babine buck in late October. I was told that the fish never had a chance. I know Carrie and I believe it. BILLY LABONTE

every cast. If you don't think you can do it, you won't, even on the best of rivers.

A large steelhead's size seems to produce a different kind of behavior, and I try to organize my presentations around this. If the fish are fit and in good condition, their size gives them a competitive edge when in the company of other fish. On the rivers I fish, the males, which are the largest and strongest steelhead, usually take the best, or one of the best, holding positions in the pool. That means I will slow down and spend more time fishing those places.

Once in its lie, a truly large fish is very aggressive in defending its territory and intolerant of competition. As such, its strike impulse may be centered around or at least partially inspired by a desire to protect that territory. I not only present my fly more slowly when I know there are large fish around, but I use a larger swimming-type pattern in hope of inducing a strike from a fish that is unwilling to share the lie.

On the other hand, this same kind of aggressive fish can still be very cautious and shy. It may seem a contradiction to say that a wild animal can be aggressive and yet shy and cautious, but I know it to be true. When they are in a familiar environment, they are strong and unafraid. When they move to the edge of their world and see that boundary, they can become cautious.

This past late season, the behavior of several large Canadian fish I hooked seemed to show exactly such a pattern. The water was cold, around 39 degrees F, but clear, and visibility exceeded five feet. Because steelhead are cold-blooded, most of them had moved into slower water to conserve energy. Thus, most were being hooked as they held in shallow and slow moving water close to shore. Almost all of these fish were small. Then I realized what was happening. The really big fish were too cautious to move into water only two feet deep because it was too clear for them to feel safe. I had a choice to make, a trade-off, and it didn't take long to decide. I changed my presentations and started to make longer casts out into current speeds that may have looked too swift for a steelhead in 39 degree water, but in fact they were not, at least for large and fit specimens.

One of these was a twenty-pound female who took at the head of a riffle in water so swift no one else wanted to fish it. During the next six days, I hooked five more large fish on long casts to deeper and swifter water. Two of these were on for over thirty minutes. We saw

The down-and-across wet-fly swing covers the most water with the least effort. Start at the uppermost part of the run that looks good. Make your first casts short, then lengthen them to a manageable and effective distance as you move downstream. The greater the angle at which you cast upstream, the deeper your fly sinks.

one of them—a large male well over twenty pounds. The others felt at least that big, for a large steelhead almost always begins to fight deliberately with a strong and sustained swimming impossible to control. Most of them also stay in the pool where they were hooked for at least ten to fifteen minutes, testing and measuring the strange pull on their jaw. Then most of them get the message and sooner or later change their strategies by leaving the pool in which they were first hooked. All of the ones I hooked did that. At the end of our trip, there had been nine large fish hooked among sixteen anglers. I had hooked six of them. By fishing this deeper and quicker water, I hooked and landed fewer steelhead than some of the other anglers, but given my weakness for big steelhead, it was a trade well made.

SIGHT-FISHING VERSUS BLIND-FISHING

Another element depends on whether you want to sight-fish or fish blind. Careful stalking and stealth remain a part of both approaches, and the need for cautious approaches and careful presentations never disappears completely. Sight-fishing requires that you use your eyes more than you use your rod. You will, therefore, make fewer casts and often wade less. It's also easier for most anglers to keep the faith when they spot their target. Sight-fishing usually requires less attention to distance casting because once you spot a fish, you can usually wade closer, if you're careful. Fishing blind requires longer casts and wider sweeps with your fly, and because you are

Sometimes the best presentations are made with a short line close to shore—especially in out-of-the-way places that are unpressured by other anglers. Remember where you are and what you are doing. You are fishing. You are not in a casting tournament, so never fall in love with a long line just for the sake of the cast.

never certain if you are fishing over a steelhead when blind fishing, you need to have more faith.

Sight-fishing is a great way to cover the water if the stream is relatively small, shallow, and clear—and if you know the stream well. Many years ago I was fishing the Sandy River in Oregon with Jim Teeny, one of the best hunter/anglers I have ever fished with. The Sandy, at that time at least, was Jim's home river, and he did know it well. We were walking and spotting fish in a side channel of the main river, and Jim spotted a pair of steelhead resting in shallow water about ten feet from shore. Jim is a master at sight-fishing, who doesn't always hide when approaching a resting fish. He often stayed in plain view, and if they did not move, he was confident he could catch them, sooner or later.

I watched as Jim approached two steelhead. Neither fish moved. Jim, only fifteen feet away from them and in full view, then proceeded to make some fifty casts with many fly changes. Finally, one of the steelhead moved slightly toward the fly. Jim looked back at me and said, "I have one interested. I'll get it." The same fish turned to the fly and took on the next cast. Jim led it downstream, released it, and then went back up and hooked the second fish after five or six more presentations. His casts were not delicate, but they were focused and well orchestrated. At the time, Jim used heavy split shot on his leader so his fly sank quickly. The lead weights dropped loudly upstream of the two steelhead, and he dead-drifted the fly to them. When they took, it was a good reminder that not all steelhead have read the same book.

It is hard not to want one of these, but to catch steelhead takes patience and effort. Savor the moment when you get one, and remember: If this was easy, no one would want to do it.

PACE

The pace of steelhead angling is unlike any other type of fishing. It is usually slower, and more deliberate, because there are usually fewer fish in the river than there would be if you were fishing for resident rainbows. Also, steelhead do not have to feed with the same sense of urgency as normal trout. There are times when you may encounter a school or pod of active steelhead grouped together in a single run of water, especially in the lower pools and runs close to the river's estuary, when they are fresh and newly arrived, but this is not something you can count on. On most days you never know where they are, unless you are sight-fishing.

When searching for fish, you normally have to cover a lot of water to catch a couple of steelhead each day.

You never know exactly when it will happen, or where, and you have to pace yourself or you'll wear out before the day is through. You may get one or two in the first pool you fish, and then nothing for the rest of the day. Or, you may make hundreds of casts all day only to finally take a fish just before darkness falls.

So, when you enter a pool, you always have to decide how much time you are going to spend there. You have to be patient and pace yourself, because nothing is worse than letting your guard down and letting the day's only opportunity slip away because you're too tired or too lazy to do it right. Perhaps the twenty-pound fish in the pool would have taken if you had just stayed focused.

Water conditions—clarity, depth, and temperature—also determine your pace. When the water is clear and I

A high rod position is a good trick for all down-and-across fishing, because it helps eliminate a belly in your line and thus will slow the drift of the fly.

Bigger water requires a slower effort because there is more of it to cover. This kind of water is a great place for a two-handed rod and sinking-tip line with a floating belly because you can sweep long sections of a run and still mend easily. This is one of my favorite runs on the Babine—a place called, appropriately enough, "Paradise."

have confidence that the fish can easily see the fly, I may move three to four feet between each cast. When the water is off-color, I will move only a couple of feet between each cast because I do not want to move so far that the fly will swing behind a fish that cannot see the swinging fly. Loud wading, including the sharp click of a wading staff, and your visible presence, including your favorite bright red shirt, all usually work against you. Be quiet, move with stealth, and blend into the surroundings as much as possible.

FOCUS

No matter your style of presentation, staying focused and confident throughout the day is critical for success and the single most important ability I have observed among expert anglers. It is not easy, but it is absolutely essential because you may have to make five hundred casts in any given day, which leaves no room for wasted effort, lost motion, wandering around, fumbling with your gear, or any kind of thinking about any subject other than the

conditions of the day and the specific demands of the particular water you are fishing—for no two pieces of water are exactly the same.

This means you must fish with studied and calculated manipulations that meet the particular demands of each and every run. This requires a sustained mental resolve and commitment to details that can be almost invisible to the untrained eye. You can take steelhead by just going through the motions, moving downstream in a series of automatic and habituated movements, always making the same basic kind of presentation to the same kind of water with the same length of line, angle of delivery, and mends done at the same time. But in this absent-minded manner, you will only take steelhead from those runs whose depth, current speeds, and direction favor that kind of presentation.

A steelheader's selective focus concentrates on finding evidence that suggests the presence of a steelhead as you simultaneously ignore everything else. When sight-fishing, this means that you are looking for a color, shape, or a movement that seems different from its immediate surroundings and out of place, rather than the complete outline of a fish. It may be only the curving edge of a fin, or a shadow, which is moving slightly, or a small sliver of pale red sandwiched in amongst all those shades of rocky brown, black, and the dark green of moss. If you are blind-fishing, it means that you must keep looking only for the things a steelhead needs—cover and relief from the fast currents.

This kind of selective focus comes from two places: from direct experience, either on your own or from side-by-side instruction, and from making contact with the hunter that resides in you. Many experienced anglers will not like what I am about to say, but it's the truth. Sometimes this selective focus transcends experience and can exist in first-time steelhead anglers who cannot cast and who know nothing about tackle and accessories. I have been fishing for steelhead for fifty years, and I have seen this phenomenon many times. These people are naturals. I have also seen the other side of the coin—anglers who have been fishing for years and who still don't get it. Hard words, but true.

Maintaining this selective focus requires desire and commitment. And you either have these or you do not. There are also a few other tips. Don't waste your time on the river performing casting maneuvers with motions better suited for fighting a bull, ballet dancing, cutting wheat, pole vaulting, or driving a Formula One racing car. Be stingy with your false casts if you fish a single-handed rod. Steelhead are not in the air. If you fish a two-handed rod, don't make three roll casts downriver to get your line straight in preparation for a good double Spey, or snap T cast, if you can do it with one cast. If you simply cannot, then take the time to get it right even if it takes five roll casts. Steelhead can't see your casting, but they certainly can see your drifting fly.

Take a break when you get tired, especially if wading has been tough and you've been throwing a long line. Pause now and then to get reorganized: it saves time in the long run and helps defeat fatigue, the great enemy of a focused angler. You have a lot of things to think about, and cutting wheat and fighting bulls with tired arms should not be among them. Be sure to choose your tackle and accessories carefully. Too many anglers carry more gear than they need, and some are so bogged down with stuff they waste effort playing with it or hauling it from pool to pool. Take only what you really need, and travel as light as you can given the circumstances. This saves time and energy and allows you to concentrate and focus on where to cast and on making a good presentation.

The day begins at place called Silver Hilton on the Babine River in northern British Columbia. The fishing here, like steelhead angling everywhere, can break your heart, or it can raise you to a level nothing else can touch. After 30 years it is home in a way, and even when it is tough going, it is still great fishing. The big ones are here.

A boat—whether it is a jet sled, raft, pontoon, or drift boat—can help you cover the water and find solitude, even on pressured rivers. Many lodges shuttle their clients to the best fishing spots in jet sleds (above).

FISHING WITHIN YOUR ABILITIES

Building the skills necessary for effective presentations is a never-ending process, and there will always be new things to learn and accomplish. It helps if you begin with tackle you can handle and straightforward, fundamental presentations, which always remain the foundation you must revisit when your casts and presentations do not go as planned. So get it right, keep it simple at first, and learn the essentials. Even advanced anglers usually have to make adjustments if and when they make a significant change in their gear, such as when crossing over from single- to two-handed rods.

Learn to cast a short line, and master mending and the elements of maintaining proper fly speed before you attempt distance casting and mending and manipulating a long line. Be frugal with your maneuvers. This is not the time for advanced casts and complicated presentations such as positive and negative curve casts, stack mending, and distance casting. Getting ahead of yourself in the beginning can create bad habits that can take years to overcome. Bad habits also create fatigue and frustration, which lead to loss of focus and poor time management. If you are fishing your fly in good water, there will generally be just as many fish within reach of a straightforward basic presentation on your side of the river as there are on the opposite shore.

Casting farther than you can fish is an almost universal temptation for all of us. Though it may be fun, over a long day it doesn't produce and can become a curse.

If conditions allow, it is usually best to present your down-and-across wet fly straight across-stream, or even upstream. This maximizes the amount of water you cover on each swing.

When I am tempted to throw a longer line than I really need, I often remind myself that the cast doesn't hook the fish. The presentation does. So don't worry too much about how far you are casting. Worry about where you are fishing and how you are wading. Worry about making your presentations effective. Worry about the speed and depth of your wet fly. Watch your dry fly, make it look alive, and keep it where it belongs—waking in the right place. Choose your pools carefully and don't waste time trying to fish lies and complicated currents that demand mending and line handling skills you have yet to master.

This can be tough because we all want to improve, and it's true that sometimes you have to push yourself and spend some time failing so that you may later succeed. I understand that. There is a certain pool on a

A prime Kispiox female steelhead took a saltwater smelt pattern on a slow-sinking tip—and then jumped eight times and peeled off a lot of line and backing. Guide David Nash told me where she would be, and when we had her, he smiled, took the photo, and said it was time for lunch. DAVID NASH

Fly lines with interchangeable tips of different densities should be in every angler's arsenal for the presentation options they provide in fishing in all types of water. In this case I am close to landing a fish taken from deep water using my favorite tip: a number eight, very fast sinking, 15-footer. JAY NICHOLS

favored stretch of the Babine fished by Silver Hilton Steelhead Lodge that has a reputation for holding big fish. It is a great run, on a great river, fished by a truly great fishing lodge, and at times there can be so many steelhead in the run that it borders on the unbelievable. In past years the lodge sometimes had late-season anglers who used conventional tackle, and I witnessed days when they took forty or more steelhead from that one run, in between breaks to warm up by the fire.

The problem was that it took a 90-foot cast just to lick the outside edges of the holding water. A 100-foot cast was even better, and I could reach it with a 10-foot single-handed rod combined with a 30-foot shooting head attached to monofilament backing. But when it came time to change my fishing style and presenta-

tion and begin fishing with a two-handed rod, I couldn't make the shot. It nearly killed me to see my presentation fail by falling well short of where it needed to be. I struggled for five years before I could make the necessary distance, and at times I considered the possibility that perhaps I should have given golf a bigger chance. Wisdom prevailed and I stayed with it, giving the pool the best I had early in the day when fatigue and loss of focus were not on the table. In the sixth season with the two-handed rod, in mid-September, I saw a beautiful fish roll in that distant seam of dark water. I waded into position, collected myself, and watched as the line sailed to 95 feet or so. When it stopped, and then started again with the strong pull of a wild steelhead, it all came back to me. Golf is OK, but I was where I wanted to be.

LANDING, REVIVING, AND RELEASING FISH

Landing a steelhead begins well before it ever reaches the shore, and your strategy for beaching your catch actually begins at that point when the fish no longer has the strength to resist your efforts. When you can begin to move the steelhead, despite its best efforts to resist, you should start increasing the pressure with your rod whenever possible and never allow it to rest. How you increase the pressure depends on simple geometry and on the distance between you and your fish. If the fish is forty feet away or more, it does little good to move your rod from one side to another as you increase your pull, because at longer distances the angle of your pull on your leader and fly does not change. You can make minor changes at forty to fifty feet by mending the floating section of your line on the water to the desired position and using water tension to exert some pull from a new direction, but this produces only a temporary and subtle change of direction.

On the other hand, if the fish is only twenty feet away, or less, the angle of your pull does change, especially with a longer two-handed rod. This pulling angle is most obvious when you have the fish within a dozen feet or so. In this case you are able to move the rod completely behind the fish and thus you can instantly change, sustain, and completely reverse the direction of your pull.

As soon as possible try to get behind the fish and stay there, always pulling in the opposite direction it is swimming. This tires them out rapidly and is the most effective position for beaching them because it gives you the greatest pressure. It usually does little or no good to pull them in the direction they are swimming unless they are entirely exhausted, and then you can lead them around as if they were on a leash. So, if they swim to the right, get behind them and pull to the left. When they go to their left, pull them back to their right. One trick is to suddenly change your direction of pull, and once they have yielded and you get them going in the direction you want, change the direction of your pull and move your rod to the other side. This confuses the fish, which causes it to expend more energy and tire sooner.

It's a little like boxing. Never keep attacking from the same direction, because your opponent will soon learn to adjust to that kind of predictable maneuver. Stay unpredictable, and they will never know what you will do next. It requires a lot more energy to struggle against an opponent whose strategy cannot be predicted.

No matter what presentation they take, a steelhead should be handled with care. Treat it properly and support it with two caring hands. This minimizes physical stress and allows the angler to both get a photo and quickly give the exhausted fish a drink of water. Never leave a steelhead out of the water for more than fifteen to twenty seconds or so.
JAY NICHOLS

ETIQUETTE

t isn't often that we have a steelhead pool all to ourselves. Sharing the water with a partner or other anglers you may not know is the norm and means that each of us should be aware of stream etiquette and good manners. When two or more anglers are sharing a pool, they line up behind one another as they fish down the run. The lead angler in first position should keep moving downstream at a reasonable pace. The last angler in line can move as slowly as she wants or stop altogether and make repeated casts to the same place. Last position is not always the worst, and if you are last in line it can pay dividends to hang back and really slow down to give the fish time to recover from all the potentially bad presentations pounding the water before you.

The angler who arrives first at a pool obviously has first choice of where to begin and can set his pace downriver. If you arrive second, you should always fish behind the angler who was there first.

As the second angler, it is considered good manners to leave at least twice the distance of your cast between you and the other angler so your fly doesn't swing into the first angler's position. Once you have chosen your position behind the first angler, the pool no longer belongs exclusively to him. From this point forward, the first angler is responsible for moving downstream as he fishes, the pace varying depending on water conditions. If the water is dirty, the pace is obviously slower than it would be if the river was clear.

Most anglers normally take two to three steps down after each cast. But since some anglers have longer legs and longer strides than others, a better way to describe the pace would be to say that an angler should move around three feet between casts. This length covers any fish resting in the run yet provides both anglers with chances to fish the bucket. The first angler fishing downstream obviously gets the bucket first, and good

manners allow a certain slowing down at this point, but not stopping and making cast after cast before moving on past the most productive part of the run. And conversely, you, as the second angler, should not crowd or push too soon. Give him a little extra time. Once past the bucket, the first angler should go back to the original pace and move three to four feet between each cast. When finished fishing through the pool, he then goes back up to the top of the run and fishes behind you or the other anglers that may have entered the lineup.

Additional anglers coming into the pool should never get in front of any of the anglers fishing their way downstream, regardless of the distance between them. Sometimes the pace and mood of the lineup is slow and easy, and extra space may grow between the individual anglers in the lineup. Squeezing in between anglers who were in the water before you arrived is a major sin. If everyone continues to move downstream at a pace appropriate for the water conditions, everyone will get to fish the entire run. No one wants to share a pool with an angler who never moves, or one who pushes too hard. Each lineup has its own psychology and movement. Take a second to look at what is going on and try to find a way to fit in.

Should someone hook a fish, the anglers behind that person should slow down and give her sufficient time to play and land the fish. Once the fish is landed, the lucky angler should again resume the pace, even if she is in the most pro-ductive part of the run. Hogging the bucket is also considered bad manners. Well-mannered anglers, after taking a fish or two, always offer to yield their spot to a second angler either by moving downstream for several yards or simply trading places, especially if they are companions.

Trading places is easier when there are only two or three anglers fishing the run and they are buddies. It becomes a much tougher decision to make if there are a lot of anglers lined up on the pool. It takes a very good person to pull out of a slot after taking a fish or two and then offer that space to a stranger, but I have seen it, and it is one of the best gestures possible for those who know and love a steelhead river. If you are in the bucket and hook a fish or two, and you do not know the other anglers in the lineup, I'd say good manners require that you speed things up a little and move farther than you ordinarily would between casts.

Well-mannered anglers, especially experienced ones, should appreciate the success of others, and if the angler in front of you hooks a fish and could use some help, give it. The other anglers in back of you should also honor your willingness to help and not see this as an opportunity to take your spot. Instead, at that point in the game, the lineup should freeze in place and simply keep fishing from the same casting position until the fish has been landed. Once the fish is landed, everyone can get back to the standard downstream pace.

Someone once said: "I like to catch a lot of steelhead because I just like to look at them." Catching a lot of steelhead can happen, and when it does, it is almost always due to an effective presentation. That's the name of the steelhead game.

Sometimes the guides get to fish. In this case Jeremy Dufton releases a nice hen taken on one of his perfect presentations. A good guide is worth his or her weight in gold. JAY NICHOLS

Once exhausted, the fish will simply give up and roll over on its side. However, steelhead are among the strongest of all fish and even when defeated, they almost always have a few lunges left in them. Never force them to quit in very shallow water, only a few inches in depth, for they can injure or kill themselves by hitting their head on a rock. Remember that the fish thinks it is about to die and will do all it can to live. Nothing reveals the character of a callous angler more than dragging a wild and valiant fish into an atmosphere in which it cannot breathe, and then watching as the helpless fish pounds against the shore.

The longer two-handed rods make landing a steelhead more difficult, especially if you are wading deep or if you are standing next to a vertical cliff or hillside. Because the longer length of these rods keeps a fish so far away from you, it is impossible to hold the rod high with one arm and then simultaneously grab the tired fish with the other hand. It is possible to let the rod slip through your hands until you are gripping it by its midsection, which in effect shortens the rod, and you may be able to then grab the fish as you keep the tip vertical. Be careful though. This is a good way to break a good rod.

Given the length of two-handed rods, it is always best if you can wade to the shore and then walk backward, as you pull the subdued fish into water around two feet deep. Then you may put the rod down and walk up to your fish. If it is truly exhausted, you have time to approach and grab it by the tail or just grasp the leader.

If you cannot move and must land your fish as you stand steady in the water, you can try the following maneuver. Pinch the line against the grip of your rod with your dominant casting hand, and bring the fish as close as possible by raising your rod tip to vertical. Hold it there. This will keep an exhausted fish as close as possible and hopefully under control. Then, as you keep the line pinched against the grip of your rod with one hand, strip about fifteen feet of line off your reel with the other.

Once you have the line stripped from the reel, release the pinched line from your rod grip and sweep your rod back over your head and down behind you to bring the stripped line close to your shoulder, where you can reach it and grab it. Now it really gets tricky. Once you have the line in your hand, tuck your rod under one of your arms, and hand-line in the fish, hand over hand, until you can tail it or grab the leader.

You can achieve the same slack-line release by taking all the drag tension off your reel and moving the rod tip well behind you and down toward the surface. This backward and downward sweep of the rod allows extra line to "play off" the reel and descend toward your arm or shoulder where you can grab it for the hand-line retrieval of your fish.

Once the fish is in your hand or the net, grasp it by the tail and hold it upright with one hand as you remove the fly with your other. Your barbless hooks will be easy to remove, which is one reason why you should use them. And a point here: Never worry about a fish throwing a barbless hook. They cannot throw a fly. Hooks only pull free.

If the fish is weak, gently hold one hand under its belly for support. As it begins to regain strength, keep it pointed into a gentle current deep enough to pass over its back. This depth guarantees sufficient current passing through its gills. Do this until you feel the steelhead's strength returning. Never let a steelhead go until it is swimming energetically in your hand. You owe it to yourself and your catch to honor this great and important moment, and to watch your fish regain its strength and composure.

There are pros and cons to either using a net or tailing the fish. On the one hand, a net shortens the struggle at a critical time, thus preventing a physical collapse from which the fish may not revive. Inappropriately light leaders are the usual problem because they do not allow you to really muscle a steelhead. When we say we are "playing" a fish, we should remember that, although it is enjoyable from the angler's point of view, the steelhead is fighting for its life. Light tackle only prolongs the struggle and may kill a fish. On the other hand, landing a steelhead in a net with hard nylon mesh removes the protective slime on a steelhead's skin. This invites disease, for the slime is a natural defense against bacteria and infection. Use nets with a rubber mesh, which do not scrape off a fish's protective coating.

I no longer weigh my steelhead unless the fish looks as if it will go twenty pounds or more; I prefer an educated estimate based on its weight and length. Formulas vary, but most are derived by length times girth squared, divided by a figure called a multiplier, which can range from 350 to 600 or more. The resulting number gives a close estimate of the weight of a steelhead, but it is not exact because much is determined by the size of their head and tail. Two steelhead may have the same length and girth measurements, but one fish may be thicker near the tail and have a larger head. If you do weigh your fish, make sure it is weighed in the net. This does not harm a steelhead because the fish is supported by the net. Hanging a fish by its tail or mouth to weigh it can cause possible tissue and muscle damage and should be avoided.

Should your fish begin to bleed excessively, stay with it and watch it carefully. If the bleeding does not stop, release it anyway. It may perish moments, hours, or days later—you never know. The manner in which you treat a subdued and helpless steelhead says more about your character and wisdom than any cast you are capable of making or equipment you own.

8

The downstream wet-fly swing covers more potential resting water than any other method because each presentation sweeps across large expanses of current. Basically you are letting the current swing your fly through the water, close enough for a resting steelhead to see it, and at a speed that makes the fly look alive and easy for the fish to intercept.

The Downstream Swing

Someone once said that when it came to trout and salmon, the downstream wet fly was the best hope for beginner and expert alike. The implication of that statement was not lost on this beginner, and over the seasons my own experiences eventually confirmed this. At times an upstream dead-drifted wet fly or nymph, as well as a dry fly fished the same way, seems almost irresistible to fish, especially summer steelhead. But if money was on the table and numbers were the name of the game, I'd still go with the fly fished slowly and carefully on a down-and-across presentation, no matter the conditions—unless there were several hundred contestants on the same stretch of water. In that case, I'd switch to a floating line, long leader, and a pair of small flies presented upstream, dead-drifted back to me, as I kept my eyes glued on the strike indicator.

The downstream wet fly presentation works so well because, on each and every pass, the fly swims through multiple current seams and more potential resting lies than with any other method. As deadly as the upstream dead-drifted fly can be, it still only drifts down one seam or current line at a time. This is fine if you can see the fish or know exactly what seam they are in, but for searching a river, under most conditions, nothing cuts to the chase like a swinging pattern. Day in and day out, especially if you are after numbers, get the fly down, and keep it there for as long as you can, fish it slowly, and let it come around as far as it can.

I also find fishing downstream more enjoyable than fishing upstream. You fish and wade by moving with the river and not against it. As you wade, you can almost lean back into the current's push against your legs and waist. The current also moves excess line safely out of the way and under control. And then there's this: The pull is not subtle or soft. It reaches you with speed and strength.

Anglers may bring their own modifications and style to this presentation, and most do. Some prefer a slight upstream pitch; others a cross-stream delivery. Still others prefer a downstream angle of one sort or another. Some

Use the wet-fly swing with all kinds of flies, leaders, and leaders, and lines, and in all water types, speeds, and depths. I carry several densities of interchangeable tips, from floating to very fast sinking, which I attach to a floating belly and running line with a loop-to-loop connection. This presentation and line system allows me to fish any place I can cast to. LANI WALLER

Catching a fish like this is always partly luck, but on trophy rivers, you can help stack the deck in your favor by keeping your fly near the bottom with a wet-fly swing and a fast-sinking tip. You should mend a lot to slow the fly down. Big bucks can get lazy and you want to make it easy for them. LANI WALLER

anglers like to mend a lot; others do not. Some depend entirely on the density of their line to reach different depths. Others use slack-line techniques to sink their fly.

My downstream presentations fall under two categories: the simple swing and the compound swing. Other styles and variations of this presentation, including mending, line handling, and slack-line techniques, are also legitimate. Most anglers have their own definition of what is "best." I did ask a well-known steelhead guide at dinner one night just what all the great anglers he had guided had in common. Did they all fish in the same way? Were they all super casters, line handlers, or strong waders? Billy Labonte paused for a moment and said

that in his experience all the great anglers had one thing in common: They all lost a lot of flies.

When fishing wet flies, you try to present the fly at the right speed and depth. The pattern should swing laterally across the currents at a speed that looks believable to the fish. Your fly is imitating life, and it must move realistically. Perhaps a long, streamlined fly that looks like a small fish or leech might be accepted by the fish on a faster swing than a pattern that looks like an insect. I do know that I have had more luck with a waking dry fly when I swing it more slowly than I would a wet fly (on the same water) and perhaps acceptable fly speed, in part, depends upon what the fish thinks the fly is.

The fly also needs to be close enough to the fish so that it can easily see and take your fly. Since most of the fish in the freestone rivers I fish are usually near the bottom, that's usually where I want my sunken fly, especially when the water is quick and over four or five feet deep.

Long casts on a wet-fly swing cover a lot of water. When the currents are deep and quick, fish a weighted fly so that the fly will sink as soon as possible. The longer your fly fishes during the swing, the more fish you will hook.

THE SIMPLE SWING

For this presentation, you cast toward the middle of the river, at an angle of your choosing, and the currents push your line, leader, and fly around in an arc. Eventually the fly comes to a stop downstream of your position, at which point you make another cast. You mend to control your fly speed and let line density, fly weight, and leader length determine the depth at which you fish the fly.

The faster the currents, the more downstream you should aim your cast, and the more you will have to mend to keep the fly swimming at the right speed. I like to err on the slow side. Steelhead will take a fly that is holding steadily, but usually only the most aggressive individuals will take a fly moving quickly across the currents. The goal of mending is to move the line without tugging or pulling the fly out of position. A perfect mend may be one that travels all the way down the line

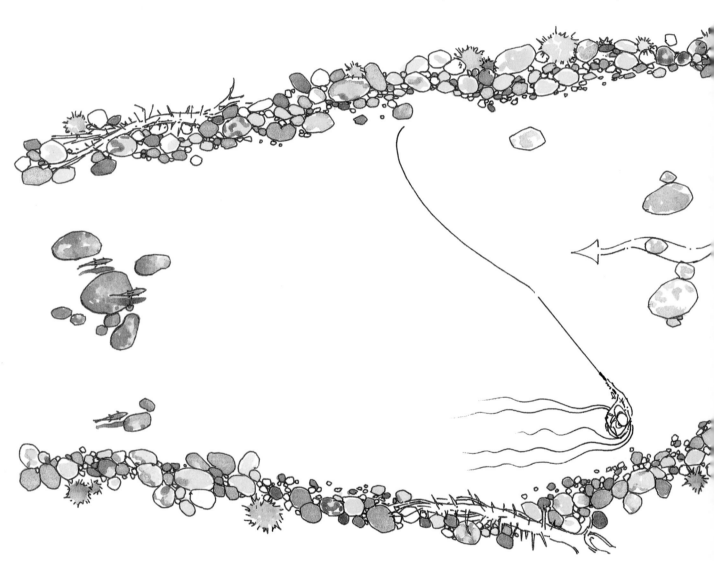

Choose your angle of delivery for the simple wet-fly swing based on water speed and current configuration. If the water currents are even and moving in a straight direction, line control will be easy and you may aim a little upstream, straight across, or slightly downstream, as in this illustration.

On the other hand, if the water is fast and has multiple currents it will be easier to mend and manage your swinging line and fly if you aim your presentation more downstream. I always push myself and try to deliver the cast as far upstream as I can manage. This kind of angle covers the most water in a single cast. That adds up to a lot of extra water covered during a long day on the water.

and the leader, stopping just before the hook eye. Not easy to do once the tip of the line has sunk, and not worth the effort. If your mend travels to within four to six feet of your fly without moving the fly itself, you have done a good job. Skilled anglers can present their flies at almost any angle because they know how to mend, add slack to the drift, and manage their line in a way that allows them to deal with almost any current speed.

To fish as much water as possible on each swing, I usually cast straight across or slightly downstream from my position. In deeper and faster water, I sometimes aim my cast upstream, giving it more time to sink. Depending on the distance of the cast, water speed, and current complexities, I usually mend line in a series of movements. I make the first mend, sometimes called a back mend, just after the line has dropped to the water. At this point, it doesn't matter if I suddenly move the fly

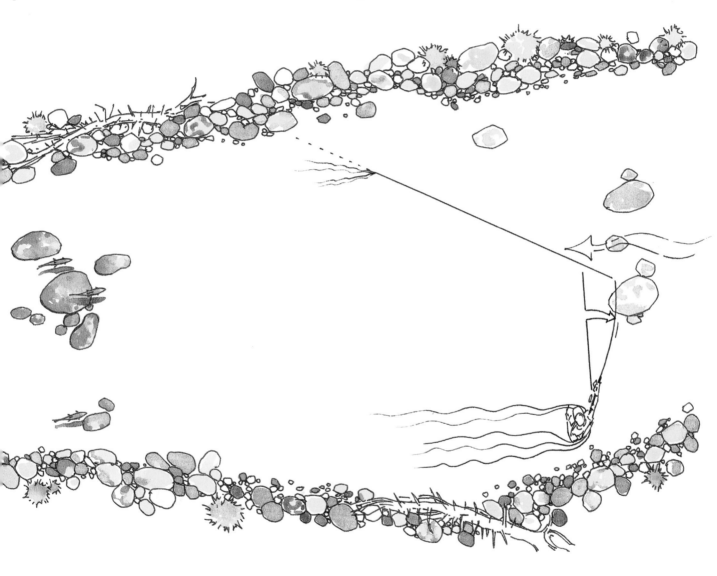

Once your line, leader, and fly have penetrated the surface, pull back and lift with your rod in an upstream direction. This gets your line straight almost from the beginning. A straight line telegraphs a strike better, it is easier to mend, and it helps reduce the amount of belly in the line as it begins to swing and the currents push against it.

On long casts, pull and lift far enough so that almost all of the line including the tip is straight. On short casts I will pull everything straight, including the leader. Sometimes I even drag my fly upstream a bit.

An upstream lift and sweep of the line is easy and is a big help to casters who do not get the line straight while it is in the air and for those who cannot make an upstream reach mend with the rod tip before the line hits the water.

because it is still so far from its target that the motion will not alarm the fish. I make this mend by lifting the rod and pulling the line back upstream until it is as straight as I can get it. On shorter casts of twenty to thirty feet, this upstream sweep and lift of the rod will actually bring the entire line leader and fly to the surface, where you can see that it is straight.

Once the line and leader are fairly straight, a bad mend can jerk a fly five or six feet at exactly the wrong time. So, when I mend after my first back mend, I usually keep the rod as low as possible by pointing the rod tip at the line on the water's surface and then flip the line with a low horizontal movement, either behind the sunken portion of line to slow the fly down in faster water or ahead of the line to speed the fly up in slower water. I often allow some excess line to slide through the guides as I make these mends to minimize the possibility of moving the fly.

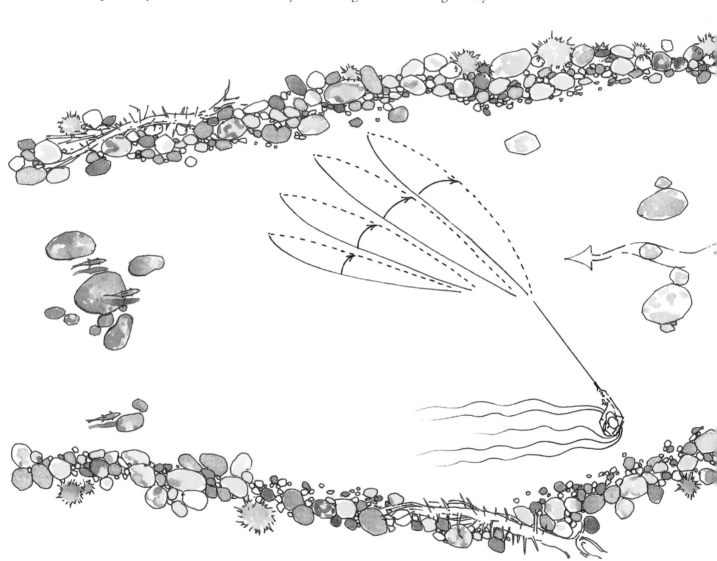

If and when your line starts to belly too much in a downstream curve, lift the rod carefully back upstream and reposition the line. How you reposition and move the line depends on how big the belly in your line is and how fast the current is pushing against it. The larger the belly in the line and the faster the water is pushing against it, the more line you have to move.

A high rod position, combined with a long upstream sweep of the rod tip, moves the most line. If the downstream belly in your line is small, you don't have to move a lot of line, and you can mend with a low rod position and a quick flip of the line back upstream.

After I mend my line back upstream, especially in faster currents, I almost always keep my rod behind the drifting line, following the swinging fly rather than leading it. By holding the rod back upstream and behind the line after you mend, you help slow down the swing. This does not completely eliminate a downstream belly on a long cast, but it helps minimize it.

The down-and-across swinging presentation in faster water demands many careful mends, each of which concludes with the rod held back upstream of the drifting line until it is time to mend again. In faster water, I never swing my rod tip back downstream after the mend, or even point my rod at the fly, because I do not want to form a belly in the line.

As the line swings around to your side of the river, this upstream reach with the rod really comes into play. Once your line has swung within fifteen feet or so from your side of the run, you can actually stop the lateral

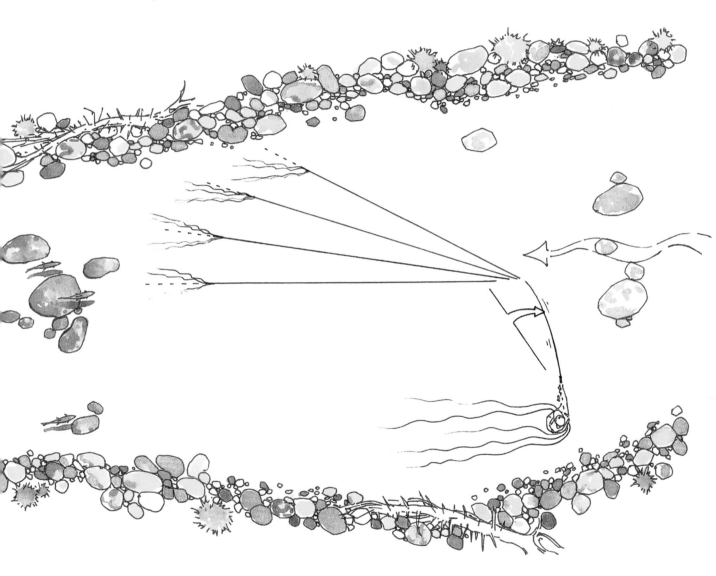

Rod position after you mend depends on current speed. If currents are fast and are pushing hard against my line, I move the rod back behind the drifting fly and I follow it after each mend, trying to slow the swing down. I call this "holding the mend." Holding your mend in fast water helps to minimize the belly in your line.

If the currents are slow, holding your mend may not be necessary. After each mend, you can keep your rod tip pointed toward the fly. If the currents are very slow, you can lead your swinging fly by moving your rod ahead of it, pulling on the line to speed up the swing.

swing of your fly and hang or suspend your fly in front of the steelheads' noses as you slowly draw it toward your side of the river. In the hands of an accomplished mender, a 14-foot rod can stop the swing of a fly when it is still twenty feet from shore.

Whatever the current speed, you must stay in control. You are always steering your drift by either holding your fly back to slow it down as it moves through faster water or leading (even pulling) your fly through slower current. In almost all cases, the swinging line should be kept fairly straight when it comes into the target area. A single broad curve in the line is acceptable, but serpentine coils will usually prevent you from feeling the take and may give the fish time to reject the fly.

The simple swing can be used with lines ranging from full floating to full sinking. My own favorites are lines in which the last fifteen feet sink. A sinking-tip line of this sort allows you to mend most, if not all, of the

As the fly swings closer to shore, it usually slows down because the currents are normally a little slower near the bank and because you are almost directly upstream of your fly. You have little or no belly in your line at this point, and you can point your rod tip toward the fly. I usually elevate my rod tip at this point to give myself some slack in case a fish takes on what I call "the hang down." My guess is that the extra slack gives a fish some time to turn and drive the hook in by its motion. If the water right next to shore looks good and I am out toward the center of the run, I will lead my fly toward shore by sweeping my rod around and pointing it toward the bank.

Fly speed is a critical element of the wet-fly swing. It is usually not possible to swing a fly too slowly for steelhead, and they will even take one that is just hanging in the current. It is possible to swing a fly so fast that it simply does not look real. I believe that you can fish long streamer flies faster than those that look like insects or salmon eggs, because streamers look like something that can swim.

floating line on the surface, and the sinking portion still holds the fly and leader in position as you lift your rod and mend. If you do have to reposition the entire line, including the tip, you can do so much more easily than you could if the entire line was submerged.

Once the fly comes around and is hanging directly below you, you can extend your arc by mending toward the shore. This is where wading becomes a part of your wet-fly strategies. I usually prefer to wade in approximately three to four feet of water, which is deep enough to hold a resting fish that may be directly below me. If the water looks good right next to my shore, I mend toward the shoreline so that my fly continues to swing and is almost touching the shore at the end of my presentation.

All kinds of lines can be used for the wet-fly swing including full floaters, full sinkers, shooting tapers, and sinking-tip lines with floating bellies. Floating lines are the easiest to handle because you can see your line position. Full-sinking lines are the most difficult because the line is under water and is harder to mend and reposition. Floating lines with interchangeable density tips are the best all-around lines to use.

Since most of the fish in the freestone rivers I fish are usually near the bottom, that's where I want my sunken fly, especially when the water is quick and over four or five feet deep. LANI WALLER

THE COMPOUND SWING

The compound swing is a term I use to describe a down-and-across swinging arc in which the fly descends toward the bottom as it swings around in the current, and mends are introduced not only to control fly speed (as in the simple swing), but also to control depth. In softer and shallower currents, the density of the line may be sufficient to sink the fly, but in deep and heavy water I like to help by taking tension off the line, leader, and fly before it starts to swing. I do not enjoy fishing tips heavier than 225 grains, and with slack-line techniques I can still effectively fish deeper runs. I add slack line by several methods, either singly or in combination, depending upon the speed and complexity of the currents, the depth of the water, and the length of line I am casting.

Since it takes time for the fly to descend to depths of five to seven feet, I lead the target and cast well to one

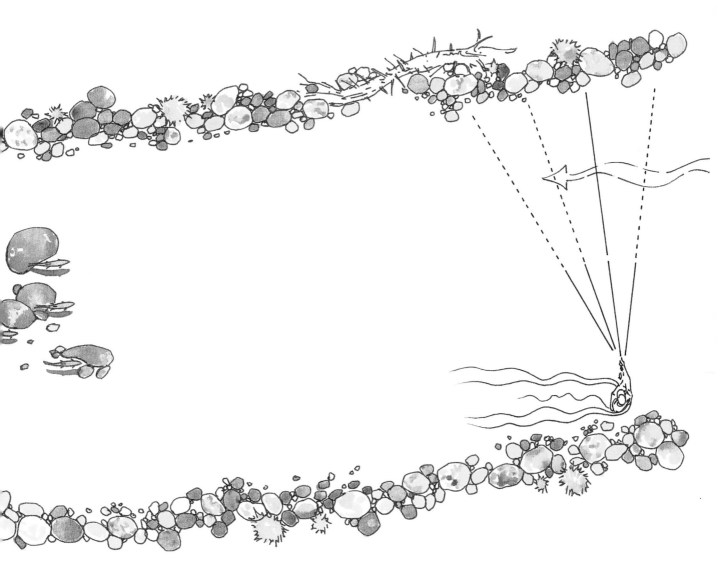

The angle for the compound swing is like that of the simple swing. You can deliver the initial cast slightly downstream, straight across, or upstream. The angle depends on water speed and depth, and your ability to control your line as it moves through the water in an arc. Most of the time I prefer an upstream angle because it gives the fly additional time to sink and because it increases the amount of water my fly will cover in its swinging arc. The deeper my target is and the faster the water is moving, the more I want to lead it.

side and well upstream of the fish's suspected lie. This usually, but not always, means a cross or slightly downstream angle. Sometimes I cast at an upstream angle to give the line even more time to sink.

Once the line settles on the surface and begins to move downstream, I usually make an initial large mend back upstream and gently pull and lift the line straight by raising my rod, just as with the simple swing. Once the line is straight, I relieve tension on the line by dropping the rod tip quickly toward the surface, and I then begin to add slack into the drift as it goes downstream. Adding slack takes more tension off the line and fly and allows your drifting pattern to sink more quickly than it would if the line was tight and straight.

You can add slack into the drift in several ways. You can strip excess line from the reel and shake the mid and tip section of the rod up and down or back and forth to allow the currents to pull the slack line through the

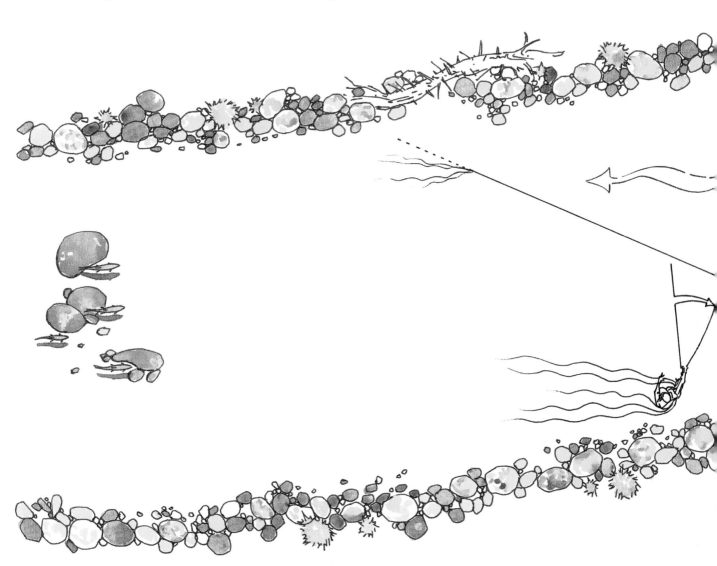

Once the fly and line have penetrated the surface, I lift my rod toward vertical and simultaneously pull it back upstream, straightening my line and leader before the swing begins. Advanced casters achieve the same thing with an aerial reach mend, and I use this maneuver on shorter casts of fifteen to fifty feet. It is harder to make a reach mend on longer casts of sixty to ninety feet. I often make the aerial mend, and once the line has settled, I finish the job of getting everything straight with the upstream lift and pull. The goal is always to set up a good drift by straightening the line as soon as possible so that you have no downstream belly.

guides. You can also take tension off the line by stack mending. First, retain the desired length of excess line in your line hand. Once the line has settled on the water, and you have it straight, quickly raise your rod tip to a vertical position, allowing the excess to slide through the guides, without pulling on the line that is in the water. Then, make a quick series of small roll casts that pile or dump themselves on top of the line just at that point where it begins to sink. This removes a lot of tension from the drifting line and allows the tip of the sinking line to descend quickly. You can make these roll casts with the length of line you had originally saved for the maneuver, or you may add more line by stripping additional line from the reel, then shaking it out of the lifting rod and adding that extra line to the series of small roll casts.

One of my favorite methods to relieve tension from the drifting line is by flipping line downstream just after

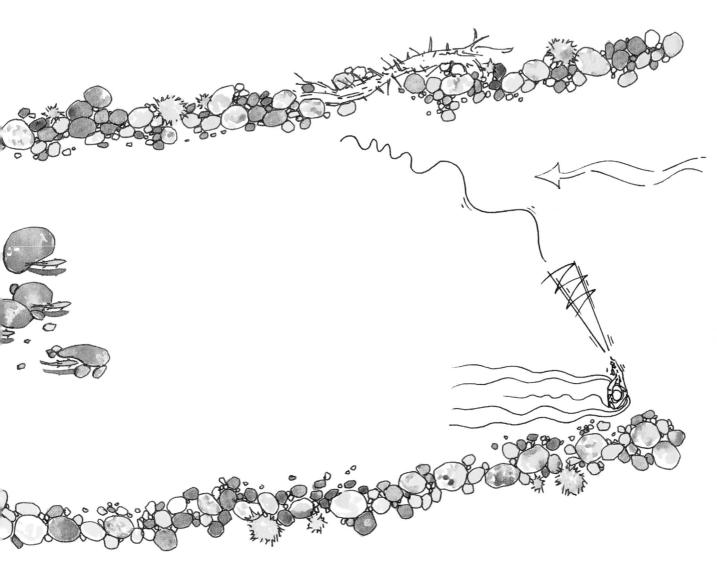

Once the drift is set up and the line is straight, I add slack in one of several ways. This illustration shows how to use the rod tip to shake extra line through the guides. Adding slack is an important part of a swinging presentation, especially in fast and deep water, because it allows the fly to sink farther and faster than it would on a straight line. Don't worry about all the slack line. If your timing is right, the fly will descend, and as it swings around, the currents will draw the line straight and tight just as it enters the target zone.

I have lifted and pulled the line straight. As soon as the line is straight, I quickly move the rod tip sharply downstream, as if in a downstream mend, which produces a sharp, pointed inside curve in the floating section of my line that travels parallel to the sinking part of my line. The amount of line I flip downstream depends on how much I want the tip, leader, and fly to sink. In some cases the downstream flip may be only two feet. In other cases, I may flip ten to fifteen feet of line downstream if I want to give the line more time to sink as deeply as possible as it travels downstream. I keep my eye on the downstream flip, and when everything comes tight, all the floating line will straighten out and be in a perfect configuration for the beginning of the fly's swing.

The particular technique I use depends on the distance of the cast. For the longest casts, I prefer to add line by simultaneously shaking line through the guides and mending. It is very difficult to make stack mends on

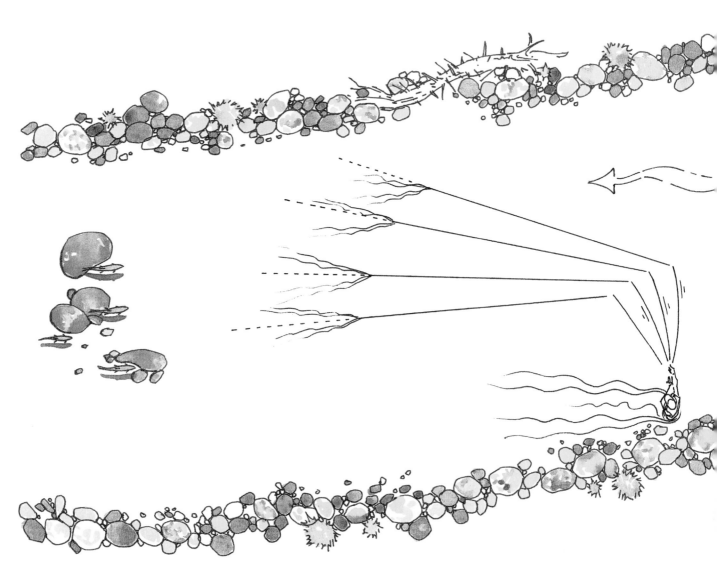

Remember that the word "mending" means fixing something. In this case, fixing problems with your fly line. The biggest problem we have as steelheaders when we fish a fly down and across is a belly in our line that makes the fly swim too fast. You can avoid this kind of problem by not leading your fly with your rod, but by following the fly with your rod. Only lead your fly when the currents are slow. The rest of the time, hold your rod back upstream to slow the drift down. This illustration shows the correct rod position as the line swings around.

casts over 70 feet because the thinner running lines on the types of Spey lines I prefer do not transmit the necessary energy to send a small loop of line rolling some 50 or 60 feet toward the point where the line is sinking. I usually stack mend on casts of 30 to 60 feet. For short casts of 20 to 30 feet, you can use any of the above mentioned techniques.

Once I have added sufficient slack and the fly is deep enough and has traveled far enough to reach the suspected lie of the fish, and when the line is tight and fairly straight, I pinch the line to halt the downstream drift and start the lateral swing toward the resting steelhead. My favorite way of pinching the line is to hold it against the grip of the rod with my pointer finger, and I keep it there as the swing is underway. Once the line begins to swim into slower water, I know I may want to retrieve the line somewhat to help keep the fly moving at the right speed. In anticipation of that, I then move

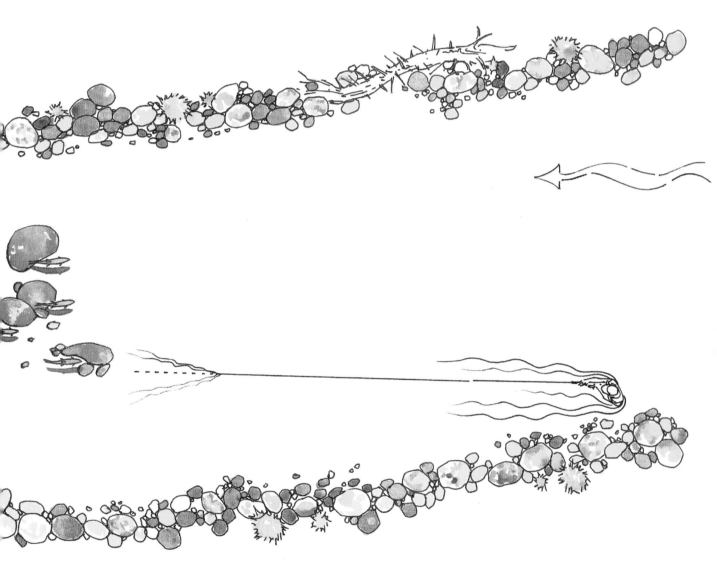

Once the fly swings below you, point the rod at the fly. I raise the rod, in case I get a take. I have not had good luck setting the hook with my rod tip pointed down toward the water and right at the fish. I also let the fly hang below me for a few seconds because there may be a steelhead resting close to shore, or a fish may have followed my fly around on its swing. After the fly has hung in the water for a few seconds, I retrieve it slowly. This telegraphs a soft take almost immediately, and it draws the casting belly close to the tip in anticipation of my next cast.

my other hand into position behind my rod-gripping hand and hold the line. This second hand is also helpful if I get a take during the slow part on the swing or on the hang down, as I will not only raise my rod for my strike, but I also simultaneously strip-set with my left hand by relaxing the pinch of my right hand against the cork grip and stripping in line with my left.

It takes some time before you can look at a piece of water and know exactly where to position your cast, how much slack to add, and when to pinch the line and begin the swing. If you stop the downstream travel of your slack line too quickly, it might swing around before the fish can see your fly. If you stop the line too late, the fly will swing behind the fish. If you get it wrong, you can either just let the fly come around all the way and then pick it up and make the necessary adjustments on the next cast, or, if you have time, pick up the line and recast before the fish has a chance to see the fly. A fly that is suddenly ripped away at the wrong time can alarm a spooky fish.

To stay in control of the swinging fly in fast water, I hold my rod upstream after making an upstream mend to help slow down the swing. This may not eliminate a downstream belly in your line on a long cast, but it will decrease it. Just as with the simple swing, there will come a time in your drift when you can hold your rod out toward the center of the river, and well upstream of your sunken fly, and actually make your fly stop and hang in front of any target that is fifteen feet or so from your shoreline. This is a great way to set up that last part of your drift—the part I call the hang-down—and finish your swinging presentation with a slow teasing drift all the way into shore.

When the fly has passed through the suspected lie of a deep holding fish, or the deepest part of the run I am searching, and begins to move toward shore where the water is slower and shallower, I often increase the tension on the fly by lifting the rod to avoid snagging on the bottom. If the line is in the correct position, and still slightly upstream of the leader and swinging fly, this lift

Always carry several spare sinking tips of the fastest densities because they are the ones most likely to wrap around a boulder during the sideways swing of a deep running fly. Even the best lines break when you try to pull them free. I carry my spares in a small pouch or fanny pack.

The downstream wet fly has been called the best hope of both beginner and expert, and it's true. It works on all rivers, at all times, and it is relatively easy to master the fundamentals. It can also be so complicated that it becomes endlessly enjoyable—a combination of slick tricks, flips, flops, aerial hoops, lifts, and pulls.

SETTING THE HOOK

I've seen all techniques for setting the hook, including but not limited to the Atomic Eruption Set, the Sickle and Heave Everything Toward the Shore Set, and of course The Great Pumping Sky Set.

My experience has been that the hook set depends on the speed your fly is traveling and its location when the fish climbs on. The easiest fish for me to hook are those that slam the fly during the swing. They seem to hook themselves at that time, and I do little except scream. Fish that take directly below, or almost directly below, me after the fly has slowed down are the most difficult to hook, and I set them pretty hard with something in between the Atomic Set and the Great Pumping Sky Set. I no longer try to set the hook by changing the direction of my pull and sweeping the rod to one side. This seems only to work on a very short cast, because you aren't going to change the angle of your pull when the fish is more than thirty feet from you.

The farther away your fly is, the more difficult it is to control its speed and depth and the more difficult it is to set the hook. This is why you always want your line to be as straight as possible during your down-and-across wet-fly swing. The bottom line is to never cast farther than you can effectively fish. Unless. Unless it has been one of those days when the river seemed almost sweet, the sky was friendly and blue, and you're on the last pool of the day, looking at the way the sun polishes the current. In that case, just wade out there, smile, and cast everything you've got, as far as you can.

brings the fly up without increasing its speed. If the current is too fast and the line has bellied far downstream of the fly, the lift will move the fly too quickly. If this is the case, mend upstream first and then slowly lift the rod to keep from snagging bottom.

At this point, the downstream compound swing is now almost finished, but if the water directly below me still looks good, I mend toward my shore to keep the fly swinging around. Once the arc is complete, or just seconds before, I strip the fly slowly toward me for about five to seven feet before I pick up for another cast. Sometimes, a steelhead will take when the fly is just hanging in the current at the end of a swing. The fish often moves directly upstream as it ingests the pattern, and you can't feel the take until the fish turns and draws the line tight. Stripping the fly at the end of the swing makes it easier to hook these fish before they have a chance to eject the fly.

In my opinion, a steelhead's strike response is triggered by a fly that looks alive and traveling at a believable speed, and not by the position from which they view it. All predators, including steelhead, have seen their prey from all possible angles, and I think movement and speed take precedence over the fly's angle when it swings toward, by, or away from them. The broadside presentation usually requires you lead, or gently pull, the fly across stream with your rod pointed ahead of the fly. This is relatively easy to do in slow and steady currents because you have plenty of time to mend, but leading the fly in swifter water invites a downstream belly and a fly speed that is too fast, at least for steelhead (perhaps not for Atlantic salmon, for which this technique seems to be popular).

For many anglers, it might not make sense that I prefer to use swinging presentations almost exclusively, especially when circumstances clearly favor dead-drifted flies and yarn indicators. But I am fishing for reasons, at long last, that have less and less to do each year with simply catching a lot of steelhead. One of the most important of these is the fact that I want the encounter I have with a steelhead, and the rivers to which they return, to be as strong as possible.

For me and for those other lost souls of similar persuasion with whom I haunt the rivers, the strength of a hard and sudden pull on a tight line is without equal. We want the heart-and-arm wrenching, electrical pull of a fish we cannot see suddenly tugging and pulling on

A swinging fly scrapes bottom now and then, so keep your hooks sharp. You'll be glad you did when you have to set up on a fish that took on a long cast. And don't be afraid to throw away wet flies with dull hooks. They are bad luck. I tie or buy flies with chemically sharpened hooks.

a tight line. The take on a swinging line is also magnified by the sensation and travel of a line that swims and crawls through imaginary landscapes of strong, dark water, distant seams, swift currents, over and around hidden boulders, drop-offs, and carved ledges of granite and shale. It seems that anything can be hidden in such places, and I've thought of them all as I've watched my line swing mysteriously around—a mermaid perhaps, a coelacanth hiding in an underwater cave, the twisted arms of ghostly trees, even immense steelhead. The swinging line not only inspires the imagination, it brings more of the river to an angler's body, hand, and rod. You can feel the currents tugging, and at times the line seems to sing with energy. The moment of the strike, your first encounter with the fish, feels like no other. "I live for the grab," one angler told me. "That's the best of it."

CHAPTER

9

Not all steelhead just lie on the bottom waiting for a fast sinking line and a short leader to come drifting by. The truly accomplished angler understands the advantages of and opportunities provided by a floating line with a long leader to get the job done. And it is effective under all water conditions—including current speed, depth of water, and its clarity.

The Greased Line

The "greased line" for steelhead took its name directly from the traditional floating fly lines used by Atlantic salmon anglers in Europe during the 1800s. These early floating lines were "good enough" but required frequent dressing to keep them floating. It would be many years before American technology produced high-floating lines that did not require continual dressing with all kinds of grease, waxes, and oils . . . including animal fats.

When I started fly fishing for steelhead in 1960, companies like Cortland and Scientific Anglers were manufacturing fly lines that were a great improvement over earlier floating lines. They did, however, require occasional cleaning and dressing with waxlike substances that kept them floating mostly high and mostly dry.

The contemporary lines now being manufactured are a dream come true; they seem to float forever, even

without cleaning and dressing with floatants. They come in a wide variety of belly lengths, weights, and taper profiles. One company, RIO Products, offers an incredible arsenal of lines for both single-handed and the longer two-handed Spey rods. Some of these are full floaters, and some are combination floating/sinking tip lines. Both types come in enough tapers to satisfy anyone who can cast. They are superb, and I have lines in my steelhead collection that I have used for several seasons and have never cleaned at all. They just keep on floating.

But these attributes and past history are not what all the fuss is about. The fuss is about something else: Steelheaders as a group are opinionated and strong willed—

floating line enthusiasts included—and their only real competition for stubborn arguments and perspectives comes from the black bass community. When I was a boy, I knew a lot of these anglers and fished with them. They caught a hell of a lot of fish, on some pretty strange lures.

Later on I gave up on bass, but I always wondered just how good pork rind "flies" would be. So I tried them once when no one else was around, and they did indeed work. So did my rubber wiggle worms for resident rainbow in Alaska and British Columbia steelhead. Nonetheless, I abandoned those types of flies for philosophical reasons that may or may not have been legitimate. But when I joined the editorial staff of *Fly Fisherman* magazine, the deal was sealed and I threw away not only my pork rind flies but my purple rubber wiggle worms, as I doubted that magazine editor John Randolph would approve.

In any event, here are some of the arguments that have supported the idea that greased line angling for steelhead is indeed a legitimate and exciting endeavor:

- The floating line is "faster on the draw" and is easier and quicker to pick up and retrieve for the next cast than a sinking line. You therefore spend more time fishing and less time picking up, dragging, and hauling a sunken line out of the river.

- You never have to worry or wonder if you have the correct density of line for the current speed and depth of water you are fishing. The line is on the top and "that's that."

- Strikes and "takes" are easier to feel or see than they are on a sinking line. For example, the subtle or "sipping" take of a cautious seagoing rainbow is easier to detect with a floating line and oftentimes you can see it—in other words, sometimes you can see the line move before you feel the pull. This can be greatly enhanced by the addition of a small, brightly colored strike indicator at the junction of your leader butt and your line tip. When the indicator moves to one side, stops, or goes under, it isn't the wind doing that. I learned this trick from one of my fishing heroes, Dave Whitlock, who uses it when he is fishing a small dry fly he can't see. I knew that a submerged steelhead fly was also impossible to see, even if it was five inches long, so I adapted Dave's trick and didn't miss many takes after that.

- You don't have to memorize all the different sink rates and colors of all the sinking lines available today. This is especially challenging when the line manufacturer decides to change the colors of the different densities, right after you've memorized them, or they make the colors so similar that they are hard to remember after a season away from the river. With a floating line there is nothing to memorize. Or forget. You just throw it out there, then mend once or twice and let it float into the bucket. What could be easier?

- The floating line responds quickly to all mending techniques, from the small flip mends to long lift mending. This helps give you close control over your fly's drifting speed, at all points in the drift.

- You don't get hung up on the bottom very often and you never have to worry about your $150 line getting wrapped around a boulder and your ability to unwrap it when it is seventy feet away in a cauldron of rushing water six feet deep.

- The "take" on a floating line is often more exciting because it is often visible. This can be heart stopping, especially if you are fishing your wet fly just under the surface film. It is an amazing thing to see a steelhead break through the surface film and take the fly in a rolling strike. There are several kinds of these responses. Some of them look like a bomb going off, and that can become addictive. Then there are some I like to call the "alligator lunge." This take includes the sight of a large white mouth opening then slamming shut with a quick snap of its gaping jaws. You have to be brain dead not to like this kind of thing, and it's even better if you end up landing the fish and your number six fly is sitting in the corner of a jaw that looks like it came from the Florida Everglades; British Columbia steelheaders know this especially well. And sometimes you can't see the take at all, even if you know exactly where your fly is swimming. It just disappears in a swirling "suck" that you thought was the river's currents swirling around.

- Some greased line steelheaders also believe the floating line and wet fly are superior for cold water temperature angling. By "superior" they usually mean that the mending capabilities of a floating line allow the angler to fish his or her fly more slowly than a sinking line can. An experienced greased line steelheader with a long rod can move forty to sixty feet of floating line all the way down to the leader butt without disturbing the drift of the fly. This is advantageous in cold water temperatures, as this condition can slow down the response of a fish and make it more lethargic. But a skilled angler with the same long rod and right kind of fly, leader, and wet tip line setup can also mend in a way that slows down the fly as effectively as a floating line angler can. So I consider this issue a "toss-up."

One more thing comes to mind here: the belly length of your floating line. RIO makes floating lines with different lengths of bellies. For example, their InTouch line has a fifty-two-foot belly, and as they say in their catalogue, "This long head and rear taper allow the angler to mend and control their fly speed at great distances." This is true. On the other hand, some of their

Spey lines have shorter belly lengths, from twenty to twenty-five feet, and the longer Spey rods do a good job of long mending with these shorter bellies. The trick is to lift the shorter belly up, get it moving in the right direction, and then use a quick mending stroke followed by a sudden stop of the rod tip. This forms a quick "mending loop" that moves the line just where you want it.

I may have left something out here, but I think this covers most of the things that floating line anglers like and believe in, and one might draw the conclusion from these perspectives that sinking lines are not necessary. And the truth is, they often are not, if the angler with the floating line is truly skilled at reading the water and knowing where he or she should or should not fish.

One of the most successful steelheaders I have ever met uses nothing but a floating line for his fishing, and the last thing I would ever want would be to fish behind the British Columbia steelheader and Atlantic salmon expert named Paul Fitzgerald. If I did, I wouldn't get much—if anything—because Paul reads water like an eagle and he simply does not fish where there are no fish. And he covers the water with an efficiency that is something to see. I have wanted to brag on Paul for a long time, as he is a legitimate expert in the best and fullest sense of the word, and because every year at Christmastime, when it's dark, cold, and rainy and all the rivers are out and I have to go with my wife to twenty-three holiday celebrations instead of steelhead fishing, Paul always sends a card with one of his incredible, brightly colored Atlantic salmon flies mounted on the inside. That helps.

I will also add that leader length for the greased line presentation is critical. I have no use for short leaders with the greased line—in other words, leaders less than ten feet. I prefer my leaders to be fairly long by steelhead standards. By this I mean tapered leaders of twelve to sixteen feet in length. Combined with a weighted fly, this leader length will allow the chosen pattern to sink deeper than a leader of, say, eight feet and gets the fly down even in deep and relatively fast currents. If I want my fly to swim closer to the surface or in shallow water, I still use the long leader but put on a slightly weighted wet fly.

No matter how shallow or deeply I am fishing my fly with a floating line, I always try for a drifting swing that creates what I think of as "the perfect vertical curve." By this I mean (1) the line is where it belongs, on the surface at the highest position of the vertical curve, or "parabola," and (2) the long leader then curves, or drops, downward, pulled into that position by my fly, which is always weighted. Unweighted wet flies, in my opinion, are close to being useless in greased line angling unless I am fishing in very shallow water. "Very shallow" means two to three feet deep, and if the water is that shallow and clear, a steelhead can see a number sixteen Adams, so my number four may be refused, but I guarantee you the fish can see it.

Dedicated wet tip anglers take note here: I feel the same way about the vertical curve if I am using a wet tip line. I still want the fly to be at the deepest position and the leader and sinking tip to be above the fly. And last but not least, the floating section of the line is still where it belongs: floating at the top of this parabola. To achieve this I often make my own ten- and fifteen-foot tips by combining two densities: The fastest sinking section is very short, about three feet, and is attached to the leader butt. The second section of the wet tip is a slower sinking material and is approximately twice the length of the short, dense section. This in turn is looped to the floating line. This combination will produce the downward drop or curving presentation that will help keep the leader (approximately three feet long) and wet tip line where they belong—above the fly, and above the rocks. Here again, if something gets snagged, it will be the weighted fly and perhaps the tippet just above the fly, but never any part of my fly line. I am not worried about losing a fly—I must have ten thousand of them by now—but I hate losing fly lines or parts of fly lines, not for financial reasons but because I hate losing any time to fixing something I think of as a "mistake."

And what about rods? Here are my feelings on the subject: In the first place, you can't have too many steelhead rods—even if you don't use them all. But I have a few that I love and use more than the others, and they all have the same things in common: (1) They do not feel like a telephone pole or a javelin. They feel like a fly rod and are light and responsive in the hand. (2) They don't merely cast the fly—they flip it on a short cast and launch it on a long one. That's because they have what I think of as a "progressive taper" in which the tip does the fifteen- to twenty-foot casts, a midsection that takes care of the thirty- to fifty-foot casts, and a butt section that kicks in for the eighty- to ninety-foot casts.

I also like rods that are easy on the eye cosmetically, and they look nice when the sun is out and it shines on

A day on a steelhead river is like no other. Our connections with the water, the forest, the mountains all around, and the sky above all come together in a way that is unique and, in my opinion, absolutely necessary.

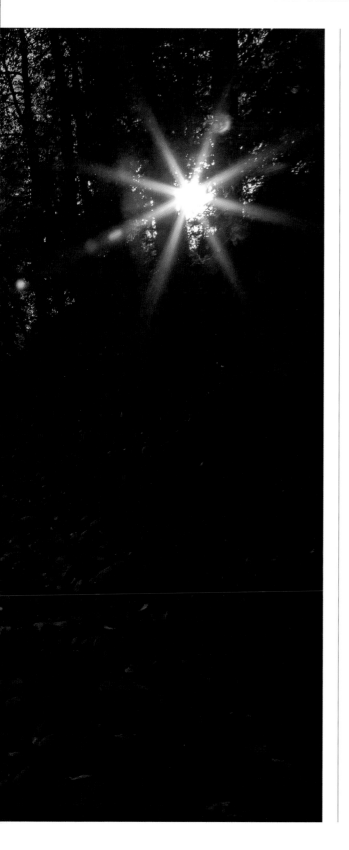

them. I also like it when they come from the dedicated hands of a master craftsperson who cares about such things and are beautifully designed, crafted, and finished.

My favorites are the "switch rods," which can be used with both hands in the traditional Spey casting method or one-handed when the wading is really tough and you have to keep one hand on your wading staff and the other on the handle of the rod. I like mine $10^1/_2$ to 11 feet in length, which I can use for standard two-handed Spey casting, regular overhand casting, or single-handed Spey casting as I make my way down the river.

Last but certainly not least, I like the rods made by a guy named Kerry Burkheimer. His $10^1/_2$-footer is the most amazingly accurate and tireless switch rod I have ever used. Period. His craftsmanship is without equal, and sometimes when I am casting, the handle of the rod is so attractively sculpted, it is hard to stop looking at the rod and start looking at where my fly has just landed.

I suppose there could be more to it than this, but after sixty years of fly fishing for steelhead, I have settled down some. I have also been coached and taught by some of the most incredible men and women I could have hoped to meet. Not all of them fished the greased line exclusively, but the ones who were adept at it showed me a thing or two that added much to my little "bag of tricks," and when I am out there and I see my floating line suddenly dart, twitch, start swimming upstream, or heading for the bottom, I get excited and thankful for all I have seen, learned, and experienced. And that, dear reader, is the best measurement of all.

CHAPTER

10

Indicators and Tugs

I don't buy the argument that fly fishers fish in a certain way only because it is traditional, or only because it always takes the most fish. We may start that way, but our years on the water eventually provide a fuller perspective; with any luck at all, we season with an appreciation for things that may have little to do with anything other than enjoyment and a basic belief in the effectiveness of the techniques we choose to use.

My own choice began innocently enough. I had no perspective from which to judge the steelheader's presentation. And it really didn't matter because, at the time, everyone simply did it the traditional way, with a down-and-across swinging fly. And that's exactly what I set out to learn.

Sometime around the early 1970s a movement began in the world of trout fishing that would eventually provide steelhead anglers with an alternative to the down-and-across presentation. My first encounter with

Fishing with an indicator can save the day in clear water and on heavily pressured waters when catching fish becomes difficult. The slow and easy drift of a smaller fly on a long leader doesn't seem to alarm jittery steelhead that have been pounded by swinging flies. The really savvy anglers I've fished with usually use a white yarn indicator on tough waters because it looks like a bubble or a bit of foam.

this movement was in the writings of Carl Richards and Doug Swisher. Their book *Selective Trout* signaled the beginning of new options for trout anglers and popularized a more scientific approach to fishing than any before it. New patterns emerged, based on both specific and generalized imitations of the natural insects, which were then married to a more natural, dead-drifted presentation. Eventually an entire generation of fly anglers picked up on the promise of that kind of fly and presentation.

In a review of *Selective Trout,* the influential American angling writer Joseph Brooks argued that the book was a revolutionary work and that the authors had proven the value of a more scientific perspective, one which included realistic dead-drifted presentations using carefully constructed nymph imitations. Brooks added that this approach had changed some of his attitudes about trout fishing, and whenever someone said that the trout in a particular stream were "uncatchable," he simply reached for his box of nymphs.

None of this was lost on me, and the success I had on northern California, Montana, and Colorado trout populations left no doubt for me about the effectiveness of a dead-drifted nymph. Years later, while angling in some of the most difficult circumstances in New Zealand, I finally reached the same conclusion as Brooks. I could go anywhere in the world and catch trout using this kind of presentation and fly. The Kiwi guides also included another innovation, a small piece of yarn attached to the leader, which was gaining favor all over the trout fishing world. No one wanted to call it a "bobber" or "float," so the name "strike indicator" became accepted. The yarn indicator would move, twitch, pause, or submerge when anything (rock, submerged tree limb, or fish) stopped the drifting fly.

Traveling American anglers took to the system, and I saw the indicator and dead-drifted fly become common on the wilderness streams of Alaska. The system centered around egg patterns, for Alaskan rainbows are famous for their weakness for salmon eggs during the annual sockeye runs in June and July.

By the late 1980s, this type of angling crossed over into the steelheaders' world, and I eventually learned of its effectiveness from anglers who fished in northern California, Oregon, and Washington. The practice eventually went north in the late 1980s to British Columbia, the last bastion of the good old wet-fly swing. The effectiveness of indicator fishing on some B.C. steelhead waters was undeniable under certain circumstances. One season, for example, during a low-water period on the

Set the hook quickly whenever the indicator does anything except move steadily downstream. Watch for the almost invisible pause, the deep plunge, the tiny twitch, or the secret swirl. Great Lakes steelheaders are masters at the game, and I'd hate to fish behind them with my swinging leech pattern.

Flies tied on light wire are a good idea because you do not have the help of a swinging line to drive the hook into the corner of a steelhead's mouth. Many anglers fish two different flies on the same terminal rigging. One favorite combination is a weighted nymph and egg pattern.

Though Great Lakes steelhead take a swung fly, especially early in the season when the water temperatures are warmer, dead-drifted egg patterns account for the bulk of the fish.
JAY NICHOLS

Kispiox River, three friends of mine who were very experienced steelhead anglers had carefully worked a pool twice without results. Their first pass through the pool was done with carefully fished swinging flies. They then went through a second time using spoons and spinners, with the same disappointing results.

As they sat resting the pool and contemplating their next move, a pair of anglers came floating around the bend in a rubber raft. The two floaters pulled to the side and asked if they could fish the pool. My friends said, "Yes, but we've gone through this run twice and we're not sure there are any steelhead here. We couldn't even get them on hardware." The anglers got out of the raft and began dead-drifting a pair of flies under yarn indicators on floating lines with long leaders of about sixteen feet, and they caught six Kispiox steelhead in front of my incredulous companions.

There have been many other examples of the effectiveness of this kind of angling on other B.C. watersheds. Late in the season, Babine water temperatures can get cold—even for that normally chilly river—and from early to mid-November I am often fishing with swinging flies and sinking lines in water temperatures in the mid-30s. During those times, after I have gone through a run carefully with a swinging fly, my guide has fished behind me with a single egg pattern under a strike indicator. Almost always, the guide will double or triple whatever I produce. If I get nothing, he will get one or two. If I take two fish, he will get three or four. This has happened so many times it cannot be a coincidence or accident.

So I have no quarrel with the effectiveness of such a presentation, and I also respect the skill and patience it requires. In fact, I consider it to be more difficult in some ways than a swinging fly, because the line handling

Narrow runs, seams, and streams too small for a swinging fly are perfect for indicator angling because most of the time, under these conditions, you only have to fish one current lane at a time. Use either double taper or weight-forward lines. Most anglers seem to prefer the weight forward because of its shooting abilities.

Jack Hanrahan drifts his egg pattern to a steelhead holding in the dark water just below a shelf. For a drag-free drift, it is necessary to mend your fly line so that it floats upstream of your indicator. If your line floats downstream of your indicator, drag will pull your fly faster than the currents.

skills are more complex and demanding. The upstream cast produces a lot of line coming downstream and back toward the wading angler. Handling this slack line is more difficult because you have two variables instead of one. You have to mend constantly, both upstream and down depending on the currents and position of the fly, as you simultaneously gather slack line. Your responsibility in the downstream swing is simply mending without regard for slack, because there is none.

The effectiveness of a dead-drifted presentation with a single fly, or pair of flies, on a long leader and with the yarn indicator is, in my experience, most effective when the water is very low and clear, when water temperature

approaches the lower tolerance levels of the particular strain of fish in a certain watershed, and when fishing pressure is intense. It is also at its best on a small stream where the relative size of the runs and pools does not allow for a swinging fly. It seems that these conditions make steelhead more cautious and more tentative.

On the rivers I fish, indicator fishing is relatively unsuccessful when water temperatures and flows are normal, especially on larger water. Some years ago I fished two major British Columbia rivers with a well-known and leading proponent of the dead-drifted fly and yarn indicator. The first of these was the Dean River, which at the time was running very low and clear, and a lot of

This angler is doing a good job of high sticking. The rod is held high to keep the floating line off the water and out of the push of faster currents between the fisherman and the target. This avoids a dragging fly and assures a dead drift.

anglers were tromping around the pools and runs of the section we were fishing. My companion did as well, or better, than I did with my swinging fly, and at times took fish behind me. Later, that same year, we went to the Babine. The water there was normal, with little public pressure. His results with the floating line, long leader, and yarn indicator were so disappointing that he put that tackle away and fished with a sinking-tip line and a swinging wet fly.

Most of the indicator angling I have seen in British Columbia is done with a 9- to 10-foot fly rod or a short two-handed rod of around twelve feet. Any good imitation of a small egg around 3/16 inch in diameter will work, though most favor a Glo Bug. Everyone has their favorite color, but it would be hard to beat pink. Another thing I have learned is that while steelhead like salmon eggs, they love their own even more.

Most anglers up north prefer a weighted fly, but some will also add a split-shot about 24 inches above the fly to ensure a deep float. Some of those Canadian anglers I have seen using indicators are absolute experts who come by it through the old tradition among bait anglers in B.C. who use conventional tackle (spinning or level wind reels of some type) combined with an adjustable cork float. The float is moved up or down the line in response to the depth of the run. When the water is cold, as it can be in winter or spring steelheading, the method can be absolutely deadly, and in the hands of an expert can produce uninterrupted perfectly dead drifts of over one hundred feet.

My own techniques have borrowed the New Zealand style of tying a relatively large weighted nymph to the end of my tippet, and then clinch-knotting a pink Glo Bug or other egg pattern to the hook bend of that nymph on a second piece of leader about twenty inches long. The larger and heavier fly helps the smaller egg fly drop down

in the current, and at times a steelhead will take the nymph. However, the fish usually prefer the egg pattern.

You have to lead your target and give your fly time to descend as it drifts. Most of the time the flies will be deepest just as they reach a point opposite you. Once they begin to drift below you, the currents will begin to lift them, and you will have to add slack into the drift as you mend to keep your rig drifting fairly deep in the water column. At some point it becomes very difficult, if not impossible, to keep the flies down as they begin to lift in the water column. At that point, you can either let them rise and fish them on the swing as they come around, or you can retrieve your line and make another cast back upstream.

Our world has long been changing. Civilization is now at the river's throat, more so than ever before. Many anglers face crowding, serious loss of stocks of steelhead, and damming and pollution of their home waters. These circumstances make angling for steelhead more difficult,

The depth that the fly drifts is set by the distance of the indicator from the fly or flies on the leader. It is important to be able to adjust your indicator because you will need to constantly adjust the depth at which you fish your fly.

A great debate rages over the relative merits of indicator angling versus the traditional down-and-across swinging fly, and the dialogue is not always friendly. My own take is this: I don't care how you catch them, as long as you treat them well and with respect. In the end that matters more than anything else.

to say the least. In truth, swinging a fly through small or crowded waters can be an exercise in futility. I recognized this a long time ago, and it was no small part of the reason I left my northern California haunts and passed both Oregon and Washington on my way to the wilderness and semi-wilderness trophy rivers of northern British Columbia. The fish there were unpressured, and angling there is (at times) certainly less challenging and difficult than steelheading in the lower 48.

Some anglers have noted, almost critically, that my experiences are therefore different than most anglers'. They say that I have had the good fortune to be able to fish for wild and trophy steelhead in unspoiled rivers and that the trophy steelhead up there are big and dumb and will take almost anything. And my reply is this: You bet they will. This is not a problem. It is a calculated solution.

On pressured streams, small water, or in low, clear conditions, anglers fishing nymphs suspended under indicators usually fare better than those who are swinging flies.

The dry fly for steelhead is most effective for stee[l]head that run the rivers in the summer and fall. These fish are troutlike, aggressive, and sometimes take natural insects. Although dead-drifted dry flies will take steelhead, most anglers use the down-and-across presentation to wake the fly across stream. Summer and fall steelhead are attracted to the surface disturbance.

Fishing the Dry Fly

As Bob Wickwire and I watched, Larry Trotter worked a steelhead with a home-tied pattern that had started out as a Green-Butted Skunk, but Larry's enthusiasm for the wing and hackle had transformed the old reliable wet fly into a floating hair-winged fortress that was nothing short of unsinkable. Larry was, in fact, trying to get the fly to sink before it came to the fish, as he himself had no idea of the possibilities for a dry fly and was simply trying to fish a wet fly on a floating line. Despite his best attempts to submerge the dragging fly, it would not sink and remained on the surface, dragging and sputtering as it swung into the target for the fourth time. Amazingly enough, each of the earlier three presentations had inspired an immense boil from something holding in front of a large boulder. I had never seen anything like this before, but I knew what I was looking at.

I remember watching the current pull the line tight on the fourth cast, and as the immense pattern began to plow into the zone like a small bird, the river blew up again. I looked at Trotter, hoping he would at least set the hook in a symbolic gesture. No such luck. He just stood there shaking as the river softened and went smooth. Wickwire was still up on the bank, hopping up and down, unable to speak. I stayed in the water behind Larry, but my mouth hung so low my bottom lip was taking water. The fish never came back, despite forty-four more casts, but it didn't matter. We'd all seen enough.

Larry spoke first. "My God you guys, how big do you think it was?"

"I don't know. Not too big. I'd say maybe twelve pounds," Wickwire said. "What do you say Waller? Did you get a good look at it?"

I thought carefully about my answer. I wasn't sure, but it looked as big as a truck. In any event, the sun would soon be down, and I was thirsty. Since Larry hadn't bought a round of drinks in a long time, only one answer seemed suitable. "Bob," I said. "It was a lot bigger than twelve. I'd give it twenty four at least."

Trotter looked at me, winding up his line. "Damn right," he said, grinning, as the sparrow finally came to rest in the top guide of his rod. "Waller is right on. It was huge."

Before that September day I had heard stories about taking a steelhead on the surface but hadn't done anything about them. British Columbia expert Jimmy Wright told stories of immense summer-run steelhead rising to a nondescript and simple fly not unlike a Muddler. Roderick Haig-Brown had also long described

Fifty percent of the steelhead that rise to your searching pattern should take it. If they rise but do not take it, your searching pattern is too large. Change to a fly that makes a much smaller surface disturbance. LANI WALLER

Undisturbed early morning steelhead in shallow water are a good bet. I took this Kispiox fish in less than two feet of water, and I could see its wake coming for the fly from fifteen feet away. This was one of several fish taken from the same run just at dawn's first light. LANI WALLER

some of his encounters with summer-run steelhead near his home of Campbell River in British Columbia. These stories interested me, but they were far from the waters I fished for winter-run steelhead in northern California. I tried Haig-Brown's technique briefly one fall on the Klamath River but without any real faith, one of the surest ways I know to fail at something you know little about, and, in fact, nothing happened. About that same time, Bill McMillan, a longtime favorite writer of mine, added additional fuel to the fire with accounts of his fishing with a floating line in the state of Washington. As I recall, this included the possibility of skating or "waking" a dry fly in the same way as Atlantic salmon anglers did for their fish. Despite the stories from Haig-Brown, McMillan, and Wright, I remained near the bottom with brightly colored egg patterns and other offerings, all fished as deeply as I could manage.

Trotter changed all that, and not long after the third round of drinks that night, we named that Babine pool after him. From then on, the dry fly became an essential part of the strategies my friends and I brought with us to the Skeena each autumn. It turned out to be a pivotal event, and several years later when Scientific Anglers 3M called with an offer to film a series of steelhead videos if I could guarantee footage of a steelhead actually taking a floater, I never hesitated. At that time, I met 3M executive and devoted steelheader Howard West, and for six years he and I and others on the Babine experimented and fished dry flies as much as we did typical wet patterns. We learned much. The wet fly is more difficult to master, but nothing surpasses the excitement of a steelhead rising to a fly on the surface.

The basic routine is simple enough. You fish downstream, taking a step or two between casts until you find a fish willing to rise. Easy enough, if you keep the faith. It is a visual game of trial and error, and patience. The ability to see everything simplifies matters—watching the descent of the floating line, watching the fly respond to the necessary manipulations and preparations, watching the swing to the target. When the fly starts skating too fast or is where you don't want it to be, you can see it and fix it. Anglers can get a jump on learning some of the intricacies of the wet fly by first seeing the drift and swing of a floating pattern as it comes around in the current. It is also a great way to learn just where steelhead lie. Fishing the dry reveals more of a river and its resting fish than the wet because even the refusal is usually

visible, unless the curious fish turns back well short of the surface.

Most signs and responses are anything but subtle as the once floating fly suddenly disappears into one of the following: "The Great White Mouth Rise," "The Quick Splash," "The Cool Sip," "The Alligator Snarf," or one of my favorites, "The Toilet Bowl Express," which is an immense flush of current large enough to swallow an entire human body. I capitalize these descriptions because I enjoy exaggerating the things I love, but if you've been there, you know what I mean. Now and then it really does become extraordinary, and you get a rise that sounds and looks like a small bomb going off.

What comes next depends on who you are and what you are made of. My own usual response—a now old and desperate habit—never fails. I freeze and make a quick but impossible estimate of the fish's size. And little has changed since that first one with Wickwire and Trotter. I almost never get it right. Seven-pound fish are estimated to be twenty, regardless of who is buying the drinks. Twenty-pounders sometimes appear to be ten to twelve pounds. The rise form can disguise the fish (so can the imagination), and for a moment you don't know. Nonetheless, some kind of hesitation or freeze is a good thing, because it gives the hook the time it needs to find a home as the steelhead closes its mouth, turns, and heads for cover. Without the pause, you simply pull the hook from a mouth that hasn't closed yet. It also helps if your hooks are sharp and have offset points.

The dry fly also seems the domain of those who fish for summer-run steelhead. As I've said earlier, the temperament—for lack of a better term—of a summer-run fish stands alone. They are more aggressive, more curious, and more troutlike than winter- or spring-run steelhead. Some have caught the occasional winter- or spring-run steelhead on a dry fly, but the reports are few. I do not believe it is a function of normally cold spring or winter water temperatures alone, because I have taken enough summer-run steelhead in water from 42 to as low as 34 degrees.

If you want one on the top, I'd take a close look at those rivers in which summer-run fish return. Exact timings vary according to specific watersheds but usually include fish that are in the rivers from June through late fall. This would include rivers in northern California, Oregon, Washington, and British Columbia. I have experimented with floating flies for October steel-

Good dry-fly water is usually around two-and-a-half to four feet deep with moderately fast currents. Sometimes, even on larger rivers, you can find these conditions a long way away, near the center of a river. If you do, don't be bashful. Fling it out there.

head in Alaska on the Lower Peninsula south of King Salmon and the Nak-Nek River system, but have had poor results.

Tackle for dry flies is not that much different from what you'd use for wets. Both single- and two-handed rods work, and I prefer a switch rod around eleven feet that can be used with one or both hands. This length of rod coupled with a weight-forward floating line easily reaches the distances required. Most of the summer-run fish I try to catch on a dry are fifty feet or less from

shore, in accessible depths of three to five feet of water, so I don't need to make exceedingly long casts.

You can easily handle these shorter casts with a floating line that has a moderately long belly. The Skagit-type floaters, with their shorter and heavier casting bellies work, but are not usually needed. My leaders usually run from twelve to sixteen feet and taper to around .010 to .012 inch diameter. I prefer this length because I do not want a resting fish to see the line. Sometimes the fish will move around between casts and may actually move toward you after rising to, and then refusing, your fly. They can become suspicious, so the less of my line they see, the better I like it. I usually prefer relatively heavy tippets, which are good insurance against chafing during a prolonged tug of water with a large and stubborn fish.

Fly design and construction are critical. When a dry fly is fished down and across it is under tension, the water pushes hard against the front of the fly, and the current may roll over the pattern, submerging it. Another problem is that the fly can be hard to see in rough water or bad light. I solve the visual problem by using dressings with fluorescent green or pink divided wings. These colors are the most visible, most of the time. Sometimes a black wing shows best if glare is strong and the surface turns bright silver.

In recent seasons, I have settled on a fly that has a foam body for good flotation and two bright and divided wings. The forward part of the fly's body forms a wedge between the wings, and both the wings and the wedge between them slant forward at approximately a 45 degree angle. This produces an inclined surface on the front of the fly, which responds to the push of currents by lifting the fly toward the surface and keeping it there.

You can help any fly stay on top by tying a half hitch behind the wing or head of the fly after tying your favorite knot to the hook eye. The push of the water against the head of the hitched fly makes the front of the fly hinge and lift toward the surface. This arrangement is called a riffle hitch, and I first came across this particular trick in Lee Wulff's great book *Atlantic Salmon*. Wulff writes that he himself first discovered the idea while fishing an eastern Canadian salmon stream called Portland Creek. One of the guides there, a man named Arthur Perry, showed Lee how to tie the knot. Perry claimed that such a fly would "out-fish a regular wet fly by a large margin." Wulff writes, "The guides were almost unanimous in believing a salmon could be taken in no other way," and goes on to say that, although he caught Portland Creek salmon with both kinds of knots, he eventually "came to prefer the hitched fly because the rise from a salmon to the surface was so exciting."

Lee also said that one reason why the fly was so effective is that it remained visible, thus making it easy for the angler to judge its speed as it swam through and across the currents. This is certainly true, and knowing how to maintain an effective fly speed by mending is a critical skill in both Atlantic salmon and steelhead fishing.

Wulff believed the riffle hitch to be a byproduct of old Atlantic salmon flies tied in the 1800s, which were dressed on hooks without eyes. The eye of the fly was constructed from a loop of twisted silkworm gut tied tightly to the front of the hook shank. Once the looped gut was in place, the fly was then tied over it, with just a loop eye of gut protruding from the forward edge of the

I do not believe that color of the dry fly matters to a steelhead, but it might to the angler. Steelhead dry-fly takes can be subtle, and it is best if you can see your fly throughout the entire drift. Bright wings on a fly are a big help. LANI WALLER

Tie your dry-fly knots carefully with dry hands, then dress your dry fly after the knot has been tied. If you dress your dry fly before you tie it on, the floatant from your fingers makes your tippet so slick that even a well-tied knot can slip and unravel when a fish takes and then runs. LANI WALLER

fly. This natural material weakened with age, and salmon anglers using these old flies would tie their tippet to the gut eye and then loop their tippet around the head of the fly in case the silkworm gut eye failed.

Lee and other salmon anglers also believed that the hitched tippet should be shifted to one side of the fly or the other, depending on which side of the river you were fishing. If you were facing downstream and fishing river left, the tippet should come from the right side of the fly. If you were fishing river right, again facing downstream, the tippet should come from the left side of the fly. This practice soon became orthodox and my own angling with a hitched fly followed this belief, but after years of fishing steelhead with a riffled fly I discovered that it made no difference at all on which side of the fly the hitch is tied, as long as the knot is tied so that the "running" part of the leader tippet remains under the head of the fly and back from the hook eye. I remember thinking that if a hitched pattern worked with the tippet

on one side or the other depending on what side of the river you were on, why couldn't you just put it in the center of the fly and kill two birds with one stone?

There was a lesson for me in this personal insight. Even though Lee Wulff was one of my heroes, and his book on Atlantic salmon angling remains one of the greatest "how to do it" angling books of all time, I eventually learned to take no man's word or experience as absolute truth under all circumstances, and that true knowledge always comes from first-hand experience. After fifty years of this kind of inquiry, I have discarded much. In the end I have found only a few absolutes, and, for better or worse, when I am in the water, I am on my own.

Most dry-fly anglers organize flies into one of two basic categories: searching patterns and closing patterns. Searching patterns are larger floating flies that are used when looking and fishing for fish you cannot see. These usually push more water, making it easier for the maximum numbers of fish to see the fly under the widest range of water depths, surface textures, clarity, and from the greatest distances.

I match the size of my searching fly to these factors: (1) how much fishing pressure the water receives (the more pressure there is, the smaller my locator will be); (2) how smooth the currents are where I am fishing (the flatter the surface, the smaller my fly); and (3) water clarity and light conditions (the clearer the water and the more light there is upon it, the smaller my fly will be). At least half of the steelhead that rise to your searching pattern should come all the way and take it. If significantly fewer fish than that actually take your searching pattern, it is too large.

If you can't see your searching pattern, you may not know something is wrong, so use one that is easy for you to see and save the smaller flies for closers. If your vision is limited and you can't be sure of what your fly is doing—because of poor light, a rough surface, or a long cast in low light—choose a dry fly that looks just as good when it is submerged. In other words avoid the bulky dressings and fish with a more streamlined fly that still looks real when it is swimming under the surface.

The best I've found for this is the Muddler Minnow. If you riffle-hitch the head of a Muddler, it throws a wake that is usually easy to see. If you lose the fly in bad light and can't see it, or if it goes under water, the fly's silhouette still looks very good and you just finish the presentation by fishing the pattern as a wet fly. I've taken a lot of steelhead with this fly under these kinds of conditions.

You cast a closing pattern to a fish that has risen to a searching pattern but refused it. Normally closing patterns are significantly smaller than searching patterns because fish that refuse a larger fly are best taken with a fly that pushes less water and makes a smaller surface disturbance. Judge the fly by the size of the surface disturbance it makes on the water and not necessarily by the volume of the pattern's body and hackle. The actual volume of the fly's body is usually only relevant in places where it can be clearly seen by a "fussy" fish.

I have seen fish that rise and refuse up to a dozen or more fly changes before they finally take. To ensure I have a pattern that interests the fish, I carry several different styles of dressings that produce a wide variety of surface disturbances. A small wet fly with an upturned eye and a riffle hitch behind the head of the pattern leaves only the smallest of a "V" in the water and can be

deadly on a fish that is hard to take with a larger dry. *The greater the difference between the fly they just refused and the next one you show them, the more likely they are to take it.* So, if they rise to a number six Muddler and you want to short circuit the process, don't choose a number eight Muddler as your next fly. Immediately go to a wet fly.

My favorite hooks for dry flies are the same I prefer for wet flies—the short-shank Japanese hooks or equivalent that have laser sharp hooks and offset points. When a steelhead closes on a fly, the hook almost always rolls over and lies flat in the fish's mouth. Once a straight-shank hook is in this position, the point often misses everything because it is lying on top of tissue, bone, or cartilage and doesn't stick into anything when the line comes tight.

With an offset hook point, the point always points toward the tissue, bone, or cartilage. In this position, it does not have to travel far at all before it sticks. And there is a difference between sticking and penetrating. A large wire hook, even one with a very sharp point, may stick, but it will not penetrate as quickly and as easily as those with a thin wire diameter. Though they look great in framed fly plates, avoid fishing flies tied on heavy wire "steelhead" and "salmon" hooks.

Where you fish the floating fly also has great bearing on your success. Normally I look for water that is between two to five feet deep, though an aggressive fish will rise farther in the water column. Current speed and depth also depend on temperature. The colder the water,

Wings for a hair-wing waking dry should slant forward about forty-five degrees and be stiff or the water will roll over the front of the fly and push it under the surface. LANI WALLER

Waller Waker (Foam)

Hook:	#4–6 Owner (short-shank, turned-up eye, offset)
Tail:	Moose body or hock
Body:	Black foam, trimmed to shape
Wing:	Fl. green or fl. orange calf tail
Throat (optional):	Moose body or hock

Tier's Note: For the body, I use ¼-inch-thick foam, which I cut into ¼-inch-wide strips. Before attaching the foam to the shank, I cut it with scissors so it is thinner toward the rear end of the fly. Once the fly is complete, I trim the foam body to make it look a little nicer and more even, although the fish do not seem to care. On the smaller foam Wakers (I call them Baby Wakers) shown in the photo, I do not tie in a beard. The foam body and wings with the foam wedge between them keep the fly up and waking.

The author's new Waller Wakers tied from foam float better and are easier to tie than the originals.

JAY NICHOLS

the less likely you will raise a steelhead in very fast currents or in deeper water. As I've said earlier, cold water temperatures themselves are relative, but normally when water gets below 45 degrees on most rivers, most steelhead slow down. Slowing down includes their willingness not only to be in fast water, but their willingness to rise to the surface for a floating fly. When water temperatures are relatively cold for the particular river I am fishing, I have found I can often get only one rise on a dry before they shut down, even ignoring a deep fly fished near the bottom on a sinking-tip line.

I also look for out-of-the-way places other anglers might ignore in their search for the perfect run. These include shallow riffles with a textured surface that provides cover, shady seams next to shore, and small pockets that can be covered with two casts. This kind of search is most important when there is pressure on the water from other anglers. In my experience, most summer

Always deliver the dry fly well to the side of the suspected lie of the fish so that they can't see your line splash. Then get your rod up, your line straight, and let it swing and wake to them steadily, slowly, and quietly.

steelhead, when pressured, will stop coming to the surface but may still take a wet fly. So, if water conditions are good and you want to stay with a dry when there are other anglers around, fish where they haven't.

The normal dry-fly down-and-across presentation is relatively straight forward. Since the fly is on the surface, fly speed is your primary concern. The quicker and more complicated the currents are, the more difficult it will be to control your fly's speed over a wide and swinging arc. If in doubt, aim your cast more downstream. By mending, you can modify the speed of the fly. Despite current speed and complexities, I always try to fish as wide an arc as possible on each presentation, and the mending capabilities of a rod eleven feet or longer help me accomplish this.

I always deliver the fly well to one side of the suspected lie—as much as twenty feet or more—away from the place I believe the fish is resting. If you cast too close, the disturbance on the water from your mending may spook the fish. Cast well away from the fish to give you time to set up the drift and make sure the current has pulled the line and leader as straight as possible before the fly arrives in the fish's vicinity. Your fly will be traveling and swinging toward your target, not away from it, and you always want the fly to appear perfectly natural when the resting fish first sees it.

A mid-air mend, or reach cast, puts the line and leader upstream of the fly while everything is still airborne and eliminates the need for on-the-water mends that might alarm the fish. If, after the mid-air mend, the line does not fall to the surface as intended, I first make an initial mend by carefully lifting the rod and pulling the line back upstream to help straighten the line. After this, I keep the rod elevated as the line tightens and drag sets in. At this point the fly is actually holding steady and waking.

As the waking fly begins its journey toward the target, I maintain this high rod position to keep some line off the water. Not only does this help slow down the fly, but the sag in your line creates enough slack, and that, combined with a pause before striking, gives the fish time to close on the fly and swim away, which draws the hook into place. Some anglers will drop their rod tip from the elevated position and bow to the fish when they take to yield additional slack and time, but I haven't found that necessary, providing I have enough of a lazy sag in the line. I just hold the rod high, and they are either on or they are not. Striking quickly, as you would for trout, only takes the fly away from them and is the surest way I know to lose almost every fish that rises to your floating pattern. If the steelhead rises to the fly but refuses, let it come around and travel well beyond the position where the fish showed before you pick it up for a second cast.

From this point forward it becomes a guessing game, and no two fish are exactly the same. After the refusal, I make a second cast with the same fly, on a slightly shorter line, in case the fish has moved forward after its response. If this second cast does not elicit a response, I cast back to the same place where the fish first showed. If the steelhead does not respond to the third cast with the same fly I began with, I assume it has lost interest in it or moved some distance away. Since I don't know exactly what is going on, I just blame the fly and play it safe by showing them something they haven't seen yet, which may rekindle their interest.

The second fly is usually a small and lightly dressed Muddler Minnow with a riffle hitch around the head. The surface disturbance is much smaller than that of the first fly. If this second pattern does not get an initial response after two or three casts, I fish a small wet fly fished with a regular knot or riffle hitch. If the small wet

If a steelhead rises to one of my larger flies fished slowly and steadily, but refuses it, I next use a low-riding Muddler Minnow, tied with a riffle-hitch through, or just behind, the deer-hair head. I keep the rod tip high and wiggle it to make the Muddler flutter. LANI WALLER

fly does not produce a rise after two or three casts, I fish a large wet fly as deeply as I can. This may involve taking the time to change from the floating line to a sinking-tip line, which rests the fish for a few moments.

By the third fly change, the game has obviously changed, and it becomes a search once more. Fish carefully and be ready. Sometimes a steelhead will rise and refuse, then swim downstream, upstream, or to one side as much as ten to fifteen feet or more, if the currents are suitable in those locations and similar to the water where it first came to the surface. They usually tend to stick around places like this longer than they do in tight holding areas surrounded by water that is too fast, shallow, or turbulent. I think this has to do with their comfort level, for lack of a better description. Large and open expanses of comfortable water speed and depth must feel safer to them than a small lie surrounded by unfavorable conditions.

It is also possible to elicit a strike by changing the drift of your dry fly from a slow and steady wake to something different. My favorite trick is to make the fly quiver or flutter as it wakes across the fish's lie by shaking the rod tip back and forth in a series of short and quick movements. I often do this with the second dry fly I show them after they have refused a previous dry. A fly that appears to be alive and struggling can be deadly, and I have raised fish to this kind of drift when a steady wake did not. These movements, however, do not increase the lateral speed of the fly. They simply make the fly twitch and flutter as it comes around. I only increase the lateral speed of the fly when I am fishing through slower or softer currents, because I believe that a fish holding in relatively slow water has a greater tolerance for a fast fly.

Sometimes all the rules seem wrong or backward, and, as I said above, it is always best to keep an open mind about just what could happen. Perhaps it is the nature of wild things to be unpredictable at times. Or perhaps we jump to conclusions out of our own habits and preferences. Years ago, I had a group of beginners with me on a famous British Columbia summer-run steelhead river. Since we arrived on the change-over day at camp, we would have no guide with us. We drew straws for the pools we would fish, and one of the anglers who really wanted to fish a dry fly asked me if a floater would work on the pool he had drawn. I said, "Yes, the upper half of the run can be OK with a dry. Do you need any help? I'll fish with you." He replied

If you can't see your waking dry fly in bad light, don't risk alarming a steelhead by ripping your line and fly out of good water. Fish the cast out, because a lot of steelhead hook themselves even if you can't see the fly. That is just what this Skeena buck did. I never saw the take. I just felt his weight. LANI WALLER

that he would be OK by himself. A second angler was afraid of bears and asked if he could fish the bottom half of the pool so that there would be two of them in case of an attack. "Of course," someone said.

At dinner that night we all talked about our experiences, and the dry fly angler was very excited, to say the least. He had taken four fish on his own with a dry fly. The other angler who had fished the lower half of the pool vouched for the guy's story. Indeed, four fish had been hooked and landed at the top of the run by the beginning angler who had not read anything about dry

DRY FLY SPEED

The correct fly speed depends upon the water you are fishing. The faster the currents are, the more slowly you should fish the waking fly. Most of the time, a fly that wakes at a rate about one half of the current speed is a good goal for your presentation, though you cannot fish a waking dry too slowly. You can, however, fish it too quickly.

To control the fly speed, choose your angle of delivery carefully. A straight-across delivery works well on slow and even currents and covers more water in a single cast. The faster or more complex the currents, the more downstream you should present the fly. Faster water almost immediately puts a downstream belly in your line, which can speed up your fly too much.

In addition to the angle at which you cast the fly, you can also control fly speed by keeping your rod tip vertical and even raising your arm as the fly wakes across stream. This lifts some of the line

off the surface, and the less line you have in the water the less chance there is of getting a downstream belly in your line.

Mending is critical to control fly speed, and the longer your rod, the more line you can manipulate. The best mends usually travel all the way down the line and stop at the leader without moving the fly. This is not always easy to do, but it helps if you start the mend with your rod high. If you begin with a low rod, you move a lot of line as you raise your rod. If the line is tight and you have to mend (and if your rod tip is low), feed a little slack with your line hand as you lift the rod. This will not move your fly and gives you a chance to reposition the floating line without changing the drifting speed of your waking fly.

Dead-drifting your dry fly will work, if you can see the fish or are certain of its position, but a down-and-across presentation covers more water. It is possible, however, to fish both a dead-drift and waking presentation on the same cast by presenting your fly upstream and letting it dead-drift down without tension. When your line swings around below you, it will come tight and the fly will start waking. Once the fly has finished its waking swing, pick it up, move a few feet downstream, and start all over again.

fly fishing for steelhead. The guy had been fishing in the "wrong" direction, casting upstream and dead-drifting his dry fly back downstream. "I thought that was how you fished a dry fly," he said. "I thought that's the way you are supposed to do it." When I asked him what fly he had used, he said, "I'm not sure, I think it was a number twelve Royal Coachman . . . you know, the one with the red body and white wings."

Three years ago, on the same river, I shared a boat with Patagonia founder Yvon Chouinard during the first week of November, which is the last week of the season. Air temperatures were rarely above freezing, and the river stayed at a cool 34 degrees. When you wade in water like that, it is obvious that it is only two degrees above freezing. Nonetheless Chouinard remained steadfast and optimistic. One morning, he is coming toward shore, blowing hot steam as we approach in the sled to pick him up for lunch. He gets in the boat and his nose is dripping, just like everyone else's. It's too cold to pull my hand out of my coat pockets, so I just point with a nod of my head over to the rather bleak looking run he had just fished. "Do any good?" I asked.

"It was interesting," he said. "Very interesting . . ."

"What happened?"

"Well, I started out with an Egg Sucking Leech, not far off the bottom. Didn't get a touch, then went through again with some fly whose name I don't know, and I scraped every inch of the bottom. Still didn't get a touch. Since you guys were so f–ing late, I took the water temperature, and decided what the hell, it's only thirty-four, and I put on a floating line and went through a third time with a dry fly."

"Get any? I asked.

"Hooked three."

Fours hours later, just before quitting time, it is even colder, so cold that freezing now sounds warm, and the

When your dry fly is under tension and waking in the zone, make careful mends that do not jerk your fly forward three or four feet. You can make these adjustment mends with a low rod tip and gentle flip of the line. Keep from jerking the fly by letting some excess line slip through your fingers as you flip the line.

four of us—me, Ron Mallory, Yvon, and Fuji Katsumi, who handles all of Patagonia's sales in Japan—are passing around a pewter flask of brandy as we call it a day and go home. When I look, there is no sun, and everything—the sky, the water, and the land—seems the same color and temperature, dark and frozen. Even the boat is covered in a hard sheath of ice. The guide says nothing. He can't talk, and for all we know he is frozen to the steering wheel. Now and then we pour some brandy on his face. Maybe some will make it to his mouth, because it's a very long way back to camp and we are running out of time and light.

When I consider our circumstances, it seems that a little philosophy mixed in with the brandy could do wonders, and as we sit there, hunched over in the boat with our teeth rattling in the frozen wind and ice hang-

ing from our chins, I decide to use the opportunity to launch yet another sermon. "Did I ever tell you guys," I begin, "what the Buddhists say about teachers and students?"

Silence. No one answers. I'm not sure whether that is a good or a bad sign, but since I need some form of exercise to avoid freezing to death, I continue talking. "Well it reminds me of teaching people how to catch more and bigger fish, because the Buddhists say that if the student does not exceed the accomplishments of the teacher, it means the teacher has failed."

More silence, and for a moment no one says anything. Then Yvon takes the flask from me, opens his mouth, and takes a big swig. He looks at all the ice, swallows the brandy, and says, "Sounds like sour grapes to me."

If you like fine-wire hooks on your dry flies, your tippet should be thick enough to resist abrasion during a long fight because you can't put the heat on a light-wire hook. I prefer standard-weight hooks on my dry flies because I can lean on a fish without opening up the hook.

Dry-fly fishing for steelhead is one of the best ways to learn where the fish are. To catch the fly, a steelhead has to move more quickly in currents like this and the speed of its response is often visible and splashy. See it once and you'll never forget it.

CHAPTER

12

Casting

A well-delivered presentation is its own reward, which is a fortunate twist of fate when you consider that a steelhead has been called "the fish of a thousand casts." And the bigger they are, the more thousands you will probably have to make. During a recent evening gathering around the walnut dinner table of a northern steelhead camp, we determined that the 31-pound buck taken the day before at Red Bandanna pool (river left, under the hanging spruce, in water temperatures of 41 degrees F) actually represented around 200,000 casts. There were several basic assumptions in our conceptual model including, but not limited to: (1) There were nine of us fishing and casting for the entire week; (2) none of us stopped when it became windy or cold, or because we hadn't had a strike in three hours, or three days; and (3) we abstained from the luxury of a forty-five-minute lunch break. You only

Good casting comes with an understanding of the basics. Train yourself to implement them. It helps to find a good teacher who is an expert caster with good communication skills. Bad habits will never transform themselves into good ones by merely pounding the river. Learn what you are doing wrong and what the solution is, and then practice.

take these when the river is really out. When it's in, you are well advised to keep your fly in the water.

What I find interesting is that most of us seem willing to study the mechanics of a good golf or tennis swing and seek advice and instruction from experts in order to improve, but when it comes to fly casting we frequently rely on fishing time as our sole practice, as if bad habits will somehow magically transform themselves into good ones if we just keep on pounding the river.

My own early efforts were no exception, and I blithely went on my not-always-merry way for years before I finally decided I had a problem.

At one time, many years ago, I decided to build fly rods for a living and eventually persuaded cane rod builder Walton Powell of Chico, California, to hire me. As part of the interview, Powell handed me a bamboo rod, and watched. About five false-casts and five tailing loops later, he grabs the rod, looks at me like a wolf, and says, "How do you expect to build a good rod if you can't even cast?" I had no respectable answer, and in order to get inside the shop, where I would spend the next year and a half immersed in the esoteric lore of splitting Tonkin culms, scraping the rind from glued-up rod sections, and polishing ferrules, I agreed to take lessons. Three years later, still a mediocre caster, I abandoned rod building and moved to the Bay Area in northern California to go into the retail fly shop trade. There, things began to get interesting as Andre Puyans, David Inks, Mel Krieger, and Steve Rajeff provided me with some insights into casting. The learning hasn't stopped, and I suppose it never will.

But what you are about to read here will not teach you how to cast. Casting cannot be learned by reading or from illustrations and photographs, because it is based on a series of interrelated motions, done in real time and space, each one dependent upon the effective implementation of the one just preceding it. And even though each individual movement may be relatively simple, when each is connected to the other, the process becomes alive, animated, subtle, and complicated. Books, diagrams, and words, including those offered here, will help. But learning how to cast, or fish for that matter, by reading a book is like trying to understand a movie by just looking at the individual frames of the film.

Secondly, no one becomes a better caster by merely improving on those parts of the process he or she has already learned. This helps, but it is insufficient. We improve most dramatically by discovering those parts of the process that are failing. You have to know what you are doing wrong, which isn't as easy as it sounds. The failures in the casting stroke for a short delivery of twenty to thirty feet may be obvious, even to you, and the short cast can be made even with relatively poor maneuvering. But it becomes a different game as you lengthen your casts. The longer the cast, the more subtle and complicated the maneuvers are, and the stroke and timing for a 90- to 100-plus-foot-long cast must be close to perfect.

Almost without exception, to improve the kinds of subtleties involved in making long casts you need to have an expert eye watch, and analyze, your casting stroke. At that point it becomes the expert's responsibility to find your mistakes and the language to convey what you are doing wrong. This may sound a little academic and obtuse, but not all great casters are great

teachers. Not all casters can find the necessary words and imagery for effective communication. For example, I struggled for years with the forward stroke of a single-handed steelhead rod, especially for distance. Despite a lot of advice, I continued to throw tailing loops, a circumstance where the line hits itself as the loop tries to unfold on the forward cast.

One day casting instructor Mel Krieger watched me for a moment as we fished for steelhead on northern California's Klamath River. Mel knew instantly what was wrong with the timing of my distance casting. In one deft sentence he gave me the imagery I needed to translate abstract words into effective motion by asking me to imagine the kind of stroke it would take to launch a tomato off the tip of my nine-foot rod. "That's what the forward cast should be," he said. "Think about it," he added, "you would have to start your forward cast slowly, accelerate smoothly, and finally stop quickly out in front of you. If you do that, the tomato will fly where you want it. If you do not, and snap the rod forward too quickly, the fruit will simply fall to the ground at your side." Bingo!

On another occasion, twenty-five years and well over a thousand steelhead later, I am in Oregon up to my waist in a cold pool fishing for winter-run steelhead with John Ferguson and Tillamook guide Scott O'Donnell. I have a two-handed rod in my hands, fishing from river right looking downstream. I am casting off my left shoulder, with my right hand still on top of the handle. Scott is with John fifty feet downriver, but he keeps looking back at me as I make the ninety-foot casts into the translucent seam I see shining just beneath the dancing reflection of a leaning pine. After a few moments, Scott comes up and says, "Not bad, Waller, but I can show you how to do it even better." He takes the rod, shows me what I am doing wrong, and hands the rod back. "Now make the same shot," he says, "but come a little farther around behind your left shoulder, about a foot or so, and then accelerate a little sooner. Stop the rod just a smidgeon more crisply, and a little sooner. By the way," he added, "the reason you sometimes 'chop wood' on your forward cast, is because you drift forward with the rod tip after your D loop is formed. Once you've done this, you have the rod extended too far in front of you, and there is no way to go but down with the rod tip." It took a few tries but I found the rhythm. Scott smiles and says, "That's better, Waller. That last cast

Casting with any rod, single- or double-handed, is effortless when you master the timing. Timing is everything, and your timing will also be one of the first things to go when you're tired. Take it easy—slow down when you sense your casting falling apart. Throwing harder and thrashing around only makes matters worse.

went around 120 feet. Now keep on fishing. Who knows? You might even get one."

I did not get one that day, but it was still satisfying fishing, even after a thousand casts. I reminded myself that I wouldn't be willing to make that many casts for a bonefish, or a trout, or any other of the great species of fish we have swimming around the fresh and salt waters of the planet. I would never have discovered the slight differences in the timing and maneuvers on my own

without the expert and critical eye of someone who could see the failure.

One of the earliest and biggest lessons I learned regarding distance casting with single-handed rods was that you don't do it with one hand. You must use your line hand to increase line speed with the double haul, because the rod hand alone cannot sufficiently load the rod or get the line as straight as quickly as you can by adding the pull of the line with your line hand. This is a

The best lines for distance casting with either a single- or double-handed rod are weight-forward tapers that are designed so the heaviest part of the line (the casting belly) is at the front. That's what loads the rod. The thin line is called shooting or running line and it goes along for the ride, following the belly out over the water.

basic but absolutely critical maneuver that you can learn through lessons and lots of practice.

The single-handed rod stroke also requires a low rod position and a straight line for the beginning of the back-cast, something many anglers, beginner and advanced, often ignore or forget. When your rod tip is low and the line is straight, you load the rod for a good backcast, and a good forward cast depends on a good backcast. Any cast over sixty feet demands a good lift of the line from the surface, followed by an accelerated backcast stroke, and a

firm stop of the rod just as it goes by your ear. Do not come forward after you stop your rod until the line has almost completely unrolled behind you. A common casting error, which some call "creeping," is drifting forward with your rod hand slightly after you stop the rod on the backcast, which introduces slack into your line and robs your cast of efficiency.

After the stop, it is possible to drift back with the rod tip almost to a horizontal position. This backward drift is a great maneuver for distance, because it sets up the forward cast by increasing the distance of travel of the rod tip during your forward cast. This increase in the forward travel of the rod tip almost guarantees that the line will be pulled straight throughout the forward stroke. This maximizes the bending of the rod, and the more a well-designed rod bends, and the more abruptly it is stopped, the more power there is in the cast. Timing is everything, and your timing will also be one of the first things to go when you're tired. Take it easy and slow down when you sense your casting falling apart. Usually, increasing your effort and simply throwing harder and thrashing around only makes matters worse. Be patient. Most of us do not learn this in a day or two.

Another easy way to improve your single-handed casting is to always use the correct grip, especially when casting for distance. Your thumb must be on top of the rod handle and not off to one side. This gives you a stronger grip because it aligns the muscles in your thumb, wrist, and forearm in a single direction. In addition, keeping your thumb on top of the rod handle helps keep your wrist from bending too much as you stop the rod on your backcast. If your wrist bends too much during your backcast, your backcast loop widens, robbing the cast of line speed that is difficult to recover with even a great forward cast. Keep the grip firm. A soft grip encourages a lazy stroke that loses power quickly. The

Many anglers believe that casting two-handed rods requires more energy and more muscle than single-handed rods, but they actually requires less muscle and energy because you have more rod working for you. Two-handed rods of 14 ½ to 15 feet are easier to learn with, but nothing equals the finesse and enjoyment of the 11-foot switch rods.

thumb on top is also a great indicator. If you have stopped your rod at the right point during your back-cast, your thumb will be pointing straight up. Once you see that, the backcast loop has been formed and you can drift back if you want.

Casting two-handed rods has a lot in common with casting single-handed rods. Learning never ends, but in the beginning I think it's helpful to remember that, when you swing the rod around to form the D loop on any cast, you are in effect making a backcast and must start as you would with the single-handed rod. In other words, begin with the proper rod position, low and pointed at the fly and water, then get the line under tension, by starting slowly, and then accelerate with a strong motion that puts the line in position and ready for the forward cast.

The forward cast with the two-handed rod also shares some common elements with that of the single-handed rod. Accelerate smoothly, stop the rod tip crisply, don't "chop wood," and don't force any part of the casting process. Most anglers, when they are starting, believe that they must use more force and more power to cast the longer and heavier two-handed rod, but the reverse is true. It takes less force and power to cast them than it does single-handed rods simply because you have more rod working for you. For years I believed that the harder I pushed the rod, the farther and faster the line would go.

The second greatest revelation came when I realized that I had more time to make the cast than I thought. I believed that the entire process had to happen very quickly, and if I paused or slowed down at anytime, a lot of bad things would inevitably happen: the sinking tip would sink too far, the floating line would drift out of position, or the cast would collapse in the air and everything would just go to hell. Faster is better, I thought,

No steelhead would ever think that the splashing water caused by the moving Spey line is a "mouse." They would say it is a very large rat, or maybe a beaver. So be careful where and how you set up your forward cast with a two-handed rod. The lines for two-handed rods have heavy bellies and they make a disturbance. Remember, you are fishing, not training rodents.

For maximum distance with large flies and heavy sinking-tip lines nothing beats the Skagit-type lines with short and heavy casting bellies. These lines are excellent for beginners because their shorter belly lengths load the rod with less motion, and the less line you have to move, the easier it is.

God bless steelhead. They do not care if you are an expert caster. They only care if your fly looks alive and if it looks easy to take. The cast may get it out there, but it is the presentation that closes the deal. So learn to cast, but when the chips are down it is your presentation that brings the fish to the net.

and I had every motion and maneuver moving so quickly it really didn't go anywhere at all. That's saying something because the sweep of an 11- to 15-foot rod moves a lot of line—even if it's being moved incorrectly—and even a bad cast with poor timing will go forty feet.

You do not have to learn every kind of Spey cast to fish effectively. Basically you have to have one cast for river right and one for river left (looking downstream). You have several options from which to choose, but I recommend the double Spey when fishing from river right and the snap T when fishing from river left. The

timing of these casts is easier than some of the other casts. There are many others, but many beginners make the mistake of trying to learn all of them at once. Just pick a cast you like (for whatever reason) for each side of the river and stay with it until you feel comfortable with it and you can cast approximately seventy feet or more with that cast. Then, try some of the others. Comfortable also means that you can make the cast repeatedly without losing the rhythm and having to abort the cast and start all over again.

Effective casting should be invisible to the fish, and it doesn't matter what it looks like. Casting should help the potential of your presentation, not diminish it. Presentation, mending, and the swing of your fly are more important than your cast. So don't worry about always making the perfect shot, and don't worry about being pretty. Worry about being effective. I have seen so many otherwise decent anglers make a less-than-perfect cast just a little short of where they think the fish is, and then rip the line back off the surface, making three or four splashy and noisy roll casts trying to get the line under control and under tension while they attempt another "better" cast. Since there may well be a fish out there that would be alarmed by all the disturbance, the caster is better off to just let the bad cast swing out of the fish's sight before making a second attempt.

When choosing a rod, beginners should probably stay away from extremes. This means single-handed rods less than eight feet and longer ones of ten to eleven feet. The shorter rod lengths require a better timing, and the longer ones put more stress on your wrist and forearm when you are learning. When learning to cast a two-handed rod, it's also best to avoid shorter rods (rods from 11 to 12 ½ feet) because they require a more sophisticated sense of touch and motion in your casting stroke. The long 15-foot rods are heavy and exert more pressure on the wrists when you are still learning the casting strokes. There is a place, however, for the 15- to 17-foot rods, and I would be the first to admit it. They do a good job of throwing a 200-foot cast during a tournament, and they would be better than a short rod for whipping a charging bear.

As I said earlier, your casting maneuvers should not diminish the effectiveness and potential of your presentation. If you are fishing a single-handed rod, minimize your false-casts, and if you are making "water casts" by casting the line on the water and using the surface tension on the line to help load the rod for a backcast, do not do them over and over again in an attempt to get the timing down or to increase the load on the rod. This only alerts a steelhead, and my advice is that if you can't get the timing down in the air you should work on your casting.

If fishing a two-handed rod, keep your downstream roll casts to a minimum as these may alarm a fish holding directly, or almost directly, below you. If I am wading fairly deeply and the water directly below me looks good, I will not throw my line there to get my line straight and set up the cast. I rotate my body somewhat and make that first "set up" roll cast away from good looking water, and toward the shore. For instance, if I am fishing river left (looking downstream) with the snap T, I rotate toward shore and make the first maneuver so close to dry land that the fish will not see it.

It is also important not to fall in love with casting a long line for the sake of distance alone. This kind of casting is a great temptation once the basics are mastered, and it is true that a steelhead caught on a long cast is very exciting. So is one caught on a short line. Even experienced anglers succumb to the temptation of the long cast (in my book, casts over 90 feet), especially on big rivers. The long line is certainly enjoyable, and sometimes necessary, if the fish have been pushed out toward the middle of a larger stream by careless anglers who wade noisily or cast poorly.

Another reminder about distance: There should be just as many steelhead on your side of the river as there are on the other. If the water doesn't look good on your side of the stream, good casting and even long deliveries won't change that, and I would respectfully suggest that you either got out of the boat on the wrong side of the river or you walked down the wrong hill. At times, you will need to be able to make long casts; just don't do so unless you have to.

Very long casts require not only very good timing but some strength in the forearms and wrists. If you have neither, you can still catch fish. Some of the best steelhead anglers I will ever fish with were not great casters, but great and quiet hunters and stalkers with a keen eye for reading the water and knowing where and how to wade and where nearby fish were holding. This kind of angler will always outfish those who only know how to cast a long line.

CHAPTER

13

Of Trophies and Heads

A young eagle pirouettes down without sound against a blue and cloudless sky and settles in the fork of an old hemlock, briefly flapping his wings as he finds his balance. Below, standing alone in a pool of cool September water, the thought crosses my mind that the young bird may have already learned that steelhead will sometimes die after release. The eagle leans into the breeze expectantly, watching, and I look at the point of light where my line descends into darkness. I feel the strong pull and look back at the eagle, wondering which of them will quit first.

I could not guess her size because her jumps were lost in the autumn glare, but I knew she weighed less than some of the others—females close to twenty pounds, strong and bright who rolled and swirled in this same light, or on days when the sky was falling and the line

All steelheaders dream of hunting a trophy, and that is a necessary ingredient of our sport. However, some days the word "trophy" takes on a meaning that goes well beyond size. It can be anything—the slip of a spotted tail in the hand, the way a steelhead leaps in the light, or the memory of something no one should ever forget.

hissed cleanly as they tore downriver as if nothing could stop them. Sometimes nothing could, and the leader would just break. This is one of the reasons why some of these watersheds get crowded at times, I thought. The big ones are here, and everyone knows it. Some years these steelhead averaged fifteen pounds or more, and always there would be many males well over twenty. Now and then someone would see, hook, or sometimes even land a real monster over thirty pounds.

In the midst of my reverie I see a grinning Karl Mauser with the fly-caught world record—an immense steelhead hanging from his two-handed grip as if it were a side of beef. It was thirty-six pounds. It took me almost ten years to finally find Mauser, but I eventually did, one October morning beside his aluminum trailer on the banks of the very river from which he pulled the immense steelhead. We drank coffee that morning, traded stories, and in the process Karl smiled and told

155

Some believe that the bigger an animal is, the more power it holds. A wild steelhead of this size does have incredible power. Hook one and you'll be a believer. Hunting for one of these is a journey of many lessons.
BILLY LABONTE

me, "There is no way to predict it. If it's size you're after, it helps if you are on a river that has them. There are still some in the rivers on the Olympic Peninsula of Washington, some in the Clearwater in Idaho, and the Smith in northern California, but my first choice would be the rivers up here. The fly doesn't matter, nor does the cast. I'm not sure about the pool, but I don't think that makes a difference. They're where you find them. I don't know, maybe I was just lucky. And besides, I never met a wild steelhead that wasn't a trophy."

After that meeting, and despite his advice, the big fish still hung in my young mind like a work of art, and my journey began. I had set out to better Mauser's incredible catch, not to diminish the older angler, but to capture something that would be life changing or magnify my power in a way otherwise impossible. The uninitiated might say that I even came close a couple of times, but four or five pounds less is not close at all.

However, what eventually became most important to me were the way the world-record-holder's eyes had brightened that day when he spoke of his seasons on the water, the way the colors of fall burned like fire along the morning banks of the river, other smaller fish that had fought harder, and for some reason, my memory of the five pairs of waders hanging from the aluminum gutters of his trailer. Mauser had dropped something into place that day that would take twenty-five years to become real. When he died, I saw a photo of him at a banquet in his honor, and when no one was looking I gently touched the man's image in a private homage before I went into the crowded hall to give a talk about wild steelhead.

"So, here we are," I shouted to the young eagle, as my line suddenly jumped again—this time seven feet to the left. Then, when the line reversed itself in a wild spin to the right, the steelhead finally yielded and came closer. In the light of late afternoon her shadow flew over the river bottom, and she reminded me that there really is something in fishing impossible to find anywhere else. Her fins stood out like wings in an atmosphere of water as she glided above the river bottom, her sides burning in the afternoon light.

A dozen revolutions of the reel handle and then a low sweep of the rod brought her almost within reach, but when she came close enough for me to see her clearly, I remember leaning forward and inhaling through my teeth—an old habit for moments when I am completely surprised. She was terribly deformed. Almost unbelievably, she had no upper jaw or nose at all, and her small eyes were crossed and not round but oval and much too close together. Her lower jaw was still intact, but it twisted badly to the left and it stood alone, holding her tongue in a cradle, pointing ahead like the calloused beak of a wounded bird. The sight of her became a question, and I wondered how she could have survived. Sadness gathered around me.

Someone will say that my response was beside the point and nothing more than misguided anthropomorphic sentiment, but I knew better. She was one of the best I had ever taken, and despite the way she had fought, her great leaps and runs, her silver sheen and rose-colored fins, her dark spots and perfect fins and tail, and her courage and resolve, no one would consider her a trophy. She was too small, barely seven pounds, if that.

How many currents has this steelhead seen? How many obstacles did it overcome before it came to the hand? It's hard to think of a fish more capable than a wild steelhead, or one more interesting.

157

She would only be thought ugly and deformed, and yet if any steelhead ever deserved the description of a trophy, she did.

"Maybe I snagged you," I thought, as she struggled to regain her breath. "And I've been dragging you around by your tail, because all of you fight like hell when you're hooked like that." But the fly was buried in the folded trench of her lower jaw. As I picked her up, I could feel the muscles in her stomach tighten.

The fly came out with a quick twist. As I held her in the water and waited for her to regain her strength, it seemed impossible not to consider her future. As I set the rod down, I moved her forward in time, with the frames of the film clicking one after the other as she lay silently next to a red stone with streaks of white quartz. Autumn began to fade.

Moments later, winter came pouring over the northern ridge of Mount Tomlinson in a blizzard of cold snow. She still didn't move, and for a moment, I wondered how much I was really seeing, how much anyone could see. Perhaps all of this went well beyond our imagination, I thought. As her gills broke loose from fatigue and began to move faster, I looked up at the hemlock, the young eagle, and the landscapes beyond and wondered, "How long can all this last?"

The wind stirred and became inseparable from my own thoughts, and it seemed I had somehow gone beyond the day and was standing inside the pages of a book. I thought I heard the water talking as it passed over the stones. "One day," it whispered, "all things will reverse, even your rivers. Some of the dead will become alive, and some of the living will disappear. It will be

Some say that everything is connected, and so it is. When salmon and steelhead die, their decomposing bodies enrich the water. The water is drawn into the roots of the trees in a wild forest. Scientists have found salmon DNA in the tips of evergreen trees.

No one gets more from a river than a steelhead angler. We wade deeper, we wade farther, and we fish harder. Sometimes we have to, centering our focus in a way that diminishes even the water. But that is not permanent. It is only a matter of moments until we feel the pull of the river again.

unrecognizable. Your children will be born in the limbs of a tree."

"No," I replied, gripping the handle of the rod, "you're wrong. We still have time." Five minutes later, near the end of April, the small steelhead moved forward imperceptibly as the sun returned, burning the ice away and warming my hands. Then, sometime in early May, a large and strong male with dark shoulders and eyes like a leopard appeared. As I stood up in the spring light, I looked at them both, then turned back toward camp as the male began to circle his mate.

When I reached the edge of the forest and disassembled my rod for the long hike back to camp, the two steelhead had moved some forty feet downstream and were now holding near the slick water tail of the pool, just above a scalloped divot. I saw their breathing, and the female's tail waiving from side to side as the male came to her side and a thousand pearl-sized eggs swirled into a mosaic of tumbled stone. Not long after the fertilized eggs had safely settled, she abandoned the male, turned to the right, and went head-first over the end of the long pool, heading once more toward the open ocean where she dissolved into time and water. But it didn't matter. "I'll never forget her," I thought. "Mauser was right."

Two days later, after the encounter with the valiant female with no nose, and on the way back home from the glacial mountains and fjords of northern British Columbia, I sat in seat number 6D, aisle row, on the evening flight to Vancouver. The other passengers, mostly autumn steelhead anglers and a few locals, sat quietly as the plane taxied and lifted from the tarmac in a rush of exhaust. Most were talking, and their words dissolved into the roar of the engines. The clouds came next, and they gathered against the cold skin of the plane. The sun began to sink. No one seemed to notice.

At a cruising altitude of 20,000 feet, and just before the soda and beer, the television monitors dropped into place with a mechanical click. I plugged in my earphones. The news—a talking head and assorted images of recent events—paraded by, punctuated by thoughts of some of the fish I had taken over the past two weeks.

Then something different. Channel 3 was showing a documentary about a young girl who was born with a portion of her cranial plates missing. Her brain lay almost exposed and vulnerable just beneath her young and fragile skin. To make it worse, her eyes were too close together and her nose was short and disfigured. And yet, during her interview there was nothing but laughter in her voice. After four major surgeries, she had not given up. Her courage and resolve were incredible. She looked at the viewers in the plane, but only a few knew what they were seeing. "Don't worry," she said. "I'm going to be all right. I'm going to make it." We can all learn from you, I thought. Every one of us.

The passenger sitting next to me seemed uncomfortable and kept moving in his seat. Perhaps needing an escape, he turned slowly from the girl and said, in a strange and prophetic voice, "Boy, oh boy, would you look at that. That's some story, eh? Say . . . you been fishing? How was it?" he asked. I smiled, but didn't say much. I was finally learning when to speak, and when not to. I turned back to the girl and the small hen at Blue Flag, and thought of the risks all living things share.

Almost to the day, five years later, on September 8, 2005, I was pounding it out on river left of a long and sinewy run called Spey. I was relaxed and moving easily, even though this pool is not easy to fish. The definition of a good cast here simply means you just do whatever it takes to make the seventy-five-foot shot with only three feet behind you for something called (optimistically) a D loop. My guide was a friend named Mark McAneeley, who is no stranger to big steelhead. I also have with me a young photographer from one of the magazines who fishes with an understanding well beyond his years. He fishes like a madman and doesn't miss much. I'd rather not fish behind him, if I had my choice.

Mark agrees, and I stand alone among a collection of greasy boulders whose arrangement could drown the unsuspecting as he heads downriver and out of sight to check on Nichols. The groove starts off well enough, I suppose. I almost fall, but save myself at the last moment. That's handy, I think. I also think I only lost one dry fly in the impossible village of trees and twigs growing behind me before I eventually poked a fresh male of ten pounds on a black foam floater with green wings. The rest of the pool produces nothing, and forty-five minutes later I am back at the top, standing next to the northern slope of the rock from hell, tying on a ferocious looking black-and-blue fly almost five inches long. You know what they say: "Big water, big fly, big fish." *What do you have to lose?* I think. *Heave it out there.* The cast isn't bad, and the fly sails out like a small crow on 220 grains of a 15-foot sinking tip and 36-inch leader. The rig sinks like a steel cable. Now and then I feel the scrape of boulders. Perfect.

On the fourth or fifth cast, Mark suddenly comes roaring back into the pool, pulls up, and drops the anchor. His face is stretched and his eyes look crazy.

"What's going on," I ask. "You look funny."

"Ohhhh, Lon," he says. "You should have seen what I saw down at the tailout as I was coming back to get you. How's it going?"

"One small buck on a dry. What did you see?"

He tells me that he flushed a really big male into the pool where I am now casting. "How big?" I ask.

"I'm not sure. Twenty five to maybe thirty pounds. You should have seen his head. "This wide," and he extends his hands to a dimension better suited for a description of a bear. "Wouldn't it be something," he added, "if you hooked it?"

I look at Mark, then back at the run. It's almost two hundred yards long, with an average width of eighty feet and about five feet in depth. I do a quick and wild guess and decide that I am looking at something that feels, at least, like fifty thousand cubic feet of water. "Yeah . . . right," I say. "That would be something. I'll tell you what. Why don't you fish? You've wanted to try this rod and now would be the perfect chance."

"No," he answers. "Not here, not now. What if I hook him? I'd never live it down."

"You're right," I said. "I wouldn't let you."

The next drift hesitates slightly, late in the swing, and I feel the scraping tick. Pulling the line in for a quick check, I can see the hook point had touched a rock and it wasn't too bad, but it really wasn't perfect either. For a moment I almost took the easy way out and just threw the fly back out there, but at the last moment common sense won over and I decided against it. A fresh hook replaced the one with the slightly curled point, and on the next cast, too early in the swing to be a rock, the line just stopped and all hell broke loose. I don't remember the first two or three words I used, but none would qualify as dignified speech or a spiritual response.

Seconds later, whatever I have attached to the fresh hook is under full steam and my line is pouring through the guides of my rod. I finally get it, from sources unknown, and it is absolutely undeniable. "It's him!" I finally scream. "It's him, Basil! It's him! I have him."

I don't remember getting in the boat, but Mark may have pulled me in with one hand. We are now running downriver as the thing thunders over the tailout like an elephant and then goes plowing downriver for fifty yards. Then it turns around and comes back into the pool, where he holds in the sunlight, just below the surface, like an olive-colored log with pectorals as big as my hands. Mark was right. It was indeed one heck of a head. When I could take my eyes off those cranial proportions and looked at the little seven-weight rod, the tip was

dangerously close to the midsection and the rod seemed a bit stressed. Three more of these piscatorial exits downriver, then back in the pool again, and forty-five minutes later we had him. Mark likes it when the tape goes to 41 by 22. His hands were shaking. "Look at this thing," he said. "Look at his head."

Silence. Then, just as the breeze changed direction, someone says something under his breath that puts an exclamation point on the whole affair, and it might have been me as Mark was the only other one there, but he wasn't doing much more than just staring. The buck looked so big and so agitated, I decided I did not want to get in the water next to him. "Look at his head," Mark says again. "Look at that thing. He's got teeth!"

"God," I said. "You're right. Get him in the net, and go get Nichols. We want a shot of this one. I'll stay here and hold him in the mesh." It took a long time for Mark to find Jay and return, about ten years it seemed. Being that close to a fish of that size for a decade doesn't happen every day. I remember staring down at him in the netting and watching his breathing to make sure it was steady. I don't think I had ever really noticed before, but the base of a steelhead's uppermost gill plates just below its head are not independent at all, and they move in

Each steelhead is an individual and worthy of respect. It is with great embarrassment that I admit that it took me too long to see them as they truly are. While they may have physical differences, they also have unmistakable similarities. JAY NICHOLS

rhythm. As I watched the buck's breathing, the rhythm seemed perfect and unspoiled, and somehow there in the solitude and silence, as I looked at the fish's breathing, I realized it was closer to mine than I would have thought.

In Loren Eiseley's brilliant book on evolution, *The Immense Journey,* he describes a civilized man thrown magically back into the beginning of time. As the man stands on the edge of a warm and ancient river, watching the water's edge, a shadowy form emerges and crawls across the muddy shore of time and biological evolution toward him. When it sees the man, it rises on its fins, which are really the beginnings of legs, and stares back at him. "There was no escape," Eiseley writes, "no hiding from the truth, for in the end the man was looking at himself. Eons ago and lost in time, his own journey had begun here, in the primordial ooze of an unfinished planet. In time the fish would become the man, through uncharted distances and immeasurable time, and the man in some ways remained irreversibly connected to something he had once been."

I'm not sure quite how to say it, and I know it sounds a bit off to one side perhaps, but I knew at that moment Eiseley had at least part of it right, if not all of it, as I watched the breathing of this magical creature suspended below me, captured in the straining mesh and steel rim. The magic and power of all life was there, palpable and obvious in our breathing. The thought crossed my mind that perhaps those of us who pursue these creatures, or others, somehow know that, whether we consciously realize it or not. Perhaps that is the magic of wild things—the possibility for the uncensored connection—and in the process, perhaps the acquisition of some of the animal's magic. For some of us, this means the bigger they are, the more power they can give.

I reached into the net, ran my hands down his sides, then took the fish by its tail and rotated it slightly. The blood-red stripe seemed to glow in the afternoon light, and I knew I was in the presence of something old and special. The little female with no nose was there with him and all the rest of them, those remembered and forgotten that were part of an odyssey I would start over again if I just had the chance.

In my more philosophical moments I wonder just what drives a steelhead angler, and the steelhead themselves. When I am casting to them, and see the way they roll and splash in the currents where I am wading, it seems as much of a rendezvous as anything else.

As it turned out, the magical buck weighed in at slightly over 27 pounds, and when I lifted him out of the net, the thought crossed my mind that everything I had ever heard about steelhead, and more, just might be true—even the words of Loren Eiseley. Nichols, oblivious to these thoughts, simply sucks in his breath and the shutter clicks. "I got 'em," he says.

So Karl Mauser was right, and I'll add this and then we can move on. If you want one (and who among us doesn't?), all you have to do is find a river to which wild steelhead still return, and fight for those rivers and for those creatures who still depend upon clean water, including your children and grandchildren. Take them and all of your life and human breath with you when you go. Fish with compassion for all you encounter. Then simply keep your line in the water and your eyes open. They'll show up. Everything will. Sooner or later.

I've taken larger steelhead than this, but none more exciting. Somehow I was in the right place at the right time—and the truth is, it was both luck and hard work. That's the way steelheading is, and neither luck nor hard work would have meaning without the other. That's part of the magic of steelheading. JAY NICHOLS

CHAPTER

14

Of Truth and Fiction

I was raised in a German fundamentalist Lutheran family in southern Missouri that believed that lying about most things was wrong but the truth could be stretched a bit when you talked about fishing. The only problem I had with that perspective was the fact that the exemption didn't apply to children and you had to wait until your eighteenth birthday before you could start telling "real" stories.

So as a six-year-old angler, I just kept my worm in the water and my eyes on my red-and-yellow bobber and caught as many bluegill, crappie, and bass as I could. I also kept my ears open and listened with great interest when my Uncle Claude—a fire-and-brimstone Bible-thumping preacher who loved to fish—claimed there were only two kinds of fish in the world: Ordinary Ones and Big Ones. I didn't know exactly when "Ordinary"

Not all fishermen are liars. It helps sometimes, especially after the fourth bottle of cold beer, but more often than not the truth is a better way to tell what really happened. The story you are about to read is the truth, the whole truth, and nothing but the truth. More or less . . .

turned into "Big," and I still don't, but I think he was right. When they are *really* big, they really are better. This means that you don't have to exaggerate their size. You just "tell the truth, the whole truth, and nothing but the truth, so help you God."

Theological perspectives aside, these are some of the reasons why I became interested in steelhead when I was fifteen. I thought of them as giant rainbow trout and they were not only beautiful, they were closer to something I couldn't quite define at the time but really liked. They became my favorites and I fished for them all through the fifties and sixties in Northern California streams.

Then, sometime in the late sixties, I started hearing stories and reading articles about the monster steelhead of British Columbia. I also knew of the large steelhead in the state of Washington but decided to hit B.C. first because there seemed to be more rivers up there and thus more big steelhead. As I've said elsewhere in this book, I eventually ended up in steelhead paradise: the one and only Skeena River system of northern British Columbia.

So, some forty-five years later, there I was, all alone and on my knees in the dark and cold water of the incredible Kispiox River. As I looked down at the steelhead lying exhausted in the water at my feet, my hands were shaking. It was indeed a big one, but how big?

My companions, Gordon Wadley and Mary Lou Burleigh, were both well upstream and around at least three or four corners, so they couldn't help me. I was on my own. I had no net and the problem was exacerbated by the fact I couldn't remember where I had put my measuring tape. To further complicate things, the fish was starting to revive and I was having one hell of a time trying to hold the immense male with one hand as I tried to find my tape with the other.

I was also running out of light and out of time. The fish was getting stronger, and the forest was getting darker. A lot darker. Even my imagination seemed to be growing, originally inspired no doubt by my early religious training, which had included some rather odd existential absurdities, including things that would sometimes hide under your bed at night if you hadn't eaten all your vegetables.

Nonetheless, as I looked up from my trophy steelhead and at all those trees, with their shaggy arms outstretched toward me, I wondered if they were pointing me out to whatever could be hiding in the dark shadows of all that shoreline vegetation. Even the Aboriginals up there said such things were true, and I had heard many stories about "Things" that were born in darkness a long time ago—"Things" with strange and hairy bodies, long powerful claws, and gnashing teeth. It is true that the local chambers of commerce scientifically dismissed such ideas, but they weren't there with me that night. The truth at that moment was the fact that I was on my own.

So I decided I better get on with it and to hell with the measuring tape. I pulled some leader material out of my waders' chest pocket and started running it from the fish's tail down to its nose. That way I could then tie a knot in the leader at the point where the monofilament reached the giant steelhead's big snout. Later on I could measure that distance with Gordy's tape. Perfect.

But when I looked down at how big that steelhead was, it seemed larger than when I first pulled it ashore in two feet of cold Kispiox water. Maybe they always do when the light is low and they are the only fish you have

hooked all day and you are so damn tired and it's the end of your year up there—and last but certainly not the least, especially when it has been five years since you got one this big.

In any event, the longer I looked at that November steelhead, the bigger it got, but I still couldn't get it to lie straight in the water as I ran the leader along its side, so I knew I had to compensate for the curvature in its body in order to get a truthful measurement. I paused and looked up at the trees but Bigfoot wasn't there yet, so I still had some time.

I began by holding the leader material at the upper tip of the steelhead's tail rather than the center of its tail, since the big fish had a deeply forked tail and I also had to compensate for that, and a measurement from the tip of its tail would give me an honest length. But as my other hand ran the leader toward the nose of the fish, I could see I needed more than just an extra inch or two. So when I reached the steelhead's huge snout, I added what I thought would be the correct and truthful length. In other words, about four, maybe five or six, inches. Maybe a little more.

As I held the fingers of my right hand at the correct point on the leader material, I let go of the steelhead's immense tail and watched it slowly swim away in the darkening coils of moving water. As the buck disappeared, I knew I would never see it again, and the farther away it got, the bigger it seemed. Its shoulders began to swell and bulge; its fins looked like wings. The last thing I saw was that tail moving back and forth in the current like the rudder of an airplane.

After it disappeared, I held the leader up with both hands to see the length I had just measured, but something was wrong. "That fish was longer than this," I said to myself. "No doubt about it."

I looked at the darkening forest. Still no Bigfoot, but there were a couple of cottonwood trees staring at me. I could see their totem faces in the bark of their tall trunks. Look at those eyes, I thought. They know how big it is. They could see it too. Who was I to argue? So I moved my fingers down the leader just a little farther— just how much I can't truthfully say—and finally tied the measuring knot.

As I wound the leader up in a coil, a final decision had to be made. I didn't clip the leader right at the knot, but rather left a little bit hanging past the knot. Then, finally satisfied that I had the right length of that steelhead, I held the coiled leader carefully in my hand as

I saw Mary Lou and Gordy coming up the cobbled shoreline.

"Get anything?" Gordon asked.

I smiled and nodded. "Oh yeah, Gordy. I got a hell of a buck."

"How big was he?" he asked.

I thought about my answer. Gordon is an expert who knows big Skeena steelhead and has caught thousands of them. One year he took a female just over forty pounds. I saw the photograph and that steelhead looked as big as a Florida tarpon. So I knew Gordy would understand how big this one was.

I spread my arms apart and showed Gordy and Mary Lou the leader. They were looking at me in a funny way. "Well, goddammit," I said. "I didn't have my tape." I kept my hands apart and Gordon reached into his front wader pocket to get his tape. I held the leader steady as he ran it down the monofilament, past the last knot I had tied on it, and to the point where I was pinching the leader material. Mary Lou's eyes widened as she leaned forward trying to read Gordy's tape.

"Good God, Waller," Gordy suddenly said, "are you sure it was this long?"

"Hell yes," I answered. "So how long was it? What does your tape say?"

Gordon hesitated. "Well, just a minute," he replied. "What about the girth? Did you measure that?"

"No," I said. "I didn't have time. It was getting too dark."

"Well, OK," he replied, as Mary Lou looked on with her mouth wide open and her eyes bulging. "Did it look fat for its length, or did it look slender?"

"It looked fat for its length," I said. "Very fat."

"Hmmm," Gordy muttered. "Then you are right. That was indeed one hell of a steelhead. That's all I can say. If it was fat for its length," he added as he held the tape, "there can be no doubt that you just released a new world record for a steelhead on the fly."

Good God. I knew what that meant. It meant that it was bigger than Karl Mausser's world record Kispiox fish. I thought about that. I had seen the famous photograph of Karl in Trey Combs's book *Steelhead Fly Fishing*, and that buck hanging from both of Karl's hands looked as big as a fifty-pound Chinook. That steelhead was so big that the thirty-foot aluminum trailer behind Karl and his big steelhead looked like a small toolshed.

"Are you kidding, Gordy?" I finally said. "How long was my fish? What does your tape say?"

"Fifty-five inches long," he replied. "Fifty-five inches."

Then silence. Thundering silence. Forbidding silence. Finally someone exhaled. Maybe it was me. Maybe it was Gordy. Maybe it was Uncle Claude. I don't know. All I knew was that Mary Lou was looking at Gordy and Gordy was looking at me as Mary Lou covered her mouth and started laughing. I knew then that things weren't going too well.

"OK," I said quietly. "Then measure the distance from the end of the leader to the knot. How long is that?" I didn't know what else to say.

Gordon ran the tape to the knot and looked at me. "Thirty-nine inches," he said. "Thirty-nine."

More silence. Then at last—thank God—Mary Lou offered salvation. "Listen up," she said, "I've got an idea. Let's go to the Kispiox River Sportsman's Lodge and have a beer or two. I know that was one hell of a fish, Lani. I can tell by how excited you are, and you can tell us all about it then, and we'll take another look at that leader. Just to be sure."

I relaxed and felt my number fifteen wading boots coming back out of my mouth. "You're the best, Mary Lou," I said as we climbed into Gordy's truck and he turned on the heater. "The absolute best. Wait until we get to the bar and have a cold one in front of us. I'll show you the fly he took. I have it right here. Tied it myself."

When we got to the lodge it was filled with local citizens, several steelhead fishermen, and not very many steelhead fisherwomen. Some of them were dancing. Some were even dancing with their spouse. A few hadn't even taken their waders off. Most of them were drunk or well on their way, and the jukebox and all those boots pounding on the wooden floor were so loud you almost couldn't hear yourself think. I found these circumstances somehow comforting as I began telling Gordy and Mary Lou the story of how that big fish had hit the fly.

"Like a shark," I said. "A shark! There's no other way to describe it." I told them how high he had jumped, hanging suspended in the November air like a silver zeppelin, "probably fifteen feet high." I told them how far downriver he had taken me—"probably a mile or two"—and how beautiful he was when he finally came to my feet in perfectly clean and clear water.

I told them about the faces I could see in the trees, and how they had inspired the Aboriginal carvings of totem poles "most likely about one thousand years ago." I described how clean the air felt against my face, and

I have often wondered what fish are thinking as we release them, but I know what I am thinking: Steelhead are one of the world's most beautiful creatures and to be this close to one is a very special event.

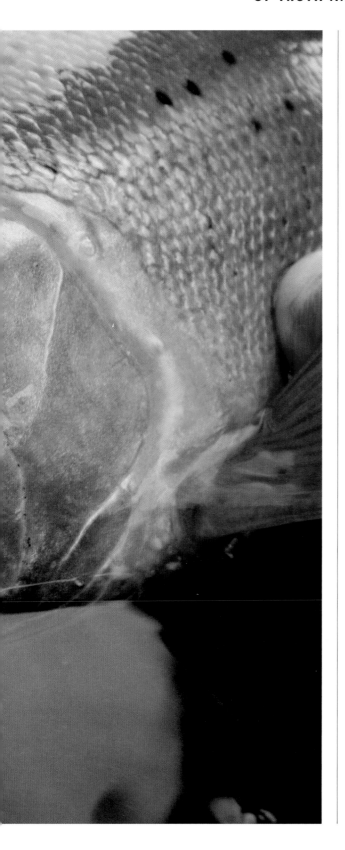

how quiet it was. I told them how beautiful the pool was and how much I loved all of it, even the stuff when I was just a six-year-old farm boy in Missouri. I told them how it had given me something I couldn't find anywhere else.

Maybe it was that fourth beer, maybe not, I don't know. Maybe it was my age at the time and my stage of life, but I couldn't shut up. I just kept talking. So I told them how important it was to keep those things safe because we need places like that, and that we were losing them all over the world, not just in British Columbia. I told them all of these feelings were the truth and there was no fiction in any of it. All of it was true. All of it was real. No matter what any politician might say, and if we ever let planet Earth fall to those kind of leaders, it wouldn't be long before we crossed a line we could never live with.

"Well then, just what are you going to do about all of that?" Mary Lou asked, leaning toward me. I looked at her, at Gordy—and at my fish, which was still swimming around in my brain. I could still feel the river pouring around my legs as I cranked that reel handle as fast as I could. I could see the eagle sitting in the tree and the dead and dying salmon lying the shallows behind me. It seemed that all of it was still there, but I wondered just how in the hell it would all turn out.

I inhaled as far as I could and then exhaled and looked at Mary Lou. "I'm going to write about it someday, Mary Lou," I replied. "That's what I'm going to do. I'm going to write about it." She was smiling and had both elbows on the table. "Well, Honey, what in the hell are you going to say about the steelhead you caught this evening? What are you going to say about that?"

"I'm not sure, Mary Lou," I answered with a grin, "but I'll think of something."

CHAPTER

15

Gearing Up

Tackle has changed tremendously over the past fifty years. Most modern steelhead equipment came from Atlantic salmon tackle, an influence still with us today. The current explosion of interest in two-handed rods is a good example. In addition, some of our early steelhead patterns and our choice of terminal tackle were also obvious reflections, if not actual copies, of traditional Atlantic salmon patterns and equipment.

Over the years, however, steelhead anglers have modified much of our early inheritance. Today, almost anything seems to be acceptable. With technical advances of the past twenty years or so such as graphite, neoprene, and Gore-Tex, today's angler has more good choices than any previous generation.

Modern steelheaders fish many different rod tapers and designs from eight to fifteen feet in length. Our lines

The two most important elements of your tackle are your rod and your line because they get the fly to the fish. Single-handed rods in the 9- to 10-foot range or two-handed rods in the 11- to 14 ½-foot range fished with a weight-forward line and interchangeable tips will do it all.

run the gamut from traditional double tapers to the latest weight-forward configurations, including relatively short-headed tapers with thin running lines and interchangeable density tips. We fish in waders scarcely thicker than a pair of jeans. Our clothing is light, warm, and immune from rainfall and extremes in temperature. Anglers have many choices, and much of the fuss is over our desire to play the game in a certain way that produces the effect we are looking for.

But a piece of tackle is more than something that is merely pleasant to use; it is a tool. Rod, lines, and flies could even be called weapons. The rod is a long and hopefully effective lever, spear, and spring that we "throw," "shoot line" with, and use to exert force on our prey, a process we refer to as "fighting a fish." Our best casts are described as being "as straight as an arrow." In my opinion, fishing is the hunt, the ancient connection between hunter and hunted, but with the luxury of a victory in which the prey is released to flourish and continue its journey. Our choice of tackle is no small part of this process.

Since I have been unable to completely escape the desire to catch as many as I can, I want all my gear to be as effective as possible under as many different circumstances as possible. Some of my best fishing comes when I have the confidence in my tackle to address any challenges I may meet on a wide variety of water conditions. To me, this means the ability to make casts from ten to ninety feet or more in almost all depths of water

and current speeds with a wide variety of sizes and types of flies, with or without a green army of trees crowding my haunches or a tangle of bushes in my face, and with the wind coming from any point on the compass. I would also like to do this from a variety of wading postures that may resemble almost anything from a pleasant walk down a summer country lane to hanging on to the north face of Mount Everest during a blizzard.

The length and weight of the longer and heavier two-handed rods took much of the pleasure out of my angling, though they are effective at casting great dis-

Most steelhead flies do not mimic any specific aquatic insect or food. Atlantic salmon flies inspired many of our current steelhead dressings. Steelheaders simplified the materials, but we still use the same construction elements: tail, body, hackle, and wing. LANI WALLER

Big steelhead don't always prefer large flies, especially in clear water. Silver Hilton guide Dave "Beano" Holland put Chris "Mad Dog" Travis on this Babine buck. Chris used a #6 Egg Sucking Leech and a 15-foot, #8 tip to get the fly near the bottom in five feet of water. LANI WALLER

All reels have to do is to store line, then let it out, then bring it back without stalling or tangling. But that is some-times a tall order when hooking into fish that can take you into your backing.

tances. The heavy 15- to 16-foot two-handed rods that started showing up on West Coast steelhead rivers in the early 1980s emerged from the traditions of European angling for Atlantic salmon, and I never liked their weight and length from the beginning. It has been inter-esting to see the gradual increase in popularity of the 11- to 13-foot rods.

The shorter rods require a better sense of timing and are not the best to learn with, but once your timing is in place, they bring back all the magic of a single-handed rod, combined with the advantages of two-handed casting. The little 11-footer I use, combined with a Windcutter-type line, brings back all the excitement of a

hard and slashing take, the sudden electric surge, the jumps and long runs downriver of a strong and vibrant fish. It also is easier to land a fish with the shorter rods. As time goes by, I think these rods will become even more popular.

Shorter rods are also called "switch rods" because you can use them with one hand when you have room for a regular backcast or two hands when there is little room behind you. Being able to use the rod one-handed is also an important part of my strategies when the wading is difficult. When I am up to my waist in swift water and sneaking around greasy boulders, I have one hand on my wading staff for stability and support as I move

TACKLE LIST

I prefer to keep things as simple as possible when traveling by foot and wading, but if I have the luxury of a boat or raft to carry extra clothing and gear, my minimalist perspective dwindles somewhat and I carry more. Here is a list of the things I would not want to be without when on a trip.

Rods. I carry two rods: a 13 ½-footer for long casts (from 70 to 90 feet or more) and fishing heavier sinking lines in deep water. My current favorite is the Sage Z Axis model #7136. I also carry a smaller and lighter 11-foot switch rod for fishing dry flies and light sinking tips at distances up to about 60 to 70 feet. My all-around favorite fishing rod is the 11-foot 7-weight Sage Z Axis, model #7110. I carry a spare of each rod.

Reels. I use large-arbor, right-hand-wind reels for maximum line retrieval. I prefer a reel with a sealed drag. In my boat bag, I carry two reels of the same model and four extra spools with different kinds of lines that are all interchangeable.

Lines. I use a Windcutter-type line for my small rod (approximately 54-foot head) and a Skagit-type line (approximately 25- to 27-foot head) for the big rod. In my boat bag, I carry two extra lines for each type in case I lose a line or two. In my fanny pack, I carry spare heavy tips, a spare of the lighter density tip, and a complete line.

Waders. I pack one pair of stocking-foot Gore-Tex and one pair of insulated bootfoot waders. I pack one extra pair of the stocking-foots in case one of the other two develops a leak. Both have a pocket at the front and top of the wader to hold my flies, hooks for tube flies, and a tippet spool.

Wading belts. One nonstretch belt goes over my waders and under my rain jacket. Another stretch belt holds my fanny pack and keeps my rain jacket tight against my waders for extra protection should I fall in. For rough and deep wading, I carry a small inflatable life preserver on the same belt with my fanny pack.

Wading shoes. I use felt soles with extra screw-in carbide tips for sure footing. My medium-weight wading socks have long uppers that I pull over my underwear. In my fanny pack, I carry a spare pair of laces for my wading shoes.

Underwear. I wear medium-weight synthetic long johns under my waders. When it gets really cold, I wear a pair of down-filled pants as a second layer under my waders.

Wading staff. I make my own out of bamboo garden poles and bring a spare metal collapsible staff in the boat in case I lose the wooden one.

Small tackle box. I bring along, but leave at camp, a soft small case to hold tackle and electrician's tape for taping the sections of my rods together, extra wader patching kits, extra carbide screw-in cleats for the soles of my wading shoes, and extra boxes of flies.

Gloves. Four pairs in my boat bag, so that when one pair gets wet I can put on a dry pair.

Hat and caps. One baseball cap with a brim and a fleece cap with long "ears" that I can put on top of my brimmed hat for warmth.

Polaroid glasses. I carry two pairs, both with amber lenses.

Rain jacket. Two jackets (one for a spare in the boat bag) both in the shorty style but long enough to fit under the belt for my fanny pack.

Shirts and jackets. I layer my clothing and start with a lightweight polypropylene long-sleeve T shirt. On top of that I put a medium fleece pullover. When it gets really cold, I add a long-sleeve down jacket.

Fanny pack. It holds extra terminal tackle, including sinking tips, leader tippet, a pair of pliers, two nippers, stream thermometer, and a Swiss Army-style pocket knife. I also keep a waterproof flashlight in here. I cinch the pack over my wading jacket to provide added security in case I go in. A tightly belted fanny pack worn over your rain jacket compresses your waterproof rain jacket against your waders and also increases the pressure of your waders against your body. This two-belted system provides additional insurance against taking in water if you should fall in.

Boat bag or small pack. I carry one complete change of clothing in a waterproof bag, matches and fire-starter material, more fly lines and extra tips, and electrician's tape for taping the ferrules. I also have a dry towel for rainy days. I hate fishing with a hood over my head because I can't see or hear as well. So I leave the hood down whenever possible, and my neck is always wet when it rains.

Miscellaneous travel. My clothing is all light-weight, non-wrinkle, and compressible, and I keep everything in small duffle bags with ID tags on the outside. The small bags are a great help because you can stuff them into the empty spaces and corners of a larger duffle.

That's it in a nutshell. Come to think of it, maybe I'm not a minimalist at all.

A smooth drag will manage a large steelhead's sudden runs and lunges. A large reel holds a large-diameter line and plenty of backing. If you have to wind in a lot of line, a large arbor does a great job of getting your string back on your reel in a hurry. LANI WALLER

A fly rod is both lever and spring. The longer two-handed rods put more pressure on the fulcrum point, which is your wrist, so help yourself during a long fight by adding your second hand to the fore-grip of the rod. This also helps keep the rod tip vertical and provides a good cushion against sudden lunges.

downstream and make two-handed casts, such as the double Spey and snap T single-handed.

I use a Windcutter-type line with this rod with a combined belly and tip length of approximately 54 feet. Today, several companies produce this kind of line, including Rio Line Company and Scientific Anglers. This line has a smaller belly diameter than the Skagit-type lines and mends easily and quietly with the 11-foot rod. This kind of line also lands more softly on the surface than the Skagit type, a real advantage in smooth currents when fishing over temperamental fish or when you have to work a fish with multiple presentations. In addition, it casts up to seventy feet with ease. It also provides a more sensitive connection to my fly and transmits even soft takes almost instantly.

All reels have to do is to store line, then let it out and bring it back without stalling or tangling, but that can sometimes be a tall order when hooking into fish that often take you into your backing. I prefer reels with large arbors that regain line quickly and that are so smooth they feel like the tumbler of an expensive bank vault when you turn the handle. On the rivers I fish, reels also have to be large enough to carry at least two hundred yards of gel-spun backing, because I can no longer run downriver as fast as a steelhead can swim.

I like to use GSP backings rather than Dacron because they are thinner and stronger and do a better job of holding big fish in rough conditions. Their thin diameter cuts through heavy currents better, thus reducing the pressure on your leader, and they hold up better when scraped against large, jagged rocks and ledges. Because of its thin diameter, you can also load more on your reel, increasing its capacity.

And at times, this line capacity becomes critical. Once, not that long ago, I hooked a fish of unknown proportions on a northern British Columbian trophy river—although I would have to say that given the emotional excitement that possessed me at the time, I would have put the fish at an honest 75 pounds. The fish eventually spooled me and broke off when I ran out of line. I never saw it. By the time the guide arrived, I was standing at the edge of at least ten feet of black water, with the roar of the rapids in my ear, unable to proceed. Now, I don't know about you, but I've never lost a small one, so now I am considering the purchase of a reel that holds 800 yards of backing.

A smooth drag is also important. I once hooked my dog as he sat patiently waiting for me to catch a summer-run steelhead from the Junction Pool of the Eel River, just off highway 101, north of Garberville, California. I hooked him on a low backcast, with a number two fully dressed Green-Butted Skunk, complete with jungle cock cheeks and a shiny wisp of polar bear hair in the wing. Trust me; you've never really heard a reel "scream," or needed a smooth drag, until you've played a 65-pound Rhodesian Ridgeback heading for the mouth of the ocean with your fly firmly embedded in his butt. I have been tempted, but have so far managed to avoid, to test a new drag by hooking a truck. Although they say it is addictive, I may yet opt for the experience, especially when the time comes that I can't wade or see very well.

If you choose a reel with a cork disc drag, make sure it is always well oiled and free from water. These drags can be very smooth, but if submerged, the lubrication on the cork disc can wash off, and the drag can become uneven and sticky. Once, Babine River guide Aaron Henderson and I had a big one on for almost thirty minutes. I had not lubed my reel in some time (pilot error), and it had been submerged several times earlier that week. Aaron and I had to get in the boat to keep up with the fish. Just at the worst moment, when the steelhead was only twenty feet away in the middle of the river, its tail finally slashed the surface. As it did so, the drag broke loose and the reel back-lashed. The steelhead didn't hesitate and turned once more to the sanctuary of

The best backing for steelhead is gel spun. These backings are thinner and stronger than Dacron backings so you can have more line on your reel and have better protection against getting cut off on a sharp rock or boulder.

heavy water in midriver, breaking 15-pound-test leader with a sound that cut both the cold October air, and our hearts. "Oh, sh—," Aaron said softly. "That was one big tail. Well, over twenty, I'd say."

I'm a right-handed caster and prefer setting my reels up with the handle on the right side of the reel so I can wind them with my right hand. On the rivers I fish, line retrieval is critical, as a very large and powerful steelhead can leave the pool anytime it wants to and make a long run downstream. In those cases I have to wind a lot of line back in—either on my own and on foot, or in the boat as the guide and I chase the fish downriver. I can regain line quicker with my dominant hand.

Lines? Several great innovations in my lifetime remain critical to this day. The first two, as I recall, came sometime in the early 1950s when Scientific Anglers of Midland, Michigan, introduced floating lines with a specific gravity less than water and a collection of sinking lines available in different densities. Before that time we had to "grease" our floating lines to make them float and rub varnish and ground-up lead particles to make them sink fast enough to be useful.

Not long after this, weight-forward tapers came into fashion and increased the distance fly anglers could cast. Anglers could then false-cast the forward casting portion of the line and shoot the remaining line through the guides. Around the same time, tournament casters from the venerable Golden Gate Angling and Casting Club discovered the advantages of a thin monofilament shooting line behind a 30-foot head, and they proceeded to break all existing distance records with the new lines. The discovery was not long a secret, and soon steelhead anglers carried them on all of the great Pacific Northwest rivers. Some anglers still do, and the lines still work.

All of these American line tapers and belly lengths were designed for one-handed rods, and lines designed

On heavily pressured steelhead waters, carry a variety of fly types, sizes, weights, shapes, and colors. Anglers on any given river often all use whatever fly is currently popular. Steelhead soon learn what that fly is, but you can fool them with something they haven't seen lately, as long as it looks and swims right.

Stocking-foot waders with lace-up wading shoes offer the best ankle support. The best traction comes by adding carbide tips to the felt soles. Don't lace your boots too tightly in cold water, or add too many socks; these "remedies" only restrict circulation and your feet will get colder, not warmer.

for single-handed rods still remain at the center of our modern lines, which now also include the option to change the tip of the line to any one of several densities and weights. As two-handed rods gain a following in this country, fly lines are being made that address their special abilities and requirements.

I like to use a line with a belly length (including the tip) that is approximately three-and-a-half times the length of my rod. This belly length is shorter than that of traditional Spey lines, but it offers some very real fishing advantages. I prefer a relatively heavy and thick belly, followed by a thin running, or shooting, line. This gives me the greatest distance and also allows me to feed slack line into the drift for additional depth in my fly swing. One of the advantages of the long-belly Spey lines is that you do not have to strip in a lot of line before you make another cast, but I do not mind having to retrieve the line at the end of my drift to prepare for the next cast. I usually like to slowly tease or strip my fly back to me as a way to induce a steelhead that may be directly below me to strike.

To keep things as simple as possible, I normally use only one density of sinking tip (a number 8). Line density refers to how quickly the line will sink and is determined by the kind and amount of material used in making the line or tip of line. The denser the material, and the more of it that is in the line, the quicker the line will sink, and the quicker it sinks the higher the number ascribed to it. Standard sinking lines comes in densities from #1 to #8. In addition to line densities, lines also have grain weights ascribed to them to measure how heavy they are. I vary the weights and carry 100, 150, and 200–225 grains in 15-foot lengths. All rods can handle more than one weight of line, and many modern fly rods have several line weights marked on their handles such as 7/8/9 or 9/10/11. The line companies understand this, so the same line is designated as being appropriate for several different rods.

I use the 100-grain tip for shallow runs and riffles, the 150-grain for deeper and faster water, and the 200-grain for dredging. In moving water, the different weights of the same density will not all sink at the same rate; the heavier they are, the quicker they sink.

If I can't get deep enough with the number 8 density in 200–225 grains combined with a short leader of around four feet, a weighted fly, and manipulating the line, I go to another pool, as I have no interest in fishing with tips heavier than 225 grains. There is nothing wrong with them, and the 300- to 450-grain tips can be a big help in scouring the bottom of deep and hard running water, but for me they aren't as pleasurable to fish as lighter lines. One of my core values as fly fisherman has always been the opportunity to use and enjoy light tackle, and if you aren't careful you can reach a point when conventional level wind or spinning tackle is actually lighter and more pleasant in the hand than throwing a heavy line with a long and heavy fly rod.

Oregon steelhead expert Scott O'Donnell, co-inventor of the Skagit type lines, also prefers one density of tip and uses mostly sections of T-14 line produced by Rio Line Company. Scott simply carries a spool of T-14 in his vest and just cuts off the required length of the sinking line material and attaches it to his casting head loop with a clinch knot. Scott will use anywhere from two to twenty feet of the sinking material, depending on how deeply he wants his fly to swim.

Jerry Siem, another friend and expert who designs rods for Sage, shares my preference for lighter tackle, and for the past season we have been discussing his choice for the business end of his casting line. In lieu of ordinary tips, Jerry uses 15-foot-long sinking leaders with a light rod such as the 11-foot Z Axis. Sinking leaders are nothing more than tapered nylon monofilament coated with the same material used for the T-14 line. Their thinner diameter cuts through the water so well that you end up with the same sink rate of a fast-sinking #8 density tip.

As far as ordinary leaders go, the best advice I've ever heard is they should be "short enough to cast well, and long enough to fool the fish." Where the fish are not heavily pressured from other anglers, my leaders for wet-fly fishing may be only a single piece of 4-foot-long monofilament, which I make short enough to keep the fly close to the sinking tip. For presenting a dry fly to these same fish, I may go to a 13- or 14-foot leader with a tippet ranging from 10- to 15-pound-test, depending on water clarity, angling pressure, and fly size.

Many anglers prefer wearing bootfoot neoprene waders when the water is cold.

Royal Treatment
(tied by Joel La Follette)

Hook:	#1–2 Daiichi 2151
Thread:	Black 70-denier Ultra Thread
Tag:	Gold oval tinsel
Butt:	Purple Floss or Dyna-Floss
Tail:	Fl. blue (teal) golden pheasant crest
Veiling (optional):	Peacock neck
Second Butt:	Peacock herl
Body:	Purple wool
Rib:	Gold oval tinsel
Underhackle:	Purple pheasant rump aftershaft feather
Hackle:	Purple guinea with blue peacock breast feather over
Throat:	Peacock sword
Wing:	Peacock sword

Summer Berry
(tied by Joel La Follette)

Hook:	#2 Daiichi 2151
Thread:	Black 70-denier Ultra Thread
Butt:	Flat silver tinsel
Tag:	Hot pink floss
Body:	Purple ostrich herl
Hackle:	Purple guinea
Wing:	Two blue peacock breast feathers

Tier's Note: This is a simple but beautiful fly. It's name comes from a tasty pie served at the world famous Steamboat Inn on the North Umpqua.

As the water drops and clears, or the fish become spooky due to angling pressure, you have to go longer and lighter. For instance, tidewater steelhead pounded for weeks in low water become impossible to catch on anything except #10–14 flies and 15- to 18-foot leaders tapered down to 4-pound-test. On the other hand, wilderness steelhead are usually unpressured and are not usually leader shy.

When selecting a pattern, choose a fly with a size and color that matches the water clarity and mood of the fish. Generally, the lower and clearer the water and the fussier the fish, the smaller and more subdued your patterns should be. I'm not sure about fly color. All colors seem to work. I've even become suspicious of the old adage of the darker they are, the easier it is for a steelhead to find them. Several seasons ago Mark McAneeley, one of the best guides I've fished with, introduced me to a long and willowy pink pattern made of marabou and long soft hackle. Mark assured me it was one of his best for dirty water and was inspired by his conventional-gear clients who had excellent angling for spring-run steelhead in cloudy water using a long, slinky pink rubber worm. My personal aesthetics aside, the idea of that color and action seemed interesting because I valued this guy's opinion. I began using Mark's long and slinky pink fly and found it to be as effective as the black and or purple patterns I had relied upon for cloudy currents. After the tenth fish or so, we decided it needed a name, and the "Pink Slammer" is now a regular in our boxes.

The Pink Slammer has remained one of my favorites for all water types, but in truth I mostly worry about color in only two circumstances. If I am following another angler or anglers through a run, I prefer to use a color none of them are using, because it seems evident that if the steelhead are there, and they refuse the color of those who are fishing before me, they very well might treat my similar fly the same way. The second circumstance is really just another form of the first. If I go through a run with one color of fly, I always change that color on the second pass through the pool, even if I have hooked a fish or two on the first time through the water. I frequently do hook a fish on the second pass using a different color, and, although I cannot prove the color change did the job, it seems a real possibility since I've already given it my best shot with the first fly. I believe steelhead can see color and differentiate between them. I also believe that, sooner or later, they can sense a cause-and-effect relationship between color and size of

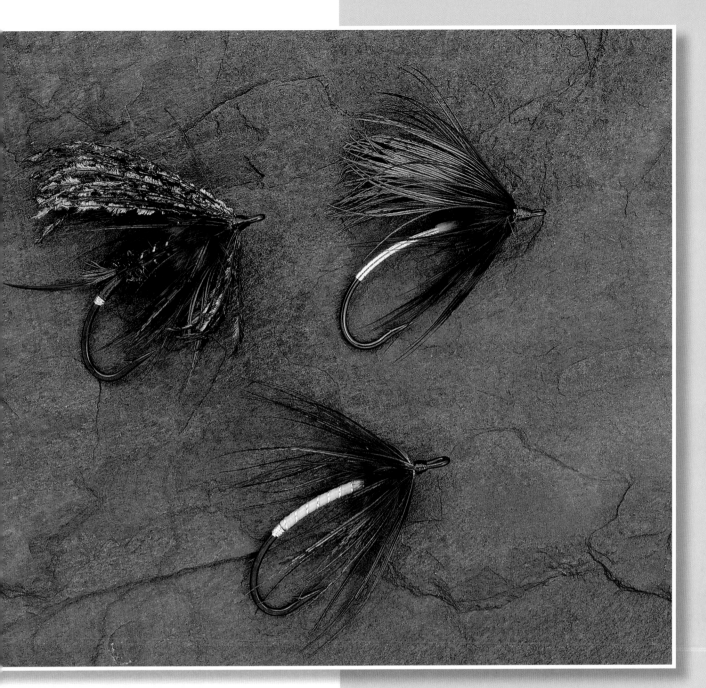

Clockwise from left: Royal Treatment, Summer Berry, and Peacock Spyder tied by Joel La Follette.

JAY NICHOLS

fly and all the fuss being kicked up when one of their neighbors takes that oddly swimming thing that keeps going by all the time.

So much for the fly dressings. Now to the heart of the matter, the bottom line, the place where the buck stops. Given a steelhead's willingness to take almost any pattern, I do not believe it's the dressing that makes the fly. It is the hook. From my point of view, the hook is the heart of the fly and reveals its most essential characteristic. It is more than a lure that attracts—it is a snare, a

Peacock Spyder

Hook:	#2 Daiichi 2151
Thread:	Black 70-denier Ultra Thread
Tag and Rib:	Silver French Tinsel
Body:	Chartreuse floss over silver Mylar
Underhackle:	Black filoplume from pheasant rump, spun in dubbing loop
Hackle:	Blue peacock breast feather

Tier's Note: When a fish comes to a fly but doesn't take, after a few more casts I go to the Spyder. It can be tied low-water style on a lighter hook.

McAneeley's Slammer tube flies. You can tie these in a wide range of color schemes to suit conditions.

JAY NICHOLS

trap, and tool. It is also the most vulnerable part of the pattern. The hook always wears out long before the hackle, cheeks, tail, or topping.

For too long most of us used heavy wire hooks for our wet flies and even relatively stout wire for our dry flies. The hooks needed major surgery to be effective, with careful re-shaping of the point until it was long and needle sharp. Once that was achieved, the first time they struck a rock or boulder they became almost useless. Rather than throw away a fancy tie, most anglers tried to re-shape and sharpen the hook, which was not easy.

For the most part, heavy-wire hooks have been replaced by short-shank, lighter-wire hooks with laser sharpened points carefully tapered to penetrate quickly. The best, in my opinion, also have offset points and turned-up eyes. A tube fly or stinger type of fly allows you to incorporate these types of hooks into your fly patterns. On tube flies, you can add a short, soft section of rubber tubing, called a junction tube, over the hard piece of plastic tubing that the fly is dressed on. Pass the leader through the tubes and tie a double surgeon's loop in the end of the tip. Then pinch the loop and thread it through the hook eye, and then around the hook. Looping the leader around the up-turned eye prevents the hook from drooping or twisting to the right or left. The loop is drawn into the soft junction tube until the knot comes to rest at the rear edge of the hard tubing, which

Slammer
(tied by Mark McAneeley)

Hook:	#1 Owner SST or Gamakatsu Octopus
Thread:	70-denier or 6/0 to match
Tube:	HMH small plastic with ½-inch junction tubing. Flare the front end of the plastic tube by scorching it with a lighter to keep the thread from slipping off.
Body:	Diamond Braid (pearl, blue, or purple) wrapped over the tube
Flash:	A few strands of Krystal Flash or Flashabou
Wing:	Rabbit strip
Collar:	Marabou

Tier's Note: Slammers are a combination of a lot of other patterns I saw tied by other anglers. The long rabbit strip wing and sparse collar of long, webby marabou provide lots of movement. The ½ inch of soft junction tubing locks the fly to the hook, preventing the tube from sliding up the leader, and prevents the stinger hook from sagging down below the fly. This fly is my main searching pattern when fishing with a sinking tip line. I tie it in many color combinations, including black, black/blue, purple, purple/pink, pink, orange, and popsicle.

Jay Nichols not only knows how to catch steelhead, but he treats them well. Note the nylon mesh glove on his right hand. That gives a firm grip without hurting the fish.
JAY NICHOLS

Morrish Medusas in black and pink, blue and black, and popsicle.

Morrish Medusa (Black and Pink)

Hook:	#1–4 Tiemco 799 (shank) and #1 Gamakatsu Octopus (trailer)
Thread:	Pink or red 6/0 or 140-denier
Tail:	Pink Krystal Flash (20–25 strands)
Wing:	Black rabbit strip and three strands on each side of black ostrich
Overwing:	Grizzly saddle hackles
Collar:	Three turns of pink marabou
Fins:	Black hen hackle
Eyes:	Small lead eyes painted white
Head:	Black crosscut rabbit spun in loop without leather. Take three turns behind the eyes, two wraps crossing eyes, and three wraps in front.

Tier's Note: I was looking for a large, weighted fly with a sculpin profile that had lots of movement and a sharp trailing hook. These flies are easier to cast than they look and are my go-to wet flies for British Columbia steelhead. Use 30-pound Berkeley Fireline for the trailing hook.

keeps the hook in place. When the point is damaged, loop a new hook in place and you're back in business. The hook does not contribute that much to the sink rate. That is the job of the sinking tip and your manipulation of slack line. You can also weight these flies with lead eyes or by using metal tubes.

For longer than I'd like to admit, my ratio of fish hooked to fish landed ran around 60 percent because the hook didn't stick and often pulled free. The offset point, the long and needle-sharp point, and the hook at the rear of the fly's wing changed that. Today I land from 80 to 90 percent of the fish I hook. These ratios become less important if you hook fifteen fish a day, but in forty years of trying, I haven't seen much of that. When you consider the possibility that you may go all day long and get only one or two good takes, it becomes critical that you do everything you can to bring the fish to hand.

In recent seasons, I have been experimenting with tube flies with wings about one inch long, some sparsely dressed, which are good for clear water and fussy fish. When conditions or my temperament changes, I can add a second tube to the first to create a bulkier fly for dirty water or simply change the color. The fly still retains its ability to hook even soft takers who "climb on" early in the swing, or those normally hard-to-hook fish that take at the end of the drift.

The stinger-type of dressing is also superb and consists of a fly tied with a loop of wire or Berkeley Fireline (30- to 50-pound-test) bound to a hook shank whose curving point has been snipped until the shaft is nothing more than a straight piece of wire with an eye. A short-shank offset hook is then looped through the loop of line or wire at the end of the straight piece of hook. Steelhead flies with stinger hooks have been perfected by Paul Miller of Ashland, Oregon, who connects the stinger hook with 50-pound Berkeley Fireline. Paul's flies look alive in the water, especially his sparser dressings, and I have used them with great results.

Other important elements of an angler's assortment of gear can include anything, and often does. But in my opinion, the items mentioned above are critical. I would describe waders in the same way, and they should be

If you have covered a run well with one color, and then decide to fish the same water a second time, change at least the color and perhaps the size of your fly on your second pass. Sometimes you can change their minds by changing your fly.

A BASIC BOX

My fly selection is based on fishing pressure and water clarity. Fishing pressure is easily five times more important than water conditions, because I've learned this about steelhead anglers: Most of them use the same kind of fly, usually the pattern that happens to be in vogue at the time for the waters they fish.

It matters little in wilderness rivers, but steelhead in heavily fished water soon wise up to this kind of consistent exposure and quickly learn how to spot a fake when they first see it. To stay successful on heavily pressured water, you must have enough types of flies so that you can use something the fish have not seen day after day. So don't think like a fisherman, think like a fish.

My inventory on lightly pressured waters for "uneducated" steelhead is simple, and I carry only a few colors in two basic sizes. I like pink, black, purple, blue, and red—either by themselves or in some combination. I prefer a large, 4-inch tube or stinger-type fly tied with materials that move in the current and make the fly look alive when it swims, and smaller flies (tubes and traditional patterns) that are from an inch to two inches long. Sometimes I mix things up and use two smaller tube flies in different color combinations or put two tube flies together for a larger fly when the water gets very murky. In these cases I usually add a one- to two-inch tube fly to a four-inch one.

Keep your tube flies separate and untangled by storing them in plastic drinking straws. It is easier to pick up just one fly because soft-hackled marabou flies like to stick to wet fingers. Extra flies always seem to fall into the water, just when your hand leaves the box. JAY NICHOLS

I most often carry my tube flies unrigged, with the fly pulled inside a clear plastic drinking straw. I then keep these unrigged tube flies organized by pattern in the compartments of a small plastic fly box. The straws keep the flies from sticking together and getting tangled, or blowing away in the wind, and since they are clear, I can see the color of the pattern. I also keep my stinger-type flies in clear drinking straws, in a compartmented plastic fly box, to keep the flies separate from one another. When the weather is cold and rigging a tube fly becomes more problematic, I prerig the tube flies, carefully coil the leader, and then put each rigged fly in a leader wallet, with one fly in each envelope. This keeps them from getting tangled and allows for instant visibility of the rigged tube fly.

Size, shape, and color of your fly in relation to the clarity of the water matters, but not as much as some believe. Steelhead have superb vision, and even in dirty water they can see any fly when it gets close enough. It is a myth, for example, that only a large, black fly works when the water is dirty. On unpressured water, I start off with almost any color, even when the water gets murky. If a fish comes to the fly but I do not hook it, I stay with that fish and change to a different color and size. You may have to change flies two or three times for some fish. On wilderness rivers, if I can't take them after two or three fly changes, with two to three presentations with each fly, I usually move on.

On heavily pressured waters, moving to another pool may only make matters worse, because you might be fishing behind an armada of anglers. In this case, you may be better off staying where you have found a fish and just keep changing your fly until it either takes or you have put it down. "Don't leave fish to find fish" is always good advice.

4-Inch Tube Flies
Popsicle
Black and Blue
Pink Slammer
Purple and Black

3- to 4-Inch Stinger Flies
Pink and Black
Black and Blue

1 ¼-inch Tube Flies
Popsicle
Black and Blue
Pink Slammer
Purple and Black

Standard Flies
Egg Sucking Leech, #4
Squamish Poacher, #4
Signal Light, #4

Staying with a fish that has responded to your fly and then refused it, or one that struck the fly but didn't get hooked, may require many fly changes before it takes. For this reason, when fishing pressured water, I carry at least twenty different patterns in different sizes (some very small ones), shapes, and colors in a foam-lined box. These include some of the tube flies mentioned above and traditional hairwing patterns, nymph patterns, a few egg patterns, and some sparse streamers.

When I am fishing unpressured waters, I carry only a few "traditional" flies (those tied on a hook in the ordinary fashion) in a compartment of a leader wallet, organized by pattern, with two to three of the same pattern stored in the same Ziploc bag. I use these for closers if I raise a fish on a tube or stinger type of fly and cannot get it to come back for the same pattern.

carefully chosen for a good fit, sure footing, and comfort. Gore-Tex waders have replaced neoprene as the material of choice, but make sure yours are tightly belted. Loose-fitting Gore-Tex waders fill up with water if you go under and get caught in the current because the current pouring into your wader tops exceeds that of the water's compression of your waders around your legs and waist, and it doesn't take long before you can find yourself in serious trouble. Felt soles on your wading boots are a must, and those combined with carbide tips are even better for navigating slippery rocks. A good wading staff is a great friend in tricky currents.

I no longer use a vest as much as I once did, because it was too easy to load up with stuff I liked to own but never used. I now wear a fanny pack with just the essentials. I can see almost everything at the same time with little searching, and the pack offers a second safety belt system on top of the belt I have around my waders. If you wear the fanny pack over a lightweight rain jacket and keep the jacket zipped to your neck and snug around the wrists, you are protected against taking in water should you slip and fall. A fanny pack also gives you good back support over a long day of wading and walking.

Polarized glasses are indispensable. They help you see things you otherwise might miss in the glare; for example, your fly line or the large rock you are about to trip over. JUD WICKWIRE

Forty years ago I owned only one rod, line, and reel, and I almost wore each out with incessant waxing, lubing, and cleaning, a ritual I used to substitute for the moments when I was actually fishing. That kind of maintenance is part of the process and seems to be a good way to prepare mentally and to keep the dream of a day in the water alive and close at hand. Today, I still dream about it all, but I have lost track of how many rods, reels, and lines I own. I see them, in part, as tools and replaceable devices designed to help me catch fish. Maintenance is minimal because most of our modern tackle needs relatively little care.

But there is no equipment like the first you owned, no rod like the rod you had when you could only afford one, and no reel quite like the first one. I fondly remember the first tackle I actually owned, if you can call it tackle—and I do—as the beginning of a life-long process and commitment to the magic of the chase. My partner in that original odyssey—my first fishing partner outside of my immediate family—was a guy named Lawrence Jones, who was, as my father used to say, "as black as coal." My mother liked to add that he "lived on the wrong side of the tracks."

None of this mattered to Lawrence and me, and when no one was looking, we would get our gear out and head for nearby water we knew and loved. Our tackle consisted of a large coffee can with holes punched in the bottom for quick and effective drainage, connected to an old broom or mop handle with two eight-penny nails.

Lawrence taught me how to make the holes in the can, and then nail it to a handle. It was intriguing, exciting preparation, punctuated by the occasional stabbing of your left hand as your right jabbed out the holes in the bottom of the can with an ice pick. Mop handles were easy, as all you had to do was unscrew the metal rigging and they were ready to go. Brooms only became a problem when my father locked his shop and I couldn't get his hand saw to cut off the bristles. We got around that with hatchets, kitchen knives, or, as a last resort, fire.

Then we would sneak over to the forbidden and oily shoals of a nearby muddy little tidal creek that had no name, although some claimed it to be nothing more than a "sewer ditch." This didn't matter either. What did matter was that with the swell of the incoming tide small fish with yellow eyes and silver sides drifted in like little luminescent submarines, with dark shadows beneath

Think of steelhead tackle and clothing as a system that helps you get what you want. It provides you with the ability to fish all day long, making effective presentations with minimal fatigue and frustration. Don't be afraid to change any part of your system if you don't enjoy it, or if it doesn't work for you. Fishing is supposed to be fun, not slave labor.

their stomachs, darting and feeding exactly like the bonefish I would see some fifty years later.

To this day, it reminds me that the best of fishing and all our attendant gear is the solid and uncensored immersion in a reality many seem to have, unfortunately, forgotten or abandoned in favor of more civilized and mundane pursuits. The memory of Lawrence and me giving them hell on an unnamed tidal ditch with tin cans and broom handles still fits perfectly into my adult perspective as a fisherman—from nearly every point of view I care to think of. The seam between one side of the tracks and the other, between the past, present, and the future, between life itself and the water's edge is always blurred, and catching any fish on a fly—wild steelhead, bonefish, or brook trout—is a capture, dissolution, and reversal of time. It is the infusion and realization of spirit and a necessary return to at least one essential component of our human identity. There is truth and meaning in it, no matter your age, partner, or gear.

So I can still see us there, a half century later, watching and silently sitting on the wooden fence that ran along the creek. So, thank you, Lawrence. You gave me a good start, and I'm not done yet. They tell me that the new rod and all the lines for it are being shipped today.

CHAPTER

16

The Evolution of Flies

The room is a mess and a little on the rustic side, with wooden beds and cracks in the ceiling that allow an occasional glimpse of starlight. It is a perfect steelhead cabin. A single light bulb burns from the center rafter, and the light falls to the floor in an orange glow that barely illuminates three fiberglass cases for three very expensive cameras, four pairs of waders, a half-dozen fly rods, and all the clothes we have worn for the past week.

Outside, British Columbia's Dean River roars by in a cacophony of water. Steelhead expert and film maker John Fabian and I have finished the shoot and are packing to go home in the morning. John is bent over in one corner of the cabin, rifling through his immense duffle. Underwear, flannel shirts, and gloves come flying out of the bag. It looks like he is swimming. *What's he want?* I wonder, as I hang on the edge of my bunk, massaging feet sore from wading shoes a bit too small.

Aesthetics aside, changes in steelhead fly design are inspired by two essential motivations that are always interconnected. First, the new fly will do a better job of triggering the strike response of a resting fish that is not in the river to feed. Second, the new fly will solve some kind of fishing or presentation problem such as rough water, dirty water, or deep water.

John finds what he is looking for then turns toward me, walks to the center of the room, and sits down in front of a chipped and worn table. His elbows grind into the pine surface and his face, which is always red, seems even more so in the incandescent light. His eyes are blazing. Clenched in his left hand is a bottle of Canadian Rye. His right hand looks like a claw and two short, but very wide and very empty glasses are held in a pincher-like grip. For a moment I feel like we are in a movie.

"I'll tell you what," he says, as he leans into the whiskey, shoving one half-filled glass toward my side of the pine table. "I got it. I really got it. The wet fly scene is off the charts. I got two solid minutes of absolutely great stuff. Wait 'til you see it."

I look at the glass, but don't say much. The rye goes down and settles on the lasagna, which is mixed with some ice cream. "God, that was a great dinner," I finally say. "I ate too much. I love lasagna and spumoni ice

Waller Waker (Original)

Hook:	#4–8 Tiemco 7989
Thread:	4/0 or 6/0 black
Tail:	Moose hair
Body:	Moose hair, spun and clipped
Wing:	Calf tail
Beard:	Moose hair

Tier's Note: The wings should be no longer than 1½ times the hook gap. If they are too long, the fly will roll over on its side, and eventually sink. The wings should also slant forward at a 45 degree angle. The moose beard provides a "keel," or smooth surface on the bottom of the fly to help the fly skim over the surface of the water.

Here's how I tie the Waker. Tie in, raise, and post the wings. Put a drop of Krazy Glue at the base of each wing to stiffen them and to help hold them in place. Fold a small piece of removable tape over each wing so you don't cut them when you later trim the moose hair body. After the wings are in place, tie in the tail, and then spin and trim the moose hair body. Tie the beard and finish the head.

The original Waller Waker was designed for the camera, since no other pattern at the time would show up on film when we wanted to record a steelhead taking a dry fly. The Waker's visibility, flotation, and its ability to create a broad wake are its strongest virtues.

JAY NICHOLS

cream. What about the dry fly sequence?" I ask. "Did you get it?"

"We need to talk about that," he answers. "You know what they want. They want some footage of a steelhead sucking in a dry. No one's ever done that. That's part of the deal and we have to get it, but I don't know about today. I'm not sure. That Bomber you had on was too hard to find in the view finder, and I kept losing it. I don't know if we got the take or not."

From this point the whiskey inspires a few stories and stories of stories of rivers fished, those still to come, of fish taken and those lost, of dry-fly dressings past and present. We talked about Harry Lemire's Grease Liner, the Muddler Minnow, tied some fifty years ago by Don Gapen (a guy no one remembers), Haig-Brown's Steelhead Bee, and a few others whose names have also faded with time.

Around eleven o'clock, John pours what must have been our third glass and says, "I can smell it, Waller.

The author works a wet fly through the strong currents of a Skeena-system steelhead run. Long, slinky, swimming flies are becoming the standard dressings in many parts of the Northwest.

This Dean River steelhead followed my Waller Waker for over forty feet during the down-and-across waking swing and finally took on the hang down. LANI WALLER

We're almost there, and it's going to be great. I just know it."

I'm not much of a drinker, but we had indeed just come off of a special week. Fortified by the rye, I decide to get philosophical about it. "John, listen to me," I say. "I'm not in this for the money. It's not about that."

"I understand," he adds, then continues in a long and uninterrupted, almost breathless statement. "Neither am I. I've been fishing steelhead all my life and I've guided for almost that long, and I've made a lot of films. But I've always wanted to make a movie about fly fishing for steelhead, and here we are. Now here is what I want you to do, because I don't know if I got that dry fly take or not because the damn Bomber rides too low in the water. None of the rest of them are any easier to see, so I want you to go home and design a new kind of dry fly, one that will show up on film."

He pauses, takes another swallow, and then adds, "And that's not all. I want you to name it, the uhh . . . the . . . uhh . . . the Waller Waker!" His eyes flash and his Adam's apple rises then drops as more of the rye hits home. "That's it," he says. "The Waller Waker. I'm going to make you famous." He lifts his glass to the ceiling, and smiles.

Now, in retrospect, I don't know what was so funny about that and maybe it was the kind of day we had and the fatigue and whiskey, but we both started to laugh. I didn't say anything, but I thought to myself that if something like that made an angler famous, then there may be something wrong with the whole idea of fishing for a living. "John," I said, "it's not about that either. I just want to tell the story."

There was another long pause, and for a moment the river came through the window and poured into the

Evolution of steelhead flies is never done by quantum leaps. One reason fly design comes slowly is that steelheaders care about the past and the accomplishments of all those who have fished before us.

dimly lit room. I thought about one particular rise ear-lier that day, on the half sunken Bomber, and how I almost blew it by taking the fly out of the water too quickly. So much of it is luck, I thought . . . just hanging in there long enough to allow it to happen on its own.

"Just go home," John says, "and design the Waller Waker for our last shoots on the Deschutes and Babine. That's all I'm asking. Just make one I can see and I'll do the rest. We'll get the shot. Then, we'll have it all."

I had a Maine Coon cat at the time named Scruffy, who used to sit on my lap, all twenty pounds of him, as I tied. Later that month, on a Sunday afternoon, the two of us finally did it. I must have used five entire calf tails and a half pound of moose hair before it all came together. I had, in fact, exhausted my entire supply of moose, and my good calf hair was down to the last small bunch. I had to be on the plane the next day and didn't have time to get any more materials.

So, the first Waller Waker was an aesthetic disaster with an insufficient amount of moose on the body and wings made with the curly stuff at the end of the calf tail—something normally discarded by serious tiers. *Go with what you've got, because it's all you've got left,* I thought, as Scruffy just sat there purring and banging on the bobbin.

When we hit the Deschutes, John liked the fly almost instantly. "Jeezus, Waller, it looks like a bass bug," he said. He changed his mind once the thing hit the water, for the white wings stood up like a flag and the wake it made could be easily seen.

As it turned out, I took only one fish on the Deschutes on the fly, just at dusk, but it didn't matter. John was holding off for "the big time," as he called it—the Babine River and a pool named Goose. That September, on the Babine, and in front of John, cameramen Gayle Lutz and Jud Wickwire, and sound man Shaun Cassidy, I raised eight steelhead on the Waller Waker and landed two of them. I was so nervous that I kept pulling it out of their yawning jaws. One of the two landed was a hen just under twenty pounds, but John, always the perfectionist, wouldn't use her because of the seal scar that ran all around her body. It didn't matter. We got the footage we wanted.

Later that fall, I took the Waker back with me to British Columbia. One morning on a piece of water named "Mauser's Riffle," Bob Clay and I watched as a half-dozen steelhead came swimming for the fly in water not much deeper than 24 inches. Some of them

There is a saying at Silver Hilton Steelhead Lodge in northern British Columbia that rings true everywhere: "If you think it is the fly that did it, then it is the fly that did it." Remember that steelhead do not read books or look at movies, and they will usually take whatever you like. So fish what you believe in, and fish it well.
MARK MCANEELEY

pushed a wake you could see from fifty feet, and they closed in on the fly like cruising sharks. It was the begin-ning of a long love affair with the floating fly, and the Waker was eventually picked up by Umpqua Feather Merchants for commercial distribution. The one-time rather shabby tie soon began taking not only steelhead in Canada, but Atlantic salmon in Russia, trophy rain-bow in Alaska, and a couple of New Zealand browns that must have thought it was a mouse. One of my biggest compliments came one day when I got a call from a bass angler in Louisiana. "The bigmouth love it," he said.

The evolution of our flies is never done by quantum leaps forward. It comes, rather, one step at a time with each new fly standing on the wings and body of those that precede it. The Waller Waker was no exception, for I wanted to keep the materials traditional and use some parts of the flies before it, especially the Bomber, which is a classic for Atlantic salmon.

Pom Skater (Nightshade)
(tied by Ken Morrish)

Hook:	#4 Tiemco 3761
Thread:	Red 6/0 or 140-denier
Tail:	Red Krystal Flash (6–8 strands)
Overbody:	Black ¼-inch foam trimmed to shape
Underbody:	Red Krystal Flash twisted around thread
Hackle:	Purple deer hair spun with tips forward and trimmed
Head:	Krystal Flash wrapped around thread

Tier's Note: Fasten the rear portion of foam with Krystal Flash wrapped around the thread and post around the base to prevent the foam from rotating on the shank. Do the same when tying down the head portion of the foam. Trim foam in front with bevels to keep the fly riding high. I created this fly for a durable, easy-to-cast skater that would not need a hitch. I also wanted a fly that rode low in back and high in front so that it would not get "pushed" away during the take.

Ken Morrish's Pompadour (Pom) Skaters float high, are easy to see, and do not require a riffle hitch to wake. JAY NICHOLS

I remember thinking that one of the things that mattered most to me was that my fly be a part of all that had come before. I also wanted to improve on past designs, so I replaced the Bomber's clipped-deer-hair body with a clipped body of moose, which floats better. For better visibility, I replaced the single wing of the old Atlantic salmon favorite with the tried-and-true divided wings of trout dry flies. The tail and throat were nothing more than a slight modification of all tails and throats of a million flies that preceded mine. In this case the stiff moose on the throat helped make the fly ride up on plane and "wake."

It wasn't perfect, but it was mine, in the sense of my commitment to at least try to do what John Fabian had asked for. I still see it in catalogs today, some thirty years later. It was a better fly than many realized. Some commercial tiers always made the wings too long and overdressed them. This diminished the floating capabilities of the pattern, because long and overly bulky wings make the fly top heavy and roll over on one side. In this position, the wings catch too much current, which can sink the fly.

In recent seasons I have replaced the moose-hair body with closed-cell foam, which does not absorb water as quickly as the moose and adds considerably to the fly's flotation. I borrowed the idea from Ken Morrish's excellent steelhead dry, the Pom. I am quite sure Ken was inspired to use foam in his pattern from another pattern somewhere.

By the more romantic among us, flies are often revered to the point of worship. Part of this comes from the mystery of a steelhead's strike response. This unpredictability can diminish the possibility of a rational and scientific explanation for the success and failure of our patterns, and some of us elevate our flies into the realm of the supernatural as magic amulets, secret concoctions, invisible allies, and fetishes. We create flies, collect flies, hoard them, hide them, and in the end we use them with hope and anticipation to catch mysterious fish. A few weeks ago I received an almost frantic phone call from an angler who told me that he had heard that only purple leeches with some kind of feathers I had never heard of were the only ones working this season in Canada. I'm not sure he was kidding.

Though I appreciate the magic of fly patterns, I keep some science in there as well. The development and evolution of steelhead flies is, in many ways, problem solving. Choosing certain materials, styles, and techniques is a response not only to the mystery of when, why, and where a steelhead bites, but to other more concrete issues such as lighting, water flow, water type, temperature, and angling pressure.

I also like to tinker with fly designs to avoid the monotony of fishing the same thing for too many seasons in a row. For example, I am currently designing a new series of small flies to be used in combination with the large and long swimming types of flies I have come to rely upon over the past eight or nine years. The process of my own reinvention as an angler is exciting for me and keeps my outlook fresh.

Most of us have been fairly conservative in our creations, and we have avoided certain kinds of patterns even if they would work. For example, Washington angler Bill McMillan has written of his successes hooking steelhead with only a bare hook painted various colors. As I recall, Bill named these creations "Toys." He added capital letters to differentiate them: "Toy A," "Toy B," etc. On at least two occasions, I have witnessed steelhead taking only a bare hook or flies, if you can call them that, with only a piece of floss tied to the shank.

These minimalist experiments reveal something about a steelhead's strike impulse, but they have not inspired any serious use because none of us have the heart for such a thing. To lose the natural furs and feathers entirely would, in my opinion, not only ignore tradition but also lose some of the magic and power inherent in these natural materials. I'm not alone. It is no coincidence that many tiers still seek, for example, polar bear hair or exotic and rare bird plumage for their flies. Not all of this is cosmetic or artistic. Some of it, for some

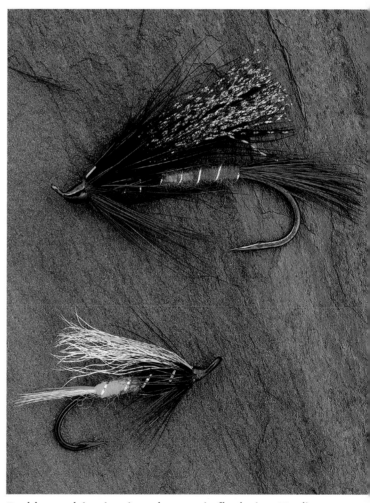

Problem solving inspires changes in fly design. Traditional fly hooks are elegant and good looking, but the heavy wire is difficult to keep sharp and does not penetrate easily. That is why many anglers moved to tube or stinger-type flies that allow them to use hooks with longer and thinner points. JAY NICHOLS

tiers, comes from a belief in the power of the animal itself.

On the other hand, I also believe that when various animals and birds become endangered, they have no place on the tier's bench, and substitutes must be found. Thus any evolutionary development should always include some reverence for the bird or animal from which the material was taken, and in order to protect endangered species, we must adopt new materials that hopefully mimic the appearance or appeal of natural materials.

Change comes slowly, and the traditional steelhead dressings are still with us, and many anglers love them above all others and will use nothing but the traditional hair- and feather-winged creations that emerged from our trout- and salmon-fishing roots. I was stuck in this perspective for decades, and I remember wondering, years before any swimming type of streamer was commonly used for steelhead, if a long streamer would be any good. I did nothing about it, however, until the day came when some of my clients and friends decided to switch from hardware to flies. They had no background in fly fishing, and no connection to any traditions of fly tying. When it came time to develop flies they could believe in, they selected only large ones tied with synthetic materials—mostly Mylar plastics—for the entire pattern.

Everything in the construction of their flies was an attempt to duplicate what they knew and believed in, which was their metal and plastic lures. Their patterns reminded me of saltwater flies for the medium- to big-game species found in blue water. Incredibly enough, at least to me at the time, the patterns worked as well or better than other types of patterns—as long as there was relatively light fishing pressure, the water was at normal or higher-than-usual levels, and was off color.

Eventually this kind of fly design gained some following among steelheaders, especially in Alaska and British Columbia, and most notably among anglers in search of big Chinook salmon in the northwest and

Flies tied with materials that wiggle and flutter in the water are effective. One of the major changes in recent wet-fly evolution is the move to these kinds of materials. Marabou and soft hackles animate the fly and make it look alive in the water.

Traditional steelhead patterns, courtesy of Joel La Follette at Kaufmann Streamborn, from top to bottom: Green Butt Skunk (originated by Dan Callaghan), Del Cooper (originated by Mike Kennedy), Freight Train (originated by Randall Kaufmann), Polar Shrimp, Signal Light (originated by Randall Kaufmann), Purple Peril, Burlap, and Silver Hilton.
JAY NICHOLS

Shrimp-Tishioner
(tied by Paul Miller)

Hook:	#3/0 Alec Jackson Spey and #1 Owner stinger
Thread:	Orange 140-denier Ultra Thread
Tail:	Bright orange Rhea Super Spey feathers
Body:	Orange Cactus Chenille
Topping:	Red golden pheasant feather tied flat
Hackle:	Bright orange Rhea Super Spey feathers
Eyes:	Black onyx beads epoxied to 40-pound-test mono

Tier's Note: This fly was born with the theory that fresh steelhead still have the prey image of prawns in their memory banks when they enter fresh water from the salt. This fly is basically a General Practitioner on steroids. The black onyx bead eyes help add some weight, making this fly an excellent pattern for pools. The hackle opens up in a slow drift. This is my favorite pattern for Dean River steelhead, as well as king salmon.

Alaska. They call it the "Flash Fly." I used my own version for several seasons, for steelhead, with excellent results, but when I had the thing in the palm of my hand and looked down at all that plastic, something was missing. Despite its success, I retired the fly around ten years ago with no regrets.

Sometime around the mid-1980s, I did begin to experiment with long and slinky streamers and came up with a pattern I called "The Invader," which was designed to trigger a steelhead's territorial response. The fly was tied Matuka-style on a long and heavy hook, and some were almost six inches long. They worked best during periods of high and cloudy water on water that was lightly fished.

About that same time, long-time Washington steelheader Harry Lemire was quoted as preferring "a long and swimming type of fly" for his steelheading on British Columbia's Dean River. I met Lemire not long after that at a trade show in Seattle, Washington, and we talked about fly design. The conversation revealed that

Paul Miller's "swimming" fly patterns come alive while swimming through the water. Many of his patterns use rhea feathers and marabou fibers, which breathe in the water. Clockwise from top: Shrimp-Tishioner, Predator, Phantom, and Prowler. Miller attaches the stinger hook with 50-pound Fireline doubled over and lashed to the hook shank. It is essential to leave a big enough loop so you can easily replace the stinger hook and to ensure the hook trails back at the rear of the fly. When you lash the Fireline to the shank with thread wraps, double back and wrap over any excess tag ends of the Fireline for extra security. Pinch the barb on the stinger. JAY NICHOLS

Predator
(tied by Paul Miller)

Hook:	#3/0 Alec Jackson Spey and #1 Owner stinger
Thread:	Fl. pink 140-denier Ultra Thread
Tail:	Rhea Super Spey feathers dyed purple
Body:	Black Cactus Chenille
Hackle:	Rhea Super Spey feathers dyed blue or purple
Flash:	Blue Electra Scale (Doug's Bugs) and Electric Blue Flashabou
Collar:	King Fisher (sky blue) marabou
Head (optional):	Pink or orange chenille

Tier's Note: This fly originated one evening at a fly tying "jam session" on the Kispiox River. Tony Stellar (who would later have unstoppable confidence in this pattern) had introduced me to a local fly tier named Wally Bolger. I introduced Wally to rhea feathers, and we each tied what we thought would be the ultimate Skeena River watershed pattern. These first flies were tied on tubes. What was evident from the start was how light these large flies were and how easy to cast. We eventually began to tie shank flies with stinger hooks, and the tubes were abandoned. In addition to having a great profile and movement in the water, these flies are durable. I recommend them for off-color and steelhead-green water.

Phantom
(tied by Paul Miller)

Hook:	#2/0 Targus 7999 and #1 Owner stinger
Thread:	Black 140-denier Ultra Thread
Tail:	Black Rhea Super Spey feathers
Body:	Black Cactus Chenille
Hackle:	Blue Chinese strung saddle hackle
Flash:	Blue Electra Scale (four strands)
Eyes (optional):	Jungle cock

Tier's Note: I originally developed this pattern for clear or low water. Though the overall coloration is black, I vary the hackle colors (pink, orange, or chartreuse). In low water, this pattern has caught fish when other large patterns would not. I also tie a smaller version on #3–5 Spey hooks.

Prowler
(tied by Paul Miller)

Hook:	#2/0 Targus 7999 and #1 Owner stinger
Thread:	Black 140-denier Ultra Thread
Tail:	Three to four olive dyed rhea filoplumes
Body:	Olive Cactus Chenille
Hackle:	Olive dyed Rhea Super Spey feathers
Flash:	Olive Electra Scale
Head:	Black deer hair, flared and clipped
Eyes:	$5/32$ gold Dazl Eyes (Spirit River)

Tier's Note: The Prowler is really a weighted underwater "waking fly" designed to give off vibrations that are picked up on by the fish's lateral-line sensors. It was originally designed for sea-run brown trout in Argentina. The weighted eyes help the fly sink and track well. Olive is an underused color for steelhead that works well from California North Coast rivers into Oregon, Washington, and British Columbia. Other variations include pink and black and an egg-sucking version. Besides steelhead, this fly is also effective for king salmon and Alaska rainbows.

Bullwinkle
(tied by Mark McAneeley)

Hook:	#4 Tiemco 105 (straight eye)
Thread:	Orange 70-denier Ultra Thread
Tube:	Small plastic HMH (burn hole into bottom to thread leader through) with ¼-inch junction tubing. Flare the front end of the plastic tube by scorching it with a lighter to keep the thread from slipping off.
Body:	Rusty orange seal's fur
Wing:	Moose hair, divided and flared back under foam
Back:	Brown closed-cell foam
Indicator:	Yellow closed-cell foam

Tier's Note: I created this pattern based on the success and increased landing ratio we were having with wet flies tied on tubes. I wanted to create a waked dry on a tube that is highly visible to the angler, buggy, low maintenance, and consistently wakes all day, in all types of water. By low maintenance I mean a fly that does not require a riffle hitch or floatant. The Bullwinkle is now my go-to searching pattern when fishing a dry.

McAneeley's Bullwinkle combines the effectiveness of a tube fly with a waking dry fly that does not require floatant or a riffle hitch. JAY NICHOLS

we both had great success with long, swimming streamers with materials that looked alive in the water.

Much of the current explosion of interest in longer, swimming flies has been generated by Ed Ward, another expert Washington steelheader. His famous Intruder also has the great advantage of a stinger hook at the rear. This kind of fly had been in use among European Atlantic salmon anglers for some time, and I had in fact seen it on the Kola Peninsula of Russia in the early 1980s, but Ward took the design to the steelhead public. The Intruder is one of the great steelhead designs.

My favorite version of this particular kind of fly is produced by a good friend and neighbor in northern California. Paul Miller's stinger patterns are as close to perfect as I have seen. He offers a series of dressings ranging from relatively sparse ties (my favorites) to bulky flies for high and dirty water. Miller's expertise is obvious, and his patterns all feature rhea feathers. What I like best about his patterns, however, is the braided line he uses to attach the stinger hook to the dressing. It is without equal, and the loop passes easily through the eye of the hook for easy changing of the hook. Equally important, it retains its stiffness, even after repeated use, which means the hook never sags or droops over time. This becomes critical in softer currents and seams because a soft loop allows the hook to sag as the fly swims through calmer currents. If you use a stinger type of pattern and some of your fish are hooked on the outside of their mouths, it is because your hook sagged away from the rear of the fly's wing.

Canadian guide Mark McAneeley's tube flies are the best I have seen. I brought tube flies to the Babine River at Silver Hilton Lodge sometime in the mid-1990s after experimenting with them with Bob Clay on the Kispiox River. Mark immediately saw the advantages of this dressing style and added a piece of soft rubber tubing to the end of the hard tube on which the fly is tied. The loop of monofilament leader is then drawn into the soft tubing until the loop's knot comes to rest at the rear end of the hard tubing the fly is dressed on. This keeps the hook suspended where it belongs, near the end of the fly's long and slinky wing. Mark's materials are all natural

Popsicle is a common attractor color scheme that you can work into your streamer patterns. The Idylwilde Bunny Tube, tied in a wide range of colors, is a versatile tube-fly design that moves in the water. JAY NICHOLS

Synthetics play an ever-greater role in steelhead fly design. They are a good way to add flash to a fly. This Alaskan peninsula steelhead took a bright and flashy wet fly without hesitation. LANI WALLER

Idylwilde Marabou Tube

Tube:	Small plastic
Thread:	6/0 or 70-denier to match
Flash:	Flashabou, approximately eight strands
Body:	Marabou wrapped around tube
Collar:	Guinea or saddle hackle

One of the great things about flies tied on short tubes is that you can stack them, increasing the length and color variations as needed. Idylwilde Marabou Tubes are simple patterns that can be tied in a wide range of colors. Flies tied in the round, such as these, never lose their orientation in the water. JAY NICHOLS

and center around soft marabou and a long rabbit-strip wing. They swim with a real come-and-get-me action.

Mark McAneeley has also developed a dry fly tied on a tube called the Bullwinkle. The leader passes through the hard section of tubing, but does not pass through the opening at the front of the hard tubing. Instead it exits out the side, through a small hole in the forward part of the hard tubing. This produces the same effect as a riffle-hitched fly because it allows the head of the fly to lift up and to one side in the current in a planing motion.

Foam has revolutionized steelhead dry flies. A collection of Titanics, tied by Jay Paulson, proves that creativity is alive and well in the realm of fly tying. JAY NICHOLS

In the mid-1990s, I sent some samples of the basic tube-style of dressing to Zack Mertens and Chris Conaty at Idylwilde Flies in Portland, Oregon, in an unabashed attempt to sweet talk them into tying some for me. They began producing a great series of patterns based on the samples that I sent and also became one of the first American companies to distribute this type of steelhead fly.

As far as the future goes, I believe we will see more and more creative expressions, with ever increasing amounts of synthetic materials. Find a way to make the fly yours. Find a way to believe in it and fish it as if it is the only fly that will work. Talk to it when it lands and when it comes around. Beg it to work and pray for the strike. I don't know how a steelhead hears these kinds of things, but somehow the message reaches the fish, and I have no quarrel with the response.

Titanic
(tied by Jay Paulson)

Hook:	#6 Tiemco 3761
Tail:	Calf tail
Body:	Brown and grizzly hackle; "hull" formed separately from closed-cell foam and glued to shank
Wing:	Calf tail

Tier's Note: Ken Morrish and I were planning for a trip to British Columbia when he challenged me to a friendly contest on who could raise a steelhead to the most unusual fly. After weeks of trying to come up with something, I woke up one morning with the idea of using a boat hull. Its design makes it literally dance over the water, even through choppy water that you normally would never dream of skating a fly. The Titanic has caught steelhead, trout, sea-run browns, and Atlantic salmon.

17

The Stinger Steelhead Fly

Every experienced steelhead angler has his or her favorite patterns and I am no exception. But after many years of throwing every possible type of fly out there, I eventually started wondering if there was a fly that would "maximize the possibilities for a response." As part of this question, I also wondered about the effects of weather and water conditions—depth, color, current speed, ambient light, and water temperature—and if those circumstances might make some kinds of flies better than others. This inquiry eventually became divided into two categories: freshly arrived coastal tidewater steelhead holding in clear and calm pools, and migrating steelhead who had left tidewater far behind them.

Forty years went by in a flash, and at one point I wasn't sure just how much of this mattered. If you know how to read water and can determine where the fish

This type of fly has it all: great action in the currents, superb hooking capabilities, and easy storage in the angler's favorite fly box. Further, the hooks are easily changed when they get dull so the fly will last a long time as the hook almost always goes bad before the feathers and hair. Last, but not least, it is also simple to change flies by simply clipping them off at the eye and putting on a new fly.

will be, maybe you just "throw it out there and they either take it or they don't." I also saw a lot of really successful steelheaders coming back at the end of the day, all of them fishing the same stretch of water under similar circumstances and none using the same kind of fly . . . and they all had their share of fish. So, as time passed, I began to think most of the "debate" was in the angler's mind and not that of the fish.

Nonetheless, I stopped using conventional hair- and feather-winged flies after I saw some tube flies, which looked so good and fished so effectively. Unlike the traditional hair-wing flies, these were tied with softer and longer materials. This kind of dressing looked alive in the water and had a swimming motion that looked good to me—much more real than the traditional short-winged flies I had grown up with.

I stayed with the tube flies for four years or so, and then stumbled across another style of dressing that included the major advantage of the tube style of fly— the long and animated swimming movement created by the use of soft feathers, marabou, and so on. It had other advantages as well, and I switched to the stinger style of dressing for several reasons. After many years of use, I still consider it my favorite and my "first fly of choice."

Stingers are relatively long, two to three inches, and like tube flies, they are tied with soft materials. And like the tube fly style, they look alive and animated as they swim on a tight line through the currents. The hook is always at the very end of the fly, looped to a short section of monofilament (or wire) that is securely tied to a hook shank that is looped at the front to receive the leader tippet. The body of the fly is tied over this monofilament or wire. When you look at this kind of dressing, it just looks like a long-bodied streamer fly, but one with an interchangeable hook at the end of the long wing.

The hook is a short shank, relatively lightweight, upturned eye model more commonly used for bait. This kind of hook performs well on a "short" take and does not twist out, as there is almost no shank for a "twisting leverage" against the jaw of the hooked steelhead. It is also quick and easy to replace.

Another advantage to this kind of dressing is that the fly lasts a long time since the hook can be un-looped and replaced when it becomes worn and dull. Lastly, this kind of dressing is easy to store and easy to change.

I carry these flies in several colors and I have my favorites, but I also believe the issue of color is more in my mind than that of the fish I am chasing. What I mostly care about are the conditions I am fishing in. When fishing in very low light or discolored waters (or both), I will use either black or a "hot" pink. I also like some bright tinsel tied in the dressing in the never-ending hope that the fluttering Mylar might reflect at least some of the ambient light in the currents I am covering. These two colors also produce in clear water, so one could argue that they are all you might need. However, I love steelhead flies and when I open my wallet I like to see a lot of different colors. They make me feel better. Other favorite colors are orange, purple, olive, rust, and combinations of other colors too random to mention.

And what about fly weight? That varies. In my opinion, it depends upon how lazy you are, how fast the currents are, how deep the water is where you are fishing, how long your leader is, what kind of line tip you are

using, and how cold or warm the river is. That's a lot to consider, but you get used to it after a while.

Irrespective of these variables, I *always* try to have the same kind of presentation with my "down and across" swinging presentation. I don't know what to call it, but this is what it looks like: The fly is always at the deepest of a curving parabola and is closest to the bottom. Next

comes a relatively short leader, usually about thirty inches long, which I want drifting *above the fly*, followed by a density of line tip that will drift *above the leader* by about two feet. Then at the very top end of this downward–curving parabola is the part of the line I can mend and move around to either speed the fly up or slow it down.

These two anglers have every right to smile at a time like this. Even on the best of rivers, a steelhead like this does not come easily or often, and such a fish has a way of making a cold day suddenly warm and happy.

For this system I almost always use a stinger fly with medium-sized lead eyes. They will get the fly down far enough in most cases, and I then decide on the weight and density of the line tip. I don't want the tip to be down where the fly is, as that will hang up too often. I want the tip above the fly and off the rocks.

The only time I use unweighted flies is when I am fishing in very shallow water—from two to perhaps three feet deep. There are more steelhead in places like that than most anglers realize, especially in the very low light of early morning and again very late in the evening when the sun is off the river, particularly if the surface is agitated and turbulent or the water is discolored.

I may have mentioned this elsewhere in the book but it is worth repeating: Another important consideration revolves around having a second fly for the times when you either can see the fish or have gone through the run without getting a response but you are convinced they are there, for those times when you miss a "short take," and when you are sharing a run with another angler and you are fishing behind that angler as you both move down the run. Fly selection under those circumstances can become a game of "cat and mouse." For example, I have had times when a single fish would respond to four or five different patterns and then simply stop responding. I have also had fish that responded to many different flies and ended up taking the first one I had shown them, and I have seen this when fishing both wet flies or skating dry flies.

For example, one balmy October afternoon, B.C. expert Bob Clay and I were fishing a certain run on the Bulkley River. I was in the lead, fishing a skating dry fly, and Bob was following me down the run with a wet fly. As I came into the "bucket," I suddenly had a large and very aggressive surface "boil" on my skating deer hair Waller Waker. As the fly disappeared in the explosive response, I paused to let the fish turn and the line tighten, and for the hook to slide in. I did all of that, but nothing was there.

I showed the fish that same fly a second time, but there was no response. I knew from experience that if they are not hooked by a second cast with the same fly, they are "off it," so I removed the Waker and tied on a smaller dry and threw it back out there.

The same fish responded with another very aggressive response, but again did not take it. If it had, I would have felt it. So I changed to a third dry fly, slowed down the drift, and watched it pass over the lie of the fish. The steelhead responded with another lunging strike at the fly but the line never tightened, and I knew he hadn't taken the pattern.

My fourth fly was a small wet fly, riffle hitched so it would swim in the surface where I could see any response. The steelhead came once more, in a lunging roll that took my breath away, but the fish did not take the fly. By this time Bob was as nervous and excited as I was, so he came down to my side and we stood there together thinking about "what the book says to do next."

"I'm out of tricks," I said, "and it's getting late. Maybe we should leave this one to someone else and go and find another. Or why don't you show it your wet fly?" I don't remember now which of us decided we should just show the fish the first fly again—the deer hair Waker—but that's what I did. As I finished the knot, I told Bob, "When the fly comes into position, maybe I just should just stop breathing, think about a cold beer later on, and then gave the fly a little twitch or two . . . that might work. What do you think?"

"Good idea," he smiled. "Throw it out there and do exactly that." So out it went and as it came into position, it seemed like the entire Bulkley River raised five inches as the fish took the fly, turned, and hooked itself as I just stood there with my mouth hanging open. "Good work," Bob said. "Now wind him in." I did as I was told, and fifteen or twenty minutes later the beautiful chrome-plated twenty-some-odd-pounder was at our feet.

As far as the wet fly is concerned, if I am in the bucket, I do the same thing, whether I can see them or not. If I think they are there, I choose a pattern that is completely different—in size, construction, silhouette, color, sink rate, and swimming motion—than the previous fly I tried. Another consideration arises if you are sharing a run with another angler. For example, if the lead angler is using a long black fly, you should follow with a fly very different from that.

My favorite lines for all of these circumstances are the RIO Skagit Max Short lines with the appropriate density of tip. These lines are quick on the draw and easily get the line and fly airborne again. And you can throw them a mile if you have to. Or want to.

I do not favor long—i.e., 13 to 15 feet—two-handed rods anymore, for two reasons: (1) they really don't feel like fly rods to me, and (2) I have always been an aggressive wader and often end up in scary places to wade, and in circumstances like these, the short Spey rods let me make all the casts I might have to with one hand. The

other hand has my wading staff held carefully in a grip sufficient to choke a bear. My favorite rod for this kind of work is one of Kerry Burkheimer's incredible creations: his 10-foot-5-inch switch rod.

For longer casts in easier water to wade, I use his 12-foot-7-inch rod, which is indeed a "rocket launcher" and makes the longest casts seem easy. In the hands of a true expert caster, hundred-foot casts are attainable, even if the angler is in waist-high currents.

In any case, Kerry's rods are a pleasure to use. Both of these rods get the line up and out of the water and in the air with minimum effort and maximum pleasure, and both are superb menders. Both know what to do when the fish pulling might be over twenty pounds. And finally, when things really slow down and I haven't had a take in a long time, even an imaginary one, I like to look at his rod handles now and then. They are indeed a sight to behold.

Dirk Wiggler (Olive)
(tied by Jon Hazlett)

Front Shank:	20mm Waddington shank by Partridge
Trailing Hook:	#2 Gamakatsu Red Octopus
Eyes:	6mm gold Dumbbell brass eyes
Joint:	30-pound Berkley FireLine
Body:	Caddis green Ice Dub
Body Flash:	Green Holographic Flashabou
Inner Skirt:	Light orange turkey flat
Outer Skirt:	Olive marabou with black stripes
Legs:	Olive Super Floss with green stripes
Collar:	Black schlappen
Head:	Black Hareline STS Trilobal Dub

Deuce Wigalo (Pink)
(tied by Jon Hazlett)

Front Shank:	20mm Waddington shank by Partridge
Trailing Hook:	#4 Black nickel Gamakatsu Octopus
Eyes:	5mm lead painted eyes in white with black pupils
Joint:	30-pound Berkley FireLine and 6mm blue pearl bead
Body:	UV hot pink Ice Dub
Body Flash:	Opal Lateral Scale
Skirt:	Whiting Black laced dyed pink Rooster cape
Legs:	Pink Super Floss
Collar:	Hot pink hackle
Head:	UV hot pink Ice Dub
Inner Tail:	Pearl Krystal Flash
Outer Tail:	Pink rabbit hide

Dirk Wiggler (Pink)
(tied by Jon Hazlett)

Front Shank:	20mm Waddington shank by Partridge
Trailing Hook:	#2 Gamakatsu Red Octopus
Eyes:	6mm gold Dumbbell brass eyes
Joint:	30-pound Berkley FireLine
Body:	Pearl Ice Dub
Body Flash:	Purple Mirage Flashabou
Inner Skirt:	Hot pink turkey flat
Outer Skirt:	Hot pink marabou with blue stripes
Legs:	Hot pink Super Floss with blue stripes
Collar:	Purple schlappen
Head:	Purple Hareline STS Trilobal Dub

Pick Yer Pocket (Pink)
(tied by Brian Kite)

Front Shank:	25mm Waddington shank by Partridge
Trailing Hook:	#2 Black nickel Gamakatsu Octopus
Eyes:	4mm silver Dumbbell brass
Joint:	30-pound Berkley FireLine
Body:	Fluorescent pink Hareline STS Trilobal Dub
Front Inner Skirt:	Pink kid goat body hair
Head:	Pink Hareline STS Trilobal Dub
Hackle:	Pink Rooster grizzly hackle
Lower Thorax:	Pink kid goat with pink guinea feather
Rear Inner Skirt:	Pink kid goat body hair
Rear Outer Skirt:	Pink guinea feather

Hobit Spey (Orange)
(tied by Clark Jennings)

Hook:	Gamakatsu C14S
Body:	Burnt orange angora goat dubbing
Butt:	Orange junction tubing
Veil:	Burnt orange Lady Amherst center tail
Body Hackle:	Burnt orange Rooster hackle
Hackle:	Burnt orange hen hackle
Tube:	2mm clear plastic tubing
Rear Skirt:	Burnt orange hen hackle
Rib:	Small gold tinsel

Hoh Bo Spey (Orange Butt/Purple)
(tied by Charles St. Pierre)

Front Shank:	25mm Waddington shank by Partridge
Trailing Hook:	#2 Black nickel Gamakatsu Octopus
Joint:	30-pound Berkley FireLine
Body:	Purple Hareline STS Trilobal Dub
Body Flash:	Purple Holographic Flashabou
Butt:	Hot orange Hareline STS Trilobal Dub
Veil:	Lady Amherst center tail fiber
Body Hackle:	Natural guinea feather
Hackle:	Blood Quill purple marabou

Hoh Bo Spey (Green Butt)
(tied by Charles St. Pierre)

Front Shank:	25mm Waddington shank by Partridge
Trailing Hook:	#2 Black nickel Gamakatsu Octopus
Joint:	30-pound Berkley FireLine
Body:	Black Hareline STS Trilobal Dub
Body Flash:	Silver Polar Flash
Butt:	Fluorescent chartreuse Hareline STS Trilobol Dub
Veil:	Lady Amherst center tail
Body Hackle:	Natural guinea body feather
Hackle:	Blood Quill black marabou

Signature Intruder (Crawdad)
(tied by Scott Howell)

Front Shank:	35mm Waddington shank by Partridge
Trailing Hook:	#2 Black nickel Gamakatsu Octopus
Rear Eyes:	5mm gold Dumbbell brass
Front Eyes:	Golden pheasant tippet
Joint:	30-pound Berkley FireLine
Inner Skirt:	Olive kid goat body hair
Inner Tail:	Thin olive ostrich feathers
Butt:	Red Hareline STS Trilobal Dub
Rib:	1/8-inch Holographic gold tinsel
Back:	Thin olive ostrich feathers
Lower Thorax:	Thin olive ostrich top with olive grizzly rabbit fur
Top Wing:	Olive-dyed Rooster grizzly hackle

CHAPTER

18

On Conservation

Today, steelhead anglers stand at a historical crossroads created from decades of environmental pressures and serious resource management failures. To further complicate matters, demand for steelhead angling opportunities continues to escalate, and there seems no end in sight. What is needed now is an honest appraisal of our problems, combined with reasonable and attainable solutions. If we fail to change, if we fail to respond to these problems with measured reason, optimism, faith, and political will, our wild rivers and the steelhead they support will continue to dwindle. As someone has noted, "If we want things to stay the same, then things have to change."

So just what has happened, and what can we do about it? The answers to both questions are numerous. They differ somewhat by region, for Alaska is certainly

Western steelhead rivers are national heritages, yet they have been dammed, silted, polluted, and misused. The forests through which they run have been clear-cut, over-roaded, and exploited beyond reasonable and sustainable limits. What does this mean for wild steelhead? Exactly this: The Pacific Northwest has lost three-fourths of our wild steelhead in only fifty years.

different from California, but a common thread runs through the Pacific Northwest in terms of our challenges, responsibilities, and possible solutions.

To begin, our Western steelhead and salmon rivers have been dammed for irrigation, drinking water, and hydroelectric power production to a point where northern California, for example, has lost over 60 percent of its wild spawning steelhead and salmon habitat. Oregon

and Washington have also suffered much of the same fate. British Columbia has escaped some of this (not all), but faces other serious threats.

Secondly, much of our watershed forests have been hit hard by inappropriate cutting and logging practices, including clear-cuts, cutting too close to mainstream waters or important tributaries, and inadequately designed access roads. A river without a diversified,

Wild steelhead are our best hope for the future. With protection, they will carry on the genetic diversity needed to survive a world that is rapidly changing in ways not always beneficial to any living thing. Hatchery steelhead are no solution. They are poor spawners, and when they do spawn with wild steelhead, they dilute the gene pool.

healthy, and sufficient forest canopy, and one with logging roads on tributaries that pour silt in the winter and spring runoff, is a river in trouble. Spawning beds become silted, oxygen levels drop, and average tributary water temperatures rise to levels unsustainable for juvenile steelhead and salmon.

These kinds of environmental changes have devastated wild steelhead and salmon populations. As biologist Bob Hooton remarked in the opening chapter of this book, "The natural production of steelhead along the Pacific Coast of North America today is around one-quarter of what it was when first documentations were made." We have lost three-fourths of our wild steelhead in about fifty years, wild fish that have been thriving for hundreds of thousands of years.

So-called solutions to this loss of wild fish and the destruction of their environment have only made matters worse. Hatchery programs, for example, have been

defined as a "sufficient, reasonable, and best solution" to replace our wild fish, and some politicians have tried to convince a naïve public that our fisheries are fine. The hatchery solution has become the central theme of management philosophies and practices in California, Oregon, and Washington. This is because hatchery production, despite significant costs, is still cheap, quick, and politically easy compared to reforming institutionalized political and economic processes that frequently resist needed change.

But hatchery steelhead are a poor replacement for wild fish. Artificially spawned hatchery steelhead have little of the innate protection from disease that wild fish have. Hatchery steelhead are poor natural spawners, and when they do spawn with wild steelhead, they distort and dilute the gene pool of the wild fish to the point where, as Hooton has also noted, even their natural biological coding that allows for diversified migration timing and patterns is all but eliminated. Thus they lose a great part of their ability to adapt to normal environmental challenges and disasters.

British Columbia has seen less of the hatchery "solution," but in the end their response to the loss of wild salmon has been, among other things, the promotion and implementation of artificially grown salmon in ocean pens. These farms, as currently designed and operated, pollute the ocean floor, spread disease, and allow for the unobstructed growth of populations of sea lice that feed on the penned salmon, then find and kill wild juvenile steelhead and salmon as they migrate from their rivers of birth out into the coastal waters occupied by penned-salmon farms. Added to this scenario is the commercial interception of steelhead by British Columbia gill-netters in search of salmon. Despite its well-deserved reputation for great numbers of wild steelhead, British Columbia steelhead and salmon have limits on the pressures they can sustain, and we must take measures to conserve what is left.

Up until now, Alaska and Russia remain somewhat off the radar for these kinds of problems and solutions, but environmental, political, and economic pressures increase each season. It is no accident that Russia has begun to limit angling pressure and public access on some of its best steelhead rivers of Kamchatka, and Alaska carefully monitors its commercial salmon harvest.

So, what do we do now? Some have argued that it's all over, and that we are past the point of no return. I disagree. Solutions are difficult, but they are not impossible if we have the political will to change the way we do business. This includes changing our resource-extraction practices (logging, mining, and commercial fishing) in a way that protects wild rivers and wild steelhead. Secondly, wild steelhead are among the strongest and most adaptable of all wild creatures. As a biologist told me one day on a population census on a California salmon and steelhead stream, "Steelhead are amazing, and do not need much. Sometimes I believe they could spawn on a damp towel."

Because their genetic coding allows them to change their migratory patterns when environmental factors such as non-stop flooding, volcanic eruption, or drought destroy their natal streams, they can either delay their migration until it is safe or temporarily return to another river. One classic example of this occurred some years ago when Mount St. Helens erupted and poured volcanic ash into the Toutle River to a point where

almost nothing could survive. Steelhead bound for the Toutle simply went somewhere else that year.

Secondly, as Mr. Hooton has also reminded us, ordinary resident rainbow trout that have never gone to sea often produce offspring who will. Thus, new steelhead can suddenly appear as if from nowhere. This is no small advantage, and it may some day be a critical one in the fight to save some steelhead from going extinct. Resident rainbows could be planted in watersheds that do not have any wild fish.

As anglers, we cannot simply fish. We must get involved and support the conservation of wild salmon and steelhead and the rivers they ascend each season. Steelhead expert and Silver Hilton Lodge owner Stephen Myers typifies the best in conservation-minded lodge owners who often lead the charge in protecting wild rivers and wild steelhead—no matter where they are found.

One of the difficulties we face is that most people have no idea what a steelhead is. More and more people, however, are beginning to care about rivers, clean water, and wild salmon. Successful steelhead conservation must ally itself with these more well-known issues.

It is thus our job to find a way to let wild steelhead live and survive as they have for thousands of years, and while it won't be easy, it is certainly possible. One of the major problems we face is the fact that we live in a world where the majority rules, and most people have no idea of what a steelhead is. And if they do, the species is simply not a priority. Secondly, experience has shown that governments are the least likely candidates to step up to the plate and do what is necessary to develop sus-

tainable economic practices. When real and meaningful help arrives, it usually comes from the private sector.

Thirdly, we will get nowhere with our efforts if we take the point of view that we are only fighting to protect our interests as recreational anglers. This narrow sentiment falls on deaf ears. Finally, we will probably never win the struggle on the basis of conservation arguments alone because these issues are overshadowed by institutionalized political and economic processes that are too

Without unspoiled rivers and wild fish, we will lose more than our fishing. In the end, we will lose ourselves and the world our children and grandchildren deserve. As someone said, "If we want things to stay the same, then things have to change."

powerful and often insensitive to needed conservation solutions.

What this all means is that we must make saving wild steelhead a part of a larger process and find ways to build alliances with other conservationists working to conserve and protect forested watersheds and the rivers flowing through them. We must also ally ourselves with the movement to protect wild Pacific salmon, especially in those rivers and watersheds where salmon and steelhead co-exist.

What is good for rivers, forests, and salmon is good for steelhead, and the fight to save forests and wild salmon has a relatively large and broadly based constituency behind it. Not many people may know of steelhead, but almost all people, regardless of their circumstance and location, have heard the story of salmon and their importance to the Northwest cultures and societies that have been using salmon for thousands of years. If nothing else, they have seen salmon on the menu and table, and the salmon's value and reputation as a food source is common knowledge.

The alliance between steelhead and wild salmon conservation efforts has paid tremendous dividends in British Columbia, for example, and today the effort to protect wild salmon is closely and successfully connected to, and allied with, the efforts to protect B.C. steelhead,

Successful steelhead conservation requires three things: time, money, and energy. Anglers who care about steelhead must find a way to contribute at least one of these elements to a conservation group. It has always been the private sector, and not the government, that has done the most to help wild steelhead and salmon.

We need to save our rivers and fish for economic reasons as well as for conservation principles and values. Sport fishing in the United States, Canada, and abroad provides real jobs for real people, and in many areas exceeds the contributions of logging, commercial fishing, mining, and hydroelectric production.

especially in the Skeena River system of northern British Columbia. This kind of alliance will work in other parts of the Pacific Rim as well.

Our rivers and fish should be saved for economic reasons as well. Sport-fishing on healthy watersheds can produce significant revenues. In northern California, for example, Klamath River steelhead and salmon sport-fishing generates more income for local, county, and state economies than almost any other activity, including hydroelectric production. In British Columbia, sport-fishing on the Babine River meets or exceeds all other watershed revenues such as timber harvesting, hunting, and whitewater rafting, and in some years it meets or exceeds sockeye salmon commercial fishing revenues.

One way to do more for salmon and steelhead is to join a conservation organization and participate in their activities. Trout Unlimited has chapters in all parts of the United States, and their track record is impressive.

California, Oregon, Washington, British Columbia, and Alaska all have chapters involved in wild steelhead and salmon restoration. California also has a hard-fighting group called California Trout that is doing an exemplary job on the West Coast. The North Coast Steelhead Alliance, Babine River Foundation, Friends of Wild Salmon, and the Skeena Watershed Coalition are in the thick of things in British Columbia and have already won many important victories.

The fight to save our wild rivers and fish is more than a collective political effort, it is also a personal struggle. Individual efforts are a fundamental and necessary part of the process to save steelhead and their rivers. There is no greater challenge than turning from the mistakes of our past and looking to a new future in which our daily lives and economic processes are a part of the solution rather than a part of the problem. We are stewards of an environment that needs us more than ever.

Colorado steelheader Bob Woods is smiling for a reason. This wild female could lay over a thousand eggs. Humans willing, some of them will always hatch and return to the rivers where they belong.

CONSERVATION GROUPS

British Columbia Steelhead
North Coast Steelhead Alliance, USA
PO Box 3940
Laguna Hills, CA 92654-3940
steelheadalliance.ca

Babine Watershed Monitoring Trust
PO Box 4274
Smithers, B.C. VOJ 2NO
babinetrust.ca

Northern Rivers Conservation Trust
PO Box 4731
Smithers, B.C. VOJ 2NO

Friends of Wild Salmon
PO Box 2803
Smithers, B.C. VOJ 2NO
friendsofwildsalmon.ca

Trout Unlimited
1300 No. 17th St., Ste 500
Arlington, VA 22209
tu.org

California Trout
870 Market St. # 528
San Francisco, CA 94102
caltrout.org

One Per Cent Planet Earth
Terry Kellog
PO Box 118
Newburyport, MA 01950
onepercentfortheplanet.org

Appendix:
Tackle and Other Resources

Patagonia, Inc.
(805) 643-8616
patagonia.com

Paul Miller Premier Flies
(541) 482-6665

Rio Products
(208) 524-7760
rioproducts.com

Sage Rod Company
(800) 533-3004
sageflyfish.com

Scientific Anglers
(888) 364-3577
scientificanglers.com

Simms
(866) 585-3570
simmsfishing.com

Teeny Line Co.
(800) 501-6602
jimteeny.com

The best part of fishing and all its trappings is the solid and uncensored immersion in a reality that many have unfortunately abandoned in favor of more civilized and mundane pursuits.

There is no substitute for time spent on the water, but good teachers, books, and DVDs such as Lani Waller's Steelhead Legacy, *that show casting, mending, and fighting fish in real time, can definitely shorten the learning curve.*

BOOKS AND DVDS

To learn more about Great Lakes steelhead, purchase *Fly Fishing for Great Lakes Steelhead* by Rick and Jerry Kustich (westriverpub.com), or by watching the Great Lakes chapter of *Lani Waller's Steelhead Legacy,* available at most fly-fishing shops across the country. The DVD includes the original three Scientific Anglers fly-fishing films as well as a recent film showing all the changes in steelheading over the past twenty-some-odd years since the first films were made.

Two other excellent steelheading books that also include in-depth decriptions of indicator tactics are *Advanced Fly Fishing for Steelhead* by Deke Meyers (Frank Amato Publications) and *Steelhead Guide: Fly Fishing Techniques and Strategies for Lake Erie Steelhead* by John Nagy (Great Lakes Publishing).

Index